SELECTED POEMS OF LUIS DE GÓNGORA

SELECTED POEMS *of* Luis de Góngora

A BILINGUAL EDITION

EDITED AND TRANSLATED BY *John Dent-Young*

THE UNIVERSITY OF CHICAGO PRESS

CHICAGO & LONDON

John Dent-Young has also translated from Chinese. He is co-author, with his son Alex, of the full English version of the Chinese classical novel the *Shuihuzhuan* (often known in English as *The Water Margin*), published in five parts under the titles *The Broken Seals, The Tiger Killers, The Gathering Company, Iron Ox,* and *The Scattered Flock.*

The University of Chicago Press, Chicago 60637
The University of Chicago Press, Ltd., London
© 2007 by The University of Chicago
All rights reserved. Published 2007
Printed in the United States of America

16 15 14 13 12 11 10 09 08 07   1 2 3 4 5

ISBN-13: 978-0-226-14059-9 (cloth)
ISBN-10: 0-226-14059-8 (cloth)

The University of Chicago Press gratefully acknowledges the generous support of the Program for Cultural Cooperation between Spain's Ministry of Culture and United States Universities toward the publication of this book.

Frontispiece—Diego Rodríguez de Silva y Velázquez, *Luis de Góngora y Argote,* 1622, oil on canvas. Maria Antoinette Evans Fund, Museum of Fine Arts, Boston. Photograph © Museum of Fine Arts, Boston.

Library of Congress Cataloging-in-Publication Data

Góngora y Argote, Luis de, 1561–1627
   [Poems, English & Spanish. Selections]
   Selected poems of Luis de Góngora : a bilingual edition / Luis de Góngora y Argote ; edited and translated by John Dent-Young.
      p. cm.
   English and Spanish text.
   ISBN 0-226-14059-8 (cloth : alk. paper)
   1. Góngora y Argote, Luis de, 1561–1627—Translations into English. I. Dent-Young, John. II. Title.
   PQ6394.A3E5 2007
   861′.3—dc22

                                                2006045514

♾ The paper used in this publication meets the minimum requirements of the American National Standard for Information Sciences—Permanence of Paper for Printed Library Materials, ANSI Z39.48–1992.

✧ *For Esther*

·❦[CONTENTS]❧·

··ҙ[INTRODUCTION]ҙ··

This selection is a limited introduction to the varied poetry of Luis de Gón-
gora, described as "the Spanish Homer" in the title of the first published
edition of his work and still considered by many to be Spain's greatest poet.
Contemporary with Shakespeare, he was both famous and controversial in
his lifetime and still is today. His name produced a literary term for an
involved and Latinate style, Gongorism, yet he was first known for ballads
and songs written in the popular tradition that runs through Spanish po-
etry from its earliest beginnings. His later style was attacked and parodied
by contemporaries like Lope de Vega and Quevedo, but it was also widely
defended and imitated, influencing, for example, Calderón and Sor Juana
Inés de la Cruz, Mexico's first Spanish-language poet. Like Cervantes, who
was a little older but published his work during the same period, Góngora
ended his life famous but impoverished. Unlike Cervantes, his fame later
underwent a partial eclipse before he was taken up again in the twentieth
century by the modernists, including García Lorca, and by one of the great
critics of the time, Dámaso Alonso. His influence can also be seen in the
work of modern Latin American poets and novelists.

After a good deal of rereading and trying at the same time to bypass tra-
ditional controversies, I have been struck by two aspects of Góngora. First
is the extent to which he lives his poetry and his poetry defines him. Al-
though, for example, he wrote a good many sonnets in the Renaissance
manner describing beautiful and unrequiting women or praising noblemen
and bishops, he also wrote a good many others dealing with quite ordinary
matters: among the subjects are gifts from friends; journeys; a gentleman
who couldn't tell a ballad from a sonnet; the poet's insulting reception by a
lady in Cuenca; a satire on a gentleman dressing for some festivities; viewing

the bulls before a bullfight; a nobleman's collection of jewels, pictures, and horses; some unusually cold weather in Andalusia with ice and snow at the time of the king's visit; and a request to a friend in Toledo to send some apricots, or if there were none left, a barbel or an eel from the Tagus. The picture that emerges has the variety and ordinariness of real life, with a Spanish perspective that would almost fit it for a modern tourist guidebook.

More important, Góngora puts himself into his poems. Sometimes, as in "Hanme dicho hermanas" (no. 14, "Sisters, they tell me . . . ," the poem addressed to some nuns) he does this directly, though it is a carefully and mischievously constructed self-portrait, obviously not to be taken at face value. Likewise, the innocence of "Hermana Marica" (no. 2, "Marica, my sister") is manipulated to create a humorous, unsentimental impression of childhood and prepare the ground for a shock at the end. The creation of a consistent poetic personality plays a big part in Góngora's poetry. Even an obviously staged performance like "Andeme yo caliente . . ." (no. 3, the *letrilla* in praise of home comforts, "Just let me be warm and easy") accords with what Jammes calls Góngora's nonconformism and announces the preference for simplicity over self-importance and artificiality that (perhaps paradoxically) is central to his complex later work (*Letrillas*, ed. Jammes, 115).

The author is also dramatically present in the humorous asides that occur when he is telling a story, in the playful choice of a word or an image, and in the occasional flourishes of pedantry that he is so fond of introducing. When Pyramus is imagining how the lion must have torn Thisbe apart and scattered her beautiful limbs, the poet muses in parentheses: "ivory, call them, divine? I'll call them divine *and* ivory" (no. 42, 11.409–10). In the *Solitudes*, probably his least playful work, there are humorous touches, apparently gratuitous, as when the pilgrim reaches shore and donates the plank that saved him to the rocks, since "even cliffs can be mollified by signs of gratitude" (que aun se dejan las peñas / lisonjear de agradecidas señas, *Solitude* I, 11.32–33). I think some of Góngora's contemporary critics found such intrusions irrelevant; objections were certainly made to some of the colloquial phrases he uses, when they add nothing to the content but are important indicators of a speaker's attitude. To us, from the other side of modernism, all this is less surprising and also may seem reminiscent of the framing fictions of *Don Quixote*.

While the relationship between the poetic personality and reality is quite confusing (as presumably Góngora wanted), on a simpler level some poems are easy to collate with his life. The sonnets on bullfighting, for example, relate to one of his lifelong interests. Or consider another sonnet in which he appears to accuse a nobleman of leaving town because of not wanting to repay some money Góngora lent him. According to an early commentator's note, this accusation of stinginess is in fact just a friendly joke. The gist of it, loosely translated, is this:

> Written when the Count of Villaflor delayed repaying Don Luis some
> money he had borrowed while gambling.
>
> The worthy Count, without more ado,
> packed his stuff and loaded the mule with baggage.
> Farewell, my ducats, I wish you bon voyage;
> obviously I've seen the last of you!
>
> He'll change you into a greyhound, just you see,
> that a page will trail behind him on a lead;
> for it all goes in support of the canine breed,
> what he gets denying the church and fleecing me.
>
> To string a man along, that's the Count's fashion,
> and as for the ladies, he leads them quite a dance.
> What a simpleton I was to lend him money!
>
> Still, if the proverb's true, you know, it's funny,
> but the more fool, the greater is my chance
> Santa Maria will come to me in a vision.

What the proverb says is that the Virgin Mary appears to simpletons, and it is used of someone who has a piece of undeserved luck. But Santa Maria was also the name of a servant of the Count who was sent round to pay his gambling debts. In addition to the neatly turned joke, the sonnet serves to remind us that Góngora was notoriously fond of gambling and other relatively frivolous pursuits.

Born into a well-off family in Córdoba, Góngora showed early promise and was sent to study law in Salamanca in 1576, when he must have been about fifteen. While there he was accused of misbehaving, devoting most of his attention to cards, profane poetry, plays, and actors. It is quite hard to relate the severe countenance in Velázquez's famous portrait to Góngora's youthful personality; but if it was painted in 1622, less than five years before his death, the subject had reasons for seeming weary and bitter. By 1581 he was back in Córdoba and had taken minor orders so he could work for the cathedral chapter, following his uncle in the post of *racionero* or prebendary. A few years later he was reprimanded by the bishop for talking during services, attending bullfights and frequenting actors, writing profane poetry, and generally behaving like *un mozo*—"a young hooligan," one might say. He seems not to have been greatly worried because he replied that it was impossible for him to have been talking during the chanting of the office since the cleric on one side of him was deaf and the one on the other never stopped singing. He admitted the bullfights but said he went to them in the company of men who were his seniors, while actors came to his house, he explained, because of his love of music. He admitted the poetry too, but said he was partly exonerated by the fact that many of the *letrillas* attributed to him were written by others.

It is not difficult to see that Góngora was determined to reserve his greatest efforts for what was always to be most important to him, the art of poetry, and that his character and interests set him on a course of opposition to authority. Given his position as a functionary of the church, he needed to be clever and stubborn to pursue his aims. It might be an exaggeration to invoke the Inquisition here, but it is worth remembering that when Góngora went to Salamanca the older poet, Luis de León, had probably just returned to the university after four years in the cells, where he narrowly escaped torture. Admittedly Góngora's sins were more worldly than theological (and therefore less seditious), but when the first collection of his poems was published by Vicuña shortly after his death it was almost immediately banned by the Inquisition.

Góngora seems to have become known as a poet quite early on, when his poems must have been sung and transmitted orally. From the 1590s his work was included in various collections of ballads. There were thirty-seven of his poems in Pedro Espinosa's famous collection, *Flores de poetas ilustres de España,* published in 1605. Probably it was his reputation as a poet that enabled him to dismiss criticisms of his way of life relatively lightly. Possibly, as his fame and poetic ambition grew, he was protected also by his love of ambiguity, punning, and metaphor, his inexplicitness. Although he was willing to have a go at almost anyone and made many enemies, it would have been difficult to attribute any really dangerous views to him. He was, after all, the son of a lawyer and had studied law himself, and the cathedral employed him on what might be described as diplomatic missions.

It seems typical of Góngora's character too that he was both meticulous in the revision of his work and careless of its preservation, so that when the poems came to be collected by Antonio Chacón, who worked on the manuscript with Góngora just before the latter's death, some had been lost and the authenticity of others was doubtful. It has been said that the Chacón manuscript would be conclusive proof of what was and was not written by

Góngora, but for one problem: Góngora himself could not always remember what he had written, and he had not kept copies. (This uncertainty worked against him in other ways, too: in the banned edition the most scurrilous poems are said to have been by other people.)

Chacón's manuscript and Vicuña's abortive edition of 1627 are the two main sources for Góngora's work. There is a story behind the banning of Vicuña's edition. One of many enemies Góngora made during his life was a Jesuit called Juan de Pineda. Pineda was one of the judges in a poetry competition, or poetic joust, held in 1610 to celebrate the beatification of Saint Ignatius of Loyola. Góngora failed to win the prize and in another sonnet (attributed rather than canonical) addresses the matter thus:

> ¿Yo en justa injusta expuesto a la sentencia
> de un positivo padre azafranado?
> Paciencia, Job, si alguna os han dejado
> los prolijos escritos de su Encia.

I take this to mean something like—

> "So in this unjust joust am I to be judged
> by an intransigent ginger Jesuit?
> Patience, Job—if you've any left
> after the prolix scribblings of His Boringness."

Father Pineda, who apparently was red-haired and had written a long book on Job, had his revenge when he denounced many poems in the Vicuña edition and it was banned.

Many of Góngora's poems can be related to journeys he made on cathedral business, or perhaps to visit patrons: Granada, Salamanca, Ayamonte near Huelva, Palencia, the court at Valladolid and later Madrid, Monforte in Galicia and Cuenca are all reflected in sonnets or ballads that he wrote. It seems also certain that the landscape and themes of *Polyphemus* and the *Solitudes* draw on sights and sounds and people he encountered on these travels. Both these long poems are much concerned with nature and country life, the *Solitudes* in particular proposing an ideal of natural simplicity in preference to the pretentiousness of court life and the greed of empire. Although this idea is closely linked to the Greek and Latin views of the classical golden age, and Góngora was especially well read in Latin, the essence of the poem is observation of real country pursuits and praise of what is not flashy or fashionable or grasping but traditional and well crafted.

These long poems, on which Góngora staked his poetic reputation, can also be linked to his life. In 1607 he was in Madrid attempting to obtain justice for his sister, whose eldest son had been killed in a street brawl in Córdoba. He had no success, and the *tercetos* he wrote at this time express his disillusionment with the court and nostalgia for country life. Some years earlier he had rented a place outside Córdoba, the Huerta de Don Marcos, where there were many fruit trees. The tenancy was for his lifetime and that of the nephew who succeeded him as prebendary; there would obviously have been a subtenant to farm the land, but it must have represented something that had a strong emotional hold on Góngora. When he returned to Córdoba in 1610, after his frustrating residence at court, he rented a house in the Plazuela de la Trinidad and shortly after handed over the cathedral job to his nephew. We can assume that it was during this period that he wrote *Polyphemus* and the *First Solitude,* the poems in which he developed the extreme form of his complicated syntax and idiosyncratic style of metaphor that would be argued over by critics and followers for the rest of his life and beyond.

While early commentators record which poems Father Pineda disapproved of on moral grounds, the real battles were more about Góngora's style than his moral content. The first and most vehement critic of this was Juan de Jáuregui, who wrote the *Antídoto contra la pestilente poesía de las "Soledades* . . . ("An Antidote to the pestilential poetry of the *Solitudes* addressed to the author in order to defend him against himself"). This was a response to the privately circulated *Solitudes* and *Polyphemus,* and it accused Góngora of writing unintelligible nonsense. It was quickly answered by Góngora's friends and allies, and battle commenced. Among Góngora's critics were two great contemporaries, Lope de Vega and Quevedo. Góngora's self-justification included claims that he sought to raise Spanish to the level of perfection of Latin, that he did not write for idiots, and that difficult poetry had the great merit of sharpening the reader's intellect. Somewhat more mysteriously he suggested that the objective of the human intellect is to know truth, and the greatest delight will be experienced when, forced to speculate by a difficult literary work, the intellect glimpses through the obscurity "asimilaciones a su concepto," which I take to mean some intimation of ultimate truth. These ideas are put forward in a letter thought to be from Góngora (though Jammes [*Soledades,* ed. Jammes, 614] expresses doubts about the authenticity of the Góngora letter, or at least part of it) replying to one by a critic, possibly Lope de Vega. What is clear is that Góngora proposed the highest possible aims for his poetry and defended it obstinately against criticism.

Although there was opposition to what became known as the new poetry and to *cultismo*, the use of unusual, Latinate syntax and vocabulary, Góngora had many admirers and defenders in his own time and after his death. Modern editions have frequent recourse to the seventeenth century commentaries of people like the Duque de Rivas, the Abad de Rute, Pellicer, and Salcedo Coronel to elucidate difficult passages. On the other hand, it cannot have escaped attention that this churchman's poetry contained little direct reference to Christianity, and "temple" is a much more frequent item in his vocabulary than "church." To some modern readers the sexual innuendo and scatological humour will probably be even more shocking, but here we must probably give some weight to changing ideas of acceptability.

The second aspect of Góngora's work that has struck me is its unity. This point is worth making simply because there has been a tendency to see Góngora in two halves: a simple Góngora of popular ballads and satires and the difficult, *culto* Góngora, author of the supposedly unintelligible later poems. Yet in the "difficult" work one comes across many expressions and images that have occurred in other Góngora poems, from all stages of his production. One of the earliest sonnets, ascribed to 1582, addresses a crack in the wall, like the one Pyramus and Thisbe spoke through, describing it as the lists where the speaker's hopes joust with his lady's disdain. Six years later he writes a sonnet in dialogue form where one of the participants is the lists of Madrid, which gentlemen should use to train their fighting skills but don't because they are too busy parading in the Paseo del Prado. The 1582 sonnet continues by begging the crack in the wall to be discreet and propitious because the speaker doesn't want his love affair to hang as a trophy on cruel destiny's tree, language that recalls ballad 10 in this collection and stanza 30 of *Polyphemus*. The sonnet ends by comparing the crack in the Babylonian lovers' wall to a *barco de vistas*, a boat used for holding international negotiations on neutral ground. The whole Pyramus and Thisbe story is told in the ballad written in 1618 (no. 42), where Góngora develops this *barco de vistas*, the ship image, as a metaphor for his go-between.

There are certain classical myths and stories that Góngora reverts to again and again, like the disaster stories of Icarus and of Phaeton, for example. Stories such as these, together with linguistic expressions from classical literature ("the snake in the grass" from Virgil is a favorite), are so firmly fixed in Góngora's mind that he continues to play with them throughout his poetic career, trying them in new combinations to make new connections and yield new ideas. In a sonnet of 1615 he advises a young man to study and strive for fame, and not let idleness be "a snake among the flowers" instead of "in the grass," flowers serving as a homage to the youth of the person he is addressing. Themes and images also repeat themselves. The praise of simplicity that later is so central to the *Solitudes* occurs in the *letrilla* of 1581 (no. 3). The *Solitudes* are partly a collage of experiences and locations that Góngora has described elsewhere: storm and shipwreck, shepherds, country food and wine, birdsong, rivers, and girls bathing, lying on the grass, and dancing. It includes many favorite sights: beautiful Andalusian horses, the flight of hawks, the color of red and white wine mixed, a river winding through fields, the rising sun dispelling mists, pools of water on the seashore sparkling in the sunlight (this last image, which occurs in the *Second Solitude,* suggests the scenery of the Coto de Doñana, the great nature reserve between Seville and the sea). The pilgrim, the protagonist of the poem, has been a subject of endless discussion—as to what exactly he is and why he is there—but the word "pilgrim" occurs in other poems, and the pilgrim's song of complaint in the *Second Solitude,* with its Icarus image, is echoed or foreshadowed in various ballads and sonnets.

All these myths, stories, and expressions are a common thread running through the different poems, the simpler ones and the more complex, the serious and the burlesque. There is also more unity of tone than one would expect between these different types: to put it simply, Góngora's serious poems contain humor and his humorous ones are serious—serious in their exuberance, in their delight in language. There is really no reason to think of two Góngoras. His entire oeuvre is pervaded by a consistent poetic personality, even if a facet of this personality is a relish for wearing different masks. Behind the role-play is the voice of one who analyzes words and ideas, not taking their meaning on trust, and believes in both the importance of his art and the beauty of the world.

Commentators have pointed out that Góngora uses every rhetorical figure there is. These rhetorical figures are not adornments but ways of examining and renewing the words that compose them. One of Góngora's tricks is to jump, with a kind of *Alice in Wonderland* logic, from a metaphorical meaning to a more literal one, which conjures up a new range of comparisons. Another is to use a metaphor in a literal way as if it were the ordinary name for the thing. Thus "boat" is "pine," and "crystal" becomes the common name for any of the following: "water," "girl," "arm," "face," and "beauty."

It may be objected that there is an inconsistency of attitude in Góngora's work that is more important than questions of language. Surely there is a world of difference between the cynicism of the Belerma ballad (no. 6), on the one hand, and on the other the romantic stories of Angelica and Medoro (no. 22) or of Acis and Galatea in *Polyphemus* (no. 41)? Many feel that Góngora's burlesque treatment of such famous love stories as Hero and

Leander or Pyramus and Thisbe somehow devalues the more serious poetry. R. O. Jones (*Poems of Góngora*, ed. Jones, 21), for one, finds the comic ballads "disturbing" because they are so different from Góngora's "exquisite poems on love." He does, however, propose a tentative solution: "Is Góngora's target the folly of useless ideals? Probably . . . " This does not seem to me to go far enough or to get the emphasis quite right. Góngora exploits or parodies all the literary conventions of his time, from pastoral and chivalresque fiction to the popular ballad and even his revered classics. He does so because they are part of the literary scene, there, like Everest, to be conquered, or to be used as materials for his craft to work on (there is no denying the competitive element in Góngora's character). The view, deriving from Romanticism, of poetry as purely the expression of emotion undervalues Góngora's technical skill and playfulness.

Even when he is not mocking, Góngora will often alter a myth for some expressive purpose. In the song near the start of the *First Solitude*, the modern Narcissus is criticized for "seeking echoes and disdaining fountains," for running after flattery and love when he would be better employed contemplating his own reflection; the original moral of the story has been turned on its head. In *Polyphemus*, Galatea is described as *pavón de Venus* and *cisne de Juno*, "Venus's peacock" and "Juno's swan." But the peacock is Juno's emblem, while the swan belongs with Venus.

There is still some cogency in the criticism that Góngora's love sonnets show little feeling. It has been noted that he manages the language and form of the Renaissance sonnet brilliantly but without any sense of real passion. Certainly many of the sonnets sound like exercises and are in part imitations, but quite often there is a twist that points the topic in a less conventional, or certainly a less amorous, direction. The earliest of the sonnets in Ciplijauskaité's edition compares the beloved with a building: foundation, walls, a coral doorway, emerald windows or portholes, which are all conventional Renaissance metaphors for beauty of face and form. It is rather mechanical, like painting with numbers. For once Father Pineda has a point when he calls it "mad exaggeration of the profane poets, which in the mouth of a priest is all the more intolerable and inexcusable, especially when combined with other excesses" (*Sonetos Completos*, 118). Yet Dámaso Alonso finds this sonnet one of Góngora's most emotional. I think Alonso must be responding to a sense of excitement in the movement of the verse, the key to which is perhaps in the fourth line: *fue por divina mano fabricado*—this beautiful building was created by a divine architect. Moving smoothly through its catalog of beauties (or architectural features), the poem reaches a conclusion in ambivalently religious and perfectly balanced terms: the poet begs the beautiful idol whom he humbly adores to hear him as he "sings your hymns, recites your virtues." Divinely created beauty has been matched by Góngora's beautiful arrangement of words and their music; this is the source of the excitement. Góngora's attitude to love poetry is probably revealed in his advice to the young man in a sonnet of 1615, when he tells him to snatch a feather from Love's most painful arrow and use it as a pen to become famous. Even so, ambition was to be weighed against a firm grasp of reality. Some of the practical difficulties of romance are strikingly epitomized in the ballad that begins with "Noble Disenchantment" (no. 10), where for instance the speaker picks up a pebble to throw at the window and gets his hands covered in filth—hardly surprising in streets that were probably not much cleaner than the cloacal rivers of Castille that Góngora enjoyed describing.

A more important question arises in relation to the Solitudes. The idyllic vision of simple life, the criticism of commercial greed and imperial ambition, and the intellectual and aesthetic excitement aroused by the new discoveries sit a little awkwardly with one another. The urge to go beyond the known world brought the cruelties of the Spanish conquest to the New World; it was also, however, a big step for mankind. Linked to the beauty of the Spice Islands anchored in the dawn sea—in the East, that is, but how expressive this is of the excitement of travel!—is irreparable loss, the old man's loss of his son and also, we might want to add, the loss of the world's innocence. We should be wary, however, of trying to reconcile contradictions that Góngora himself could not solve or to clarify the mysteries that he himself suggested it might not be possible to view clearly. Góngora and his contemporaries were brought up in the spirit of humanism and despite the general seventeenth-century tendencies toward cynicism and religious reaction that historians have observed, there must surely have been a genuine tension between admiration for human advances and revulsion toward some of the results. These are, after all, equations that we have not solved in our own time. Perhaps if Góngora had completed the Solitudes he would have reflected more light on such problems.

In much of Góngora's poetry awareness of transience and death underlies other human concerns, while nature holds the balance, converting the busy deceptions of the world into tranquillity or the festive contemplation of beauty. Time gives "green consolations (as I have translated line 221 of Soledad I)." But in the poems of the 1620s the mood seems increasingly sombre. In a sonnet of 1620 about the portrait a Flemish artist was painting of him, Góngora expresses fears that the portrait will not last, but then concludes that things last better than men:

Los siglos que en sus hojas cuenta un roble,
árbol los cuenta sordo, tronco ciego;
quien más ve, más oye, menos dura.

[The centuries an oak tree counts in its leaves,
it counts them dumbly, as a tree it's deaf and blind;
man sees and hears, and yet lasts so much less.]

In the great sonnets of 1622–23 the disillusionment seems to be heartfelt. These are perhaps the most deeply emotional poems Góngora wrote. His sojourn in Madrid had proved a failure. The patrons who were his last hope were dead or disgraced. His own life was on a steep downward curve. Before the end, unable to pay the rent, he was thrown out of his house. According to the story it was his old enemy Quevedo who owned the house, having bought it and several others in the same street, then Calle del Niño, now called Calle de Quevedo. After suffering a stroke, Góngora finally returned to Córdoba, where he died in 1626. It is not even clear where he was buried. Much later, a body that was found and dug up was thought to be his. There was originally no plaque to commemorate him.

The difficulty of Góngora has been exaggerated. He can be simple and direct, even in later poems: one has only to look at sonnet no. 23, the 1603 sonnet on arriving in Valladolid, or "A Carnation Has Fallen" (no. 34), the 1621 Christmas carol. Even in his complex style, the difficulties of the word order can be mitigated by paying close attention to the system of balance and contrast; the significance of allusions and myths can often be elucidated by further reading in Góngora's work because one poem illuminates another. Startling metaphors require us to look closely at the objects and situations being described. Góngora's preoccupation with words led to a heightened observation of ordinary objects. His style may seem abstract, but closer reading shows simple objects revealed under an intense light. The effect is almost the reverse of Velázquez's skill with paint, which produces at a distance an impression of heightened reality, but in close-up is as unrepresentational as an abstract painting. This is not the only parallel between poet and painter, who must have met when Velázquez, visiting Madrid for the first time as a young man not much known outside his native Seville, painted the portrait. In his earlier work Velázquez also uses mythological subjects, like Bacchus, Vulcan, and Ariadne but accomodates them so completely to the life around him that people hesitate to give them their original titles: the painting of Bacchus is commonly known as *The Drinkers*, that of Arachne, as *The Spinners*. The impression most viewers take away from these paintings is of the faces of ordinary people and a sense of the vitality of their involvement in work.

In its forms, ideas, and vocabulary Góngora's poetry draws heavily on precedent and yet it manages to be intensely personal. He became famous because he was popular; his poetry was earthy and traditional as well as witty and learned and in its peculiar way avant-garde. He himself believed he was writing for an élite. Nowadays that is unfashionable, and perhaps we can change it in a way that Góngora himself might have appreciated if we say that his poetry is for the alert.

Finally, a brief note on the translation. My aim has been to produce versions that can be read on their own, and in the more difficult works like the *Solitudes* to clarify the narrative without oversimplifying or losing all the richness of metaphor. My hope was that I could rescue Góngora from his role as textbook example of the Baroque and give him a human voice. I have tried not to sentimentalize the poems or to make too big a change in their form. Different poems have required different strategies, according to their center of gravity and different possibilities and impossibilities: I have indicated some of the reasons in the notes. I have cross-referenced some of the notes in order to support my sense of a joined-up Góngora. What I would like above all is to have caught the down-to-earth aspect of Góngora's poetry and the seriousness of his approach, whatever the mood and tone of a particular poem.

Special thanks are due to all my patient and encouraging readers and advisers, and particularly Martin Murphy, Simon Ellis, and Maria-Elena Pickett, to all of whom I owe many good suggestions.

"For remember, fools, from behind / Opportunity's shown bald" (poem no. 8).
Alciato's was one of the books of emblems that were popular in the sixteenth
and seventeenth centuries, especially as a source of poetic images.
Alciato, *On Opportunity* (1621), emblem no. 122.

Introduction

The ballads (*romances*), sonnets, and *letrillas* in this section are printed in chronological order, as given in the editions of Antonio Carreño, Biruté Ciplijauskaité, and Robert Jammes, respectively. I have selected poems that I hope will show not only the variety of Góngora's poetry but also the continuity: forms and images are repeated throughout a poetic career that continued until almost the end of his life, and although his style develops in complexity it is as recognizably his in the earlier as it is in the later poems.

For ease of reference, I have given titles to the English versions, although there are usually no titles in the Spanish.

1. Romance (1580)

La más bella niña
de nuestro lugar,
hoy vïuda y sola
y ayer por casar,
viendo que sus ojos
a la guerra van,
a su madre dice
que escucha su mal:
dejadme llorar
orillas del mar.

Pues me distes, madre,
en tan tierna edad
tan corto el placer,
tan largo el pesar,
y me cautivastes
de quien hoy se va
y lleva las llaves
de mi libertad,
dejadme llorar
orillas del mar.

En llorar conviertan
mis ojos de hoy más

1. [But yesterday married]

The loveliest creature
in all our town,
but yesterday married,
now widowed, alone,
    seeing that her lover
to the wars is gone,
says to her mother,
who hears her complain:
    *Give me leave to cry
    on the seashore.*

Mother, you gave me
away so soon
to such brief pleasure,
to such long pain;
    since you bound me
to one who's gone,
taking the keys that
end my freedom,
    *give me leave to cry
    on the seashore.*

Let my eyes from now on
to tears convert

el sabroso oficio
del dulce mirar,
pues que no se pueden
mejor ocupar,
yéndose a la guerra
quien era mi paz.
    Dejadme llorar
    orillas del mar.

    No me pongáis freno
ni queráis culpar,
que lo uno es justo,
lo otro por demás.
Si me queréis bien
no me hagáis mal;
harto peor fuera
morir y callar.
    Dejadme llorar
    orillas del mar.

Dulce madre mía
¿quién no llorará,
aunque tenga el pecho
como un pedernal,
y no dará voces,
viendo marchitar
los más verdes años
de mi mocedad?
    Dejadme llorar
    orillas del mar.

Váyanse las noches,
pues ido se han
los ojos que hacían
los míos velar;
váyanse y no vean
tanta soledad,
después que en mi lecho
sobra la mitad.
    Dejadme llorar
    orillas del mar.

the agreeable practice
of looks that enchant,
    for what occupation
can they have more,
since he who was peace
is gone to the war?
    Give me leave to cry
    on the seashore.

    Don't seek to stop me,
or hold me to blame,
one may be just
but the other's extreme;
    if truly you love me,
why do me this harm?
Or would you prefer me
dead or struck dumb?
    Give me leave to cry
    on the seashore.

    Who wouldn't cry,
sweet mother of mine,
even had she
a heart of stone,
    who wouldn't shout
to see wither and wane
the greenest years
of my youthful season?
    Give me leave to cry
    on the seashore.

    Let the nights hide away,
since the eyes are gone
that kept mine always
open till dawn,
    let the nights not see
me so alone,
now half my bed's
not needed again.
    Give me leave to cry
    on the seashore.

2. *Romance (1580)*

Hermana Marica,
mañana que es fiesta,
no irás tú a la amiga,
ni yo iré a la escuela.
    Pondraste el corpiño,
y la saya buena,
cabezón labrado,
toca y albanega;
    y a mí me pondrán
mi camisa nueva,
sayo de palmilla,
media de estameña;
    y si hace bueno
trairé la montera,
que me dio la Pascua
mi señora abuela,
    y el estadal rojo
con lo que le cuelga,
que trajo el vecino
cuando fue a la feria.
    Iremos a misa,
veremos la iglesia,
daranos un cuarto
mi tía la ollera.
    Compraremos de él
(que nadie lo sepa)
chochos y garbanzos
para la merienda;
    y en la tardecica,
en nuestra plazuela,
jugaré yo al toro,
y tú a las muñecas,
    con las dos hermanas,
Juana y Madalena,
y las dos primillas,
Marica y la tuerta;
    y si quiere madre
dar las castañetas,

2. [Marica, my sister]

Marica, my sister,
tomorrow is fiesta,
you won't go to school
nor I to the college.

You'll put on your bodice
and your best skirt,
the embroidered collar,
your headscarf and hairnet;

and I will be dressed in
my newest shirt,
my gown of blue cloth,
and my worsted stockings;

and if it's a fine day,
I'll wear the smart cap
dearest Grandma
gave me for Christmas

and the red sash
with the holy stuff on it
which our neighbour brought back
when he went to the fair.

We'll go to mass
and see the church,
our aunt the potter
will give me a penny.

With it we'll buy
(but don't tell anybody)
beans and chickpeas
for our picnic;

in the afternoon
in our little square
I'll play at bulls,
and you with your dolls,

with the two sisters,
Juana and Magdalena,
and the cousins, Marica
and the one with one eye;

and if Mother will get
the castanets,

podrás tanto de ello
bailar en la puerta;
    y al son del adufe
cantará Andrehuela:
No me aprovecharon,
madre, las hierbas;
    y yo, de papel
haré una librea,
teñida con moras,
por que bien parezca,
    y una caperuza
con muchas almenas;
pondré por penacho
las dos plumas negras
    del rabo del gallo,
que acullá en la huerta
anaranjeamos
las Carnestolendas;
    y en la caña larga
pondré una bandera
con dos borlas blancas
en sus tranzaderas;
    y en mi caballito
pondré una cabeza
de guadamecí,
dos hilos por riendas;
    y entraré en la calle
haciendo corvetas;
yo y otros del barrio,
que son más de treinta,
    jugaremos cañas
junto a la plazuela
porque Barbolilla
salga acá y nos vea;
    Bárbola, la hija
de la panadera,
la que suele darme
tortas con manteca,
    porque algunas veces
hacemos, yo y ella

you can dance till you drop
in front of the door,
    while Andrehuela
sings to the tambourine:
"The herbs, Mother,
they did me no good."
    And I will make
from paper a livery,
stained with blackberry
to make it look good,
    and a cap cut out
with jagged edges;
I'll wear for a plume
the two black feathers
    from the tail of the rooster
we stoned with oranges
out there in the orchard
during Carnival,
    and on my lance
I'll have a flag
with two white tassels
where it's tied on,
    and for my horse
I'll have a head
of colored leather,
two strings for reins;
    I'll enter the square,
prancing, curvetting,
and with the rest of the gang—
there's more than thirty—
    we'll joust with canes
next to the square,
so young Bárbola
will come out and see us,
    Bárbola (you know her,
her mother's the baker),
she likes to give me
cakes and pastries,
    because of the thing
we do together,

las bellaquerías
detrás de la puerta.

3. *Letrilla (1581)*

Ándeme yo caliente
y ríase la gente.

Traten otros del gobierno
del mundo y sus monarquías,
mientras gobiernan mis días
mantequillas y pan tierno,
y las mañanas de invierno
naranjada y aguardiente,
    y ríase la gente.

Coma en dorada vajilla
el príncipe mil cuidados,
como píldoras dorados;
que yo en mi pobre mesilla
quiero más una morcilla
que en el asador reviente,
    y ríase la gente.

Cuando cubra las montañas
de blanca nieve el enero,
tenga yo lleno el brasero
de bellotas y castañas,
y quien las dulces patrañas
del Rey que rabió me cuente,
    y ríase la gente.

Busque muy en buena hora
el mercader nuevos soles;
yo conchas y caracoles
entre la menuda arena,
escuchando a Filomena
sobre el chopo de la fuente,
    y ríase la gente.

she and I,
behind the door.

3. [Let them laugh]

Just let me be warm and easy,
and let them laugh, if they will.

Let others of the governance
of the world speak and its kingdoms,
I'd rather my days were ruled
by fresh rolls and butter;
and if in winter I've my fill
of orange conserve and brandy,
let them laugh, if they will.

Let princes eat from golden plates
a thousand tribulations,
gilded like a pill;
I at my simple cottage board
prefer a nice black pudding,
spitting and hissing on the grill.
Let them laugh, if they will.

When the mountaintops are covered
in January's white snows,
I'm happy seeing my brazier full
of acorns and sweet chestnuts,
with one beside me who can tell
tales of the mad king's exploits.
Let them laugh, if they will.

The merchant can go, and welcome,
to seek his new horizons;
while I stay here and search the sands
for any pretty seashell,
and listen to the nightingale
in the poplar beside the well
and let them laugh, if they will.

Pase a medianoche el mar,
y arda en amorosa llama
Leandro por ver su Dama;
que yo más quiero pasar
del golfo de mi lagar
la blanca o roja corriente,
    y ríase la gente.

Pues Amor es tan crüel,
que de Píramo y su amada
hace tálamo una espada,
do se juntan ella y él,
sea mi Tisbe un pastel,
y la espada sea mi diente,
    y ríase la gente.

4. *Letrilla (1581)*

Da bienes Fortuna
que no están escritos:
    cuando pitos flautas,
    cuando flautas pitos.

¡Cuán diversas sendas
se suelen seguir
en el repartir
honras y haciendas!
A unos da encomiendas,
a otros sambenitos.
    cuando pitos flautas,
    cuando flautas pitos.

A veces despoja
de choza y apero
al mayor cabrero;
y a quien se le antoja
la cabra más coja
parió dos cabritos.

Let Leander burning
with desire for his lady love
struggle to pass the midnight sea,
but as for me, I'd rather swim
in floods that from my winepress spill
their red and white sparkling tides.
Let them laugh, if they will.

While Love so cruelly lets a sword
make the marriage bed
where Pyramus and his love
are to be joined forever,
let a pastry be my Thisbe,
my teeth the murdering steel,
and let them laugh, if they will.

4. [Flutes for whistles]

Fortune gives gifts
that aren't what you asked for:
flutes for whistles,
and whistles for flutes.

How different are the routes
followed by Fortune
in her distribution
of honors and possessions:
great estates to some,
to others the Inquisition.
Flutes for whistles,
and whistles for flutes.

Sometimes she will strip
the most important goatherd
of his home and all his goods;
sometimes for the poor man
the lame goat gives birth
to a pair of kids.

cuando pitos flautas,
cuando flautas pitos.

En gustos de amores
suele traer bonanza
y en breve mudanza
los vuelve en dolores.
No da a uno favores,
y a otro infinitos.
    cuando pitos flautas,
    cuando flautas pitos.

Porque en una aldea
un pobre mancebo
hurtó sólo un huevo,
al sol bambolea;
y otro se pasea
con cien mil delitos.
    cuando pitos flautas,
    cuando flautas pitos.

5. Soneto (1582)

¡Oh claro honor del líquido elemento,
dulce arroyuelo de corriente plata,
cuya agua entre la hierba se dilata
con regalado son, con paso lento!,

pues la por quien helar y arder me siento
(mientras en ti se mira), Amor retrata
de su rostro la nieve y la escarlata
en tu tranquilo y blando movimiento,

vete como te vas; no dejes floja
la undosa rienda al cristalino freno
con que gobiernas tu veloz corriente;

que no es bien que confusamente acoja
tanta belleza en su profundo seno
el gran Señor del húmedo tridente.

Flutes for whistles,
and whistles for flutes.

In matters of love she'll give
a thousand joys one day,
then, with a sudden turn,
take them all away:
to one countless favors,
to another none.
    Flutes for whistles,
    and whistles for flutes.

In the village one
poor boy because he stole
just a single egg
is dancing in the air;
the author of a hundred crimes
is strolling in the sun.
    Flutes for whistles,
    and whistles for flutes.

5. [O shining stream]

O shining stream, O you who grace
the liquid world with flowing silver,
whose waters through the meadows wander
with pleasing sound, unhurrying pace,

since she for whom I burn, I freeze,
looks and presents for Love to seek
the snow and scarlet of her cheek
mirrored on your smooth surface, please

watch how you go; hold tight the reins
and regulate with crystal bit
the restless steeds of your swift current;

for it's not right that in disarray
her beauty should go down to meet
the great Lord of the dripping trident.

6. Romance (1582)

Diez años vivió Belerma
con el corazón difunto,
que le dejó en testamento
aquel francés boquirrubio.
    Contenta vivió con él,
aunque a mí me dijo alguno
que viviera más contenta
con trecientas mil de juro.
    A verla vino Doña Alda,
viuda del conde Rodulfo,
conde que fue en Normandía
lo que a Jesucristo plugo.
    Y hallándola muy triste
sobre un estrado de luto,
con los ojos que ya eran
orinales de Neptunio,
    riéndose muy despacio
de su llorar importuno,
sobre el muerto corazón
envuelto en un paño sucio,
    le dice: "amiga Belerma,
cese tan necio diluvio,
que anegará vuestros años,
y ahogará vuestros gustos.
    "Estése allá Durandarte
donde la suerte le cupo;
buen pozo haya su alma,
y pozo que esté sin cubo.
    "Si él os quiso mucho en vida,
también le quisistes mucho,
y si tiene abierto el pecho,
queréllese de su escudo.
    "¿Qué culpa tuvistes vos
de su entierro, siendo justo,
que el que como bruto muere,
que le entierren como a bruto?
    "Muriera él acá en Paris
a do tiene su sepulcro,

6. [Belerma]

Ten years Belerma lived
with the dead heart
that half-baked Frenchman
left her in his will.

She was quite happy with it,
though I've heard a rumor
she'd have been happier still
with three thousand a year.

Doña Alda came to see her,
Count Rudolph's widow—
that was a count in Normandy
for as long as God willed it.

Finding her very sad
on a mound of black cushions,
with eyes that were truly
like Neptune's urinals,

Doña Alda laughed most deliberately
at such incontinent grief
over a dead heart
wrapped in a dirty cloth,

and said: "Belerma, my dear,
put an end to this foolish flood;
it can only destroy your youth
and drown all your pleasures.

Let Durandarte remain
where fate decreed;
let him rest in peace,
in his foreign field.

He loved you a lot, no doubt,
but you loved him the same;
if there's a hole in his chest,
his shield's to blame,

His burial's not your fault,
it's only reasonable
that he who dies like a brute
should be buried like one too.

Why couldn't he die here in Paris,
where there's a grave for him?

que allí le hicieran lugar
los antepasados suyos.
    "Volved luego a Montesinos
ese corazón que os trujo,
y enviadle a preguntar
si por gavilán os tuvo,
    "Descosed y desnudad
las tocas de lienzo crudo,
el monjilón de bayeta
y el manto basto, peludo;
    "que, aun las viudas más viejas,
y de años más caducos,
las tocas cubren a enero,
y los monjiles a julio,
    "cuanto más a una muchacha,
que le faltan días algunos
para cumplir los treinta anos,
que yo desdichada cumplo.
    "Seis hace, si bien me acuerdo,
el día de Santiñuflo,
que perdí aquel mal logrado
que hoy entre los vivos busco.
    "Holguéme de cuatro y ocho,
haciéndoles dos mil hurtos,
a las palomas de besos,
y a las tórtolas de arrullos.
    "Sentí su fin, pero más
que muriese sin ver fructo,
sin ver flujo de mi vientre,
porque siempre tuve pujo,
    "mas no por eso ultrajé
mi buena tez con rasguños,
cabal me quedó el cabello,
y los ojos casi enjutos.
    "Aprended de mí, Belerma,
holguémonos de consuno,
llévese el mar lo llorado,
y lo suspirado el humo.
    "No hiléis memorias tristes
en este aposento obscuro,

Those ancestors of his
could have made room.

Now give Montesinos back
that heart he brought
and write to ask him,
did he think you're a hawk
        or what? Undo, tear off
that coarse linen toque,
that nunnish robe,
and the rough hairy mantle,

        for even in the oldest widows,
the most decrepit and gray,
it the toque covers January,
the robe conceals July.

        let alone in a young girl
who has not yet arrived
as I, worse luck, have,
at the ripe age of thirty.

        It's six years, if I'm right,
the day of St. Humphrey,
that I lost that hapless wretch
whom I've yet to replace.

        I had a great time of it,
stealing two thousand
kisses from the lovebirds,
cooings from the doves.

        I was sad at his death,
sadder still he died childless,
no fruit from my womb;
I was always too anxious.

        But I still didn't scratch
my complexion to pieces,
and my hair stayed intact,
my eyes all but dry.

        Now Belerma, listen to me,
let us have fun together,
let the sea wash away the tears
and the sighs vanish like smoke.

        Don't sit weaving sad memories
in this gloomy old room,

que cual gusano de seda
moriréis en el capullo.
    "Haced lo que en su fin hace
el pájaro sin segundo,
que nos habla en sus cenizas
de pretérito y futuro.
    "Llorad su muerte, mas sea
con lagrimillas al uso;
de lo mal pasado nazca
lo por venir más seguro.
    "Pongámonos a la par
dos toquitas de repulgo,
ceja en arco, manos blancas,
y dos perritos lanudos.
    "Hiedras verdes somos ambas,
a quien dejaron sin muros
de la muerte y del amor
baterías e infortunios.
    "Busquemos por do trepar,
que, a lo que de ambas presumo,
no nos faltarán en Francia
pared gruesa, tronco duro.
    "La iglesia de san Dionís
canónigos tiene muchos
delgados, cariaguileños,
carihartos y espaldudos.
    "Escojamos como en peras
dos déligos capotuncios,
de aquestos que andan en mulas,
y tienen algo de mulos;
    "destos Alejandros Magnos,
que no tienen por disgusto,
por dar en nuestros broqueles,
que demos en sus escudos.
    "De todos los Doce Pares
y sus nones, abrenuncio,
que calzan bragas de malla
y de acero los pantuflos.
"¿De que nos sirven, amiga,
petos fuertes, yelmos lucios?

or else like the silkworm
you'll stifle in your cocoon.

Take your cue from the end
of the peerless creature
which in its ashes tells of
the past and the future.

Mourn his death, if you will
but with customary tears;
from past misfortune see that
a securer future appears.

We'll both have the same
neatly sewn caps,
well-painted eyebrows,
white hands, and lapdogs.

We are both like green ivy:
the demands and the sorrows
of death and of love
left us nothing to cling to.

Let us seek a support,
for if I know us at all,
in France we won't lack for
a strong trunk or firm wall.

The abbey of Saint Denis
has canons aplenty,
slim and hawk-nosed or
round-cheeked and broad shouldered.

Let's have ourselves now
two rollicking clerics,
the kind who ride mules
and have the same bent,

two such Alexanders
who won't shrink in the least
from falling on our shields,
or covering us with theirs.

I renounce the twelve Peers,
odds, evens, the whole pack,
with their slippers of steel
and their chain-mail pants.

What do *we* want, my dear,
with breastplates and helmets?

armados hombres queremos,
armados, pero desnudos.

"De vuestra Mesa Redonda
francos paladines, huyo,
donde ayunos os sentáis,
y os levantáis más ayunos;

"la de cuatro esquinas quiero,
que la ventura me puso
en casa de un cuatro picos,
de todos cuatro picudo,

"donde sirven, la Cuaresma,
sabrosísimos besugos,
y turmas en el Carnal,
con su caldillo y su zumo."

Más iba a decir Doña Alda,
pero a lo demás dio un nudo,
porque de Don Montesinos
entró un pajecillo zurdo.

7. *Soneto (1582)*

Mientras por competir con tu cabello
oro bruñido al sol relumbra en vano,
mientras con menosprecio en medio el llano
mira tu blanca frente el lilio bello;

mientras a cada labio, por cogello,
siguen más ojos que al clavel temprano,
y mientras triunfa con desdén lozano,
del luciente cristal tu gentil cuello,

goza cuello, cabello, labio y frente,
antes que lo que fue en tu edad dorada
oro, lilio, clavel, cristal luciente,

no sólo en plata o víola troncada
se vuelva, mas tú y ello juntamente
en tierra, en humo, en polvo, en sombra, en nada.

We'll have our men armed,
armed, yes, but naked.
    You can keep your Round Table
and its chivalrous knights,
who sit down to eat fasting
and rise again starving.
    Let mine have four corners;
for I'm to be in the house
of a four-cornered hat,
pricked by all four of them,
    where in Lent they serve up
fine bream and in Carnival
sheep's testicles with all
their broth and their juices."
    Doña Alda would have said more,
but she put a sock in it,
when Montesinos's left-handed page
came in without knocking.

7. [Now while to match your hair . . .]

Now while to match your hair bright gold must know
it seeks in vain to mirror the sun's rays,
and while amid the fields with envious gaze
the lily regards the whiteness of your brow;

and while on each red lip attend more eyes
than wait on the carnation, as if intent
on plucking it, and while your graceful neck
outdoes bright crystal with disdainful ease,

enjoy them all, neck, hair, lip, and brow,
before the gold and lily of your heyday,
the red carnation, crystal brightly gleaming,

are changed to silver and withered violet,
and you and they together must revert
to earth, to smoke, to dust, to shadow, to nothing.

8. Romance (1582)

¡Que se nos va la pascua, mozas,
que se nos va la pascua!

Mozuelas las de mi barrio,
loquillas y confiadas,
mirad no os engañe el tiempo,
la edad y la confianza.
No os dejéis lisonjear
de la juventud lozana,
porque de caducas flores
teje el tiempo sus guirnaldas.
¡Que se nos va la pascua, mozas,
que se nos va la pascua!

Vuelan los ligeros años
y con presurosas alas
nos roban, como harpías,
nuestras sabrosas vïandas,
La flor de la maravilla
esta verdad nos declara,
porque le hurta la tarde
lo que le dio la mañana.
¡Que se nos va la pascua, mozas,
que se nos va la pascua!

Mirad que cuando pensáis
que hacen la señal de la alba
las campanas de la vida,
es la queda y os desarma
de vuestro color y lustre,
de vuestro donaire y gracia,
y quedáis todas perdidas
por mayores de la marca.
¡Que se nos va la pascua, mozas,
que se nos va la pascua!

Yo sé de una buena vieja
que fue en un tiempo rubia y zarca,
y que al presente le cuesta

8. [The party's over]

The party's ending, girls,
the party's over!

Hey there, you girls of my parish
with your wild airs and your flaunting,
watch out, you'll be deceived by time,
by age and over-confidence.
    Don't let yourselves be flattered
by the magic charms of youth
because from fading flowers
Time weaves the funeral wreath.
The party's ending, girls,
the party's over!

    Lightly the years fly by
and in their hurried flight
like harpies snatch away
our most enticing sweets.
    The tiger flower, the marvel
of Peru reveals this truth,
because afternoon steals from it
the bloom that morning gave.
The party's ending, girls,
the party's over!

    Look out because when you think
dawn prayers are being sounded
by the tolling bells of life,
it's the curfew, which divests you
    of all your color and shine,
your precious wit and grace,
and all of you are lost
and past your sell-by date.
The party's ending, girls,
the party's over!

    I know of one good woman
once blue-eyed and fair,
who now can't find it in her

harto caro el ver su cara;
    porque su bruñida frente
y sus mejillas se hallan
más que roquete de obispo
encogidas y arrugadas.
    ¡Que se nos va la pascua, mozas,
    que se nos va la pascua!

    Y sé de otra buena vieja,
que un diente que le quedaba
se lo dejó, estotro día,
sepultado en unas natas;
    y con lágrimas le dice:
"Diente mío de mi alma,
yo sé cuando fuistes perla,
aunque ahora no sois nada."
    ¡Que se nos va la pascua, mozas,
    que se nos va la pascua!

    Por eso, mozuelas locas,
antes que la edad avara
el rubio cabello de oro
convierta en luciente plata,
    quered cuando sois queridas,
amad cuando sois amadas;
mirad, bobas, que detrás
se pinta la ocasión calva.
    ¡Que se nos va la pascua, mozas,
    que se nos va la pascua!

9. *Romance (1583)*

    Amarrado al duro banco
de una galera turquesca,
ambas manos en el remo
y ambos ojos en la tierra,
    un forzado de Dragut
en la playa de Marbella
se quejaba al ronco son

to look at her own face,
    because of her blackened forehead,
because of her sunken cheeks,
more gathered and more pleated
than a bishop's rochet.
The party's ending, girls,
    the party's over!

    I know too of another
who lost the other day
the one tooth she still boasted
in the cold grave of a custard
    and said to it through her tears:
"Dear tooth, I still remember
the days when you were a pearl,
you who are nothing now."
The party's ending, girls,
    the party's over!

    So then, you crazy girls,
before the miserly years
transform your mane of gold
into shining silver,
    give love in return for love,
and don't stint those who love you.
For remember, fools, from behind
Opportunity's shown bald.
The party's ending, girls,
    the party's over!

9. [Anchored to the hard bench]

    Anchored to the hard bench
of a Turkish galley
with both hands on the oar
and both eyes on the land,
    a Spanish slave of Dragut
off Marbella's beach complains
in time to the harsh rhythm

del remo y de la cadena:
"¡Oh sagrado mar de España,
famosa playa serena,
teatro donde se han hecho
cien mil navales tragedias!

"Pues eres tú el mismo mar
que con tus crescientes besas
las murallas de mi patria,
coronadas y soberbias,

"tráeme nuevas de mi esposa,
y dime si han sido ciertas
las lágrimas y suspiros
que me dice por sus letras;

"porque si es verdad que llora
mi captiverio en tu arena,
bien puedes al mar del Sur
vencer en lucientes perlas.

"Dame ya, sagrado mar,
a mis demandas respuesta,
que bien puedes, si es verdad
que las aguas tienen lengua;

"pero, pues no me respondes,
sin duda alguna que es muerta,
aunque no lo debe ser,
pues que vivo yo en su ausencia.

"Pues he vivido diez años
sin libertad y sin ella,
siempre al remo condenado,
a nadie matarán penas"

En esto se descubrieron
de la Religión seis velas,
y el comitré mandó usar
al forzado de su fuerza.

10. Romance (1584)

Noble desengaño,
gracias doy al cielo
que rompiste el lazo

of the oars and the chains:
"Oh sacred sea of Spain!
Oh serene and lovely shore!
how many marine tragedies
have played out here before!

Since you are the same sea
that kisses with its tides
the walls of my native town
with their ramparts and their towers,

bring me tidings of my wife
and tell me she's not lying
when she tells me in her letters
of her tears and her sighing;

if it's true that on your sands
for my bondage she sheds tears,
then you can boast your beaches
surpass the South Sea in pearls.

Answer me, sea, I pray you,
that's something you can do,
since water has a tongue,
if what they say is true.

But since you don't reply
it must mean she is dead,
although it's hardly possible
that without her I still live.

If without her and liberty,
for ten years I've lived on,
always chained to this oar,
then grief never killed anyone."

But just then on the horizon
six Christian sails were sighted,
and the overseer ordered
the slave to put his back into it.

10. [Noble disenchantment]

Noble disenchantment,
I give thanks to heaven
that you severed the bond

que me tenía preso.
   Por tan gran milagro
colgaré en tu templo
las graves cadenas
de mis graves yerros.
   Las fuertes coyundas
del yugo de acero,
que con tu favor
sacudí del cuello,
   las húmedas velas
y los rotos remos,
que escapé del mar
y ofrecí en el puerto,
   ya de tus paredes
serán ornamento,
gloria de tu nombre,
y de Amor descuento.
   Y así, pues que triunfas
del rapaz arquero,
tiren de tu carro
y sean tu trofeo
   locas esperanzas,
vanos pensamientos,
pasos esparcidos,
livianos deseos,
   rabiosos cuidados,
ponzoñosos celos,
infernales glorias,
gloriosos infiernos.
   Compóngante himnos,
y digan sus versos
que libras captivos
y das vista a ciegos.
   Ante tu deidad
hónrense mil fuegos
del sudor precioso
del árbol sabeo.
   Pero ¿quien me mete
en cosas de seso,
y en hablar de veras
en aquestos tiempos

that kept me a captive.
    For such a miracle
I will hang in your shrine
the oppressive manacles
of all my grave sins.
    The cumbersome harness
of the heavy iron yoke
that with your assistance
I learned to shake off;
    the waterlogged sails
and the splintered oars
I retrieved from the sea
and offered in the port
    will go to adorn
the walls of your temple
in your name's honor,
to Love's confusion.
    And so, in your triumph
over the boy archer,
let your carriage be pulled by
these, as your trophies:
    crazy expectations,
vain cogitations,
misdirected steps,
libidinous desires,
    raging concerns,
poisonous jealousies,
infernal glories,
and glorious hells.
    Let hymns be sung to you
whose verses will tell
how you rescue captives
and give sight to the blind.
    Before your deity
may a thousand fires be
fed by the precious sweat
of the Sabaean tree.
    But who told me to speak
of serious matters,
to say what I mean,
when we live in such times

donde el que más trata
de burlas y juegos,
ese es quien se viste
más a lo moderno?

Ingrata señora,
de tus aposentos,
mas dulce y sabrosa
que nabo en adviento,

aplícame un rato
el oído atento,
que quiero hacer auto
de mis devaneos:

¡qué de noches frías
que me tuvo el hielo
tal, que por esquina
me juzgó tu perro,

y alzando la pierna
con gentil denuedo,
me argentó de plata
los zapatos negros!

!Qué de noches de estas,
señora, me acuerdo
que andando a buscar
chinas por el suelo,

para hacer la seña
por el agujero,
al tomar la china
me ensucié los dedos!

¡Qué de días anduve
cargado de acero,
con harto trabajo,
porque estaba enfermo!;

como estaba flaco,
parecía cencerro:
hierro por de fuera,
por de dentro hueso.

¡Qué de meses y años
que viví muriendo
en la Peña Pobre
sin ser Beltenebros;

that he who would appear
most up-to-date
must deal in nothing
but trifles and jokes?

Unmerciful lady,
enthroned in your boudoir,
with more sweetness and savor
than turnip at Advent,

lend me for a moment
an attentive ear,
while I make a confession
of all my bufoonery:

those freezing cold nights
whose icy grip had me
in such state that your dog
thought me a gatepost

and raising his leg
with elegant insolence
plated my best
black shoes with silver!

How many nights, lady,
do I remember
that scratching around
for pebbles on the floor

to throw at your window
for giving the signal
I took one in my hands
that was covered in filth!

How often I went
weighed down with steel,
which caused me great hardship
because I was ill,

being then so thin,
I was just like a bell:
iron on the outside,
inside a bare clapper.

What months and what years
I roamed Peña Pobre
more dead than alive,
though no Beltenebros;

donde me acaeció
mil días enteros
no comer sino uñas,
haciendo sonetos!

¡Qué de necedades
escribí en mil pliegos,
que las ríes tú ahora
y yo las confieso!

Aunque las tuvimos
ambos, en un tiempo,
yo por discreciones
y tú por requiebros.

¡Qué de medias noches
canté en mi instrumento:
Socorred, señora,
con agua a mi fuego!

Donde aunque tú no
socorriste luego,
socorrió el vecino
con un gran caldero.

Adiós, mi señora,
porque me es tu gesto
chimenea en verano
y nieve en invierno,

y el bazo me tienes
de guijarros lleno,
porque creo que bastan
seis años de necio.

11. *Romance* (*1585*)

Entre los sueltos caballos
de los vencidos cenetes,
que por el campo buscaban
entre la sangre lo verde,

aquel español de Oran
un suelto caballo prende,

for sometimes a thousand
days I ate nothing
but my own fingernails,
writing you sonnets!
  How many idiocies
I committed to paper,
which now you will laugh at
and I have to blush for!
  Although at the time we
both saw them differently:
I thought them witty,
you took them for compliments.
  How many midnights
I sang to the lute:
"Rescue me, lady,
pour water on my fire!"
  When, although you never
came to the rescue,
the neighbour helped out
with a whole panful.
  Farewell now, my lady,
for to me your service
is ice in midwinter,
a fireplace in summer,
  and all my reward is
a bellyfull of stones;
and I think it's enough:
six years of foolishness.

11. [Among the riderless horses]

  Among the riderless horses
of the scattered Berber troop
that were seeking about the field
green grass in all that blood,
  the Spanish knight from Oran
chooses one riderless steed,

por sus relinchos lozano,
y por sus cernejas fuerte,
    para que lo lleve a él,
y a un moro captivo lleve,
un moro que ha captivado,
capitán de cien jinetes.
    En el ligero caballo
suben ambos, y él parece,
de cuatro espuelas herido,
que cuatro alas lo mueven.
    Triste camina el alarbe,
y, lo más bajo que puede,
ardientes suspiros lanza,
y amargas lágrimas vierte.
    Admirado el español
de ver, cada vez que vuelve,
que tan tiernamente llore
quien tan duramente hiere,
    con razones, le pregunta,
comedidas y corteses,
de sus suspiros la causa,
si la causa lo consiente.
    El captivo, como tal,
sin excusas le obedece,
y a su piadosa demanda
satisface de esta suerte:
    "Valiente eres, capitán,
y cortés como valiente;
por tu espada y por tu trato
me has captivado dos veces.
    "Preguntado me has la causa
de mis suspiros ardientes,
y débote la respuesta
por quien soy y por quien eres.
    "En los Gelves nací, el año
que os perdistes en los Gelves,
de una berberisca noble
y de un turco matasiete.
    "En Tremecén me crié
con mi madre y mis parientes,

whose neighing denotes mettle,
and its fetlocks strength,
     to carry him and another:
a captive he has taken,
a Moorish prisoner, captain
of a hundred Berber horsemen.
     Both of them mount the charger
and urge him on his way,
so with four spurs to goad him
he seems to have wings and fly.
     Sadly goes the Arab,
and hoping that no one hears
he sighs passionate sighs
and weeps bitter tears.
     Each time he turns his head
the Spaniard is amazed to see
how one who dealt such blows
can weep so tenderly,
     and so he asks politely,
with grave and courteous words,
what is the cause of these sighs,
if it's something that can be told.
The Moor, as honor requires,
obeys without hesitation,
and the compassionate query
is answered in this fashion:
     "You're a brave soldier, Captain,
and courteous as you are brave;
by your sword and by your treatment
you have captured me twice over.
     You ask what is the reason
why I groan and sigh;
for what I am and what you are,
I owe you a reply.
     I was born in Djerba the year
your side was defeated there,
son of a noble Berber
and a prodigious Turk.
     I grew up in Tremecen
with my mother and my kin,

después que perdí a mi padre,
corsario de tres bajeles.

"Junto a mi casa vivía,
porque más cerca muriese,
una dama del linaje
de los nobles melioneses,

"extremo de las hermosas,
cuando no de las crueles,
hija al fin de estas arenas,
engendradoras de sierpes.

"Cada vez que la miraba
salía un sol por su frente,
de tantos rayos ceñido
cuantos cabellos contiene.

"Juntos así nos criamos,
y Amor, en nuestras niñeces,
hirió nuestras corazones
con arpones diferentes.

"Labró el oro en mis entrañas
dulces lazos, tiernas redes,
mientras el plomo en las suyas
libertades y desdenes.

"Apenas vide trocada
la dureza de esta sierpe,
cuando tú me captivaste:
¡mira si es bien que lamente!"

12. *Soneto (1585)*

A Córdoba

!Oh excelso muro, oh torres coronadas
de honor, de majestad, de gallardía!
¡Oh gran río, gran rey de Andalucía,
de arenas nobles, ya que no doradas!

¡Oh fértil llano, oh sierras levantadas,
que privilegia el cielo y dora el dia!
¡Oh siempre gloriosa patria mía,
tanto por plumas cuanto por espadas!

after I'd lost my father,
who led three pirate ships.
    Next to my house there lived,
in order that I should die,
a lady of the lineage
of the nobles of Meliona.
    Of beauties she was the summit
and also one of the cruellest,
a true child of the desert
that breeds the most venomous serpents.
    When I looked at her it seemed
the sun was shining there,
and every ray of that sun
was streaming from her hair.
We grew up side by side,
and Love in our childhood days
wounded both our hearts
but in quite different ways.
    His golden arrow forged
in my heart tender snares;
liberties and disdain
his leaden one in hers.
    But I'd seen a sudden change,
a softening of her heart,
just before I became your prisoner;
now judge if I've cause to lament!"

12. [To Córdoba]

To Córdoba
O lofty wall, O towers nobly crowned
with honor and majesty, with grace and daring,
O mighty river, great Andalusian king,
with sands that are noble, even if not gold-bearing!

O steeply rising hills, O fertile plain,
which heaven smiles on and the sunshine gilds.
O ever glorious native land of mine,
as famous for your pens as for your swords,

Si entre aquellas ruinas y despojos
que enriquece Genil y Dauro baña
tu memoria no fue alimento mío,

nunca merezcan mis ausentes ojos
ver tu muro, tus torres y tu río,
tu llano y sierra, i oh patria, oh flor de España!

13. *Romance (1587)*

Servía en Orán al Rey
un español con dos lanzas,
y con el alma y la vida
a una gallarda africana,
    tan noble como hermosa,
tan amante como amada,
con quien estaba una noche,
cuando tocaron al arma.
    Trecientos cenetes eran
de este rebato la causa,
que los rayos de la luna
descubrieron sus adargas;
    las adargas avisaron
a las mudas atalayas,
las atalayas los fuegos,
los fuegos a las campanas;
    y ellas al enamorado,
que en los brazos de su dama
oyó el militar estruendo
de las trompas y las cajas.
    Espuelas de honor le pican,
y freno de amor le para;
no salir es cobardía,
ingratitud es dejalla.
    Del cuello pendiente ella,
viéndole tomar la espada,
con lágrimas y suspiros
le dice aquestas palabras:

if among those ruins and remains
the Genil enriches and the Dauro bathes
your memory ever ceased to feed my soul,

may it never to my absent eyes be granted
to see your walls, your towers, your river again,
your plain and hills, O my land, O flower of Spain!

13. [In Oran]

    In Oran a Spanish knight
with two lances did his duty
to the King; but body and soul
he gave to an African beauty,
    a lady of noble blood
who loved as truly as he did;
he was with her one night when
the call to arms was sounded.
    Three hundred Berber horsemen
had caused this hue and cry,
their glinting shields revealed
by the moon in the sky.
    The shields it was that gave
the silent watchers warning,
the watchers lit the fires,
the fires set the bells tolling,
    and the bells aroused the lover,
who lying in his lady's arms
heard the martial clamor
of the trumpets and the drums.
    If honor pricks him on,
love applies the brake;
not to go is cowardly,
yet loyalty holds him back.
    She hangs about his neck
as he reaches for his sword;
and amid tears and sighs
she speaks these bitter words:

"Salid al campo, señor,
bañen mis ojos la cama;
que ella me será también,
sin vos, campo de batalla.

"Vestíos y salid apriesa,
que el general os aguarda;
yo os hago a vos mucha sobra,
y vos a él mucha falta.

"Bien podéis salir desnudo,
pues mi llanto no os ablanda;
que tenéis de acero el pecho
y no habéis menester armas."

Viendo el español brïoso
cuánto le detiene y habla,
le dice así: "Mi señora,
tan dulce como enojada,

"porque con honra y amor
yo me quede, cumple y vaya,
vaya a los moros el cuerpo,
y quede con vos el alma.

"Concededme, dueño mío,
licencia para que salga
al rebato en vuestro nombre,
y en vuestro nombre combata."

14. Romance (1587)

Hanme dicho, hermanas,
que tenéis cosquillas
de ver al que hizo
a Hermana Marica.

Por que no mováis,
el mismo os envía
de su misma mano
su persona misma;

digo, su aguileña
filomocosía,
ya que no pintada

"Go, then, go to your battle
and leave me here to weep,
in this bed, that if you're absent
allows me no peace in sleep.

"Go on, get dressed and go,
don't keep the general waiting;
I'm nothing to you, I know,
and he can't do without you.

"You may as well go naked;
since my tears can't win you over,
your heart is cased in steel,
you'll need no other armor"

When the impetuous Spaniard sees
how she clings to him so fiercely,
he says to her, "My lady,
so lovely and so angry,

"so that I to both honor and love
may give the service due,
let my body go forth to fight,
while my soul remains with you.

"Grant me this boon, my mistress:
give me leave to depart from you,
to go in your name to the field,
and to fight in your name too."

14. [Sisters, they tell me]

Sisters, they tell me
that you're just itching
to see him that produced
To Marica my sister.

So to spare you a movement,
he himself sends you,
by his very own hand,
his own personal self;

to wit, his aquiline
physiontology,
if not famed in painting,

al menos escrita,
　y su condición
que es tan peregrina
como cuantas vienen
de Francia a Galicia.
　Cuanto a lo primero,
es, su senoría,
un bendito zote
de muy buena vida,
　que come a las diez
y cena de día,
que duerme en mollido
y bebe con guindas;
　en los años, mozo,
viejo en las desdichas,
abierto de sienes,
cerrado de encías;
　no es grande de cuerpo,
pero bien podría
de cualquier higuera
alcanzaros higas;
　la cabeza al uso
muy bien repartida,
el cogote atrás,
la corona encima;
　la frente espaciosa
escombrada y limpia,
aunque con rincones,
cual plaza de villa;
　las cejas en arco,
como ballestillas
de sangrar aquellos
que con el pie firman;
　los ojos son grandes,
y mayor la vista,
pues conoce un gallo
entre cien gallinas;
　la nariz es corva,
tal, que bien podría
servir de alquitara

at least well described,
   and his general character
quite as peculiar as
anything a pilgrim finds
between France and Galicia.
   Now, as far as he goes,
His Worship is
a blessed idiot
with a fine lifestyle,
   who lunches at ten
and dines before dark,
sleeps in soft beds and
has cherries in his drink;
   in years a mere boy,
an old man in misfortunes,
with a broad forehead
and a tight mouth;
   he's not very big
but he could easily
reach you down a fig
from any old fig tree.
   The head is quite normal,
but very well organized,
with the back behind,
and the crown on top;
   the forehead's wide,
smooth and uncluttered,
though with some odd corners,
like an old town square;
   the eyebrows are arched
like the little bows
they use for bleeding
those who sign with their foot;
   the eyes are great,
his sight even better:
he can pick out a cock
among hundreds of hens;
   the nose has on it
a curve so big
it'd serve an apothecary

en una botica;
la boca no es buena,
pero, al mediodía
le da ella mas gusto
que la de su ninfa;
la barba, ni corta,
ni mucho crecida,
porque así se ahorran
cuellos de camisa;
fue un tiempo castaña,
pero ya es morcilla:
volveránla penas
en rucia tordilla;
los hombros y espaldas
son tales, que habría
a ser él San Blas
para mil reliquias;
lo demás, señoras,
que el manteo cobija,
parte son visiones,
parte maravillas.
Sé decir, al menos,
que en sus niñerías
ni pide a vecinos
ni falta a vecinas.
De su condición
deciros podría,
como quien la tiene
tan reconocida,
que es el mozo alegre,
aunque su alegría
paga mil pensiones
a la melarquía.
Es de tal humor,
que en salud se cría
muy sano, aunque no
de los de Castilla.
Es mancebo rico
desde las mantillas,
pues tiene (demás

for an alembic;
  the mouth's not great,
but with lunch on the table
it gives him more pleasure
than that of his sweetheart;
  the beard's neither too
short nor too bushy,
which in shirt collars
makes for economy;
  once it was brown
but now it's gone black:
cares will soon turn it
pepper and salt;
  his shoulders and back
are such there'd be plenty
were he Saint Blaise,
to fill a reliquary;
  as for the rest, ladies,
what's under the cloak,
well, it's partly visions
and partly wonders.

  I can assure you anyway
that for certain requirements
he doesn't borrow from neighbors
or disappoint neighbors' wives.

  As to his disposition,
I can certainly tell you,
as one who knows it
only too well,
  he's a cheerful chappy
though often his jollity
pays a big forfeit
to melancholy.

  His constitution is such
as to make him feel
he's in good shape, though not
like "those of Castille."

  He's been in clover
since his infancy,
for he has in addition

de una sacristía),
    barcos en la sierra,
y, en el río, viñas,
molinos de aceite,
que hacen harina,
    un jardin de flores,
y una muy gran silva
de varia lección,
adonde se crían
    árboles que llevan,
después de vendimias,
a poder de estiércol
pasas de lejía.
    Es enamorado
tan en demasía,
que es un mazacote,
que diga, un Macías;
    aunque no se muere
por aquestas niñas
que quieren con presa,
y piden con pinta;
    dales un botín,
dos octavas rimas,
tres sortijas negras,
cuatro clavellinas;
    y a las damiselas,
mas graves y ricas,
costosos regalos,
joyas peregrinas,
    porque para ellas
trae cuanto de Indias
guardan en sus senos
Lisboa y Sevilla.
    Tráelas de las huertas
regalos de Lima,
y de los arroyos
joyas de China.
    Tampoco es amigo
de andar por esquinas
vestido de acero,

to a sacristy,
boats in the mountains,
vines on the river,
some olive mills
that grind out flour,
    a flower garden,
and a very big wood
of miscellaneous delights
richly endowed
    with trees that bear
after the harvest
with the aid of manure
big black raisins.
    He's so incessantly
engaged in some love affair
that he's a total bore,
I mean a troubadour;
    though he won't pine away for
the girls who are always
taking tricks or
upping the stakes:
    as booty he gives them
one boot, two lines
of heroic verse, three
black rings, and four pinks;
    and for the other madams,
of more weight and substance
needing costlier gifts
and gems of rare brilliance,
    to them he brings
such treasure of the Indies
as Lisbon and Seville
hold in their vaults:
    from the orchards,
presents from Lima,
and from the streams,
diamonds of China.
    He's little inclined to
hang about on street corners
dolled up in steel

como de palmilla,
    porque, para él,
de la Ave María
al cuarto de la alba
anda la estantigua;
    y porque a su abuela
oyó que tenían
los de su linaje
no más de una vida,
    así desde entonces
la conserva y mira
mejor que oro en paño,
o pera en almíbar.
    No es de los curiosos
a quien califican
papeles de nuevas
de estado o milicia,
    porque son (y es cierto,
que el Bernia lo afirma)
hermanas de leche
nuevas y mentiras.
    No se le da un bledo,
que el otro le escriba,
o dosel le cubra,
o adórnelo mitra;
    no le quita el sueño
que de la Turquía
mil leños esconda
el mar de Sicilia;
    ni que el Inglés baje
hacia nuestras islas,
después que ha subido
sobre quien lo envía.
    Es su reverencia
un gran coronista,
porque en Salamanca
oyó Teología,
    sin perder mañana
su lección de prima,
y al anochecer,

as if it were velvet,
    because in his view
from the evening bell
till the dawn watch
ghosts and ghoulies
    are abroad, and it was
his grandma's belief
that those of his clan
have only the one life,
    and since she said it
he keeps his wrapped up
like gold in cotton,
pears in syrup.
    He's no nosey parker,
doesn't make a big thing
of news sheets describing
state affairs and battles:
    for, as the Italian
poet affirms,
news and lies
are from the same womb.
    He cares not a whit to be
theme for a writer,
or given a throne
or crowned with a miter.
    He's not kept awake
by fears of the Sicilian sea
concealing a thousand
vessels from Turkey
    nor dreams of the Englishman
bearing down on our islands
after getting on top of
the mistress who sends him.
    His Reverence is also
a great chronicler,
because in Salamanca
he read theology,
    never missing
a lecture at prime
or an evening class

lección de sobrina;
    y así es desde entonces
persona entendida,
si a su oído tañen
una chirimía.
    De las demás lenguas
es gran humorista,
señor de la griega
como de la escitia.
    Tiene por más suya
la lengua latina
que los alemanes
la persa o la egipcia.
    Habla la toscana
con tal policía,
que quien le oye dice
que nació en Coimbra;
    y en la portuguesa
es tal, que dirías
que mamó en Logroño
leche de borricas.
    De la Cosmografía
pasó pocas millas,
aunque oyó al Infante
las Siete Partidas;
    y así, entiende el mapa,
y de sus medidas
lo que el mapa entiende
del mal de la orina.
    Sabe que en los Alpes
es la nieve fría,
y caliente el fuego
en las Filipinas;
    que nació Zamora
del Duero en la orilla,
y que es natural
Burgos de Castilla;
    que desde La Mancha
llegan a Medina
más tarde los hombres

with a niece,
    and has been ever since
one who doesn't miss much:
play the bagpipes in his ear
and surely he'll hear it.

    When it comes to your languages,
he's a great humorist:
a master of Greek
and even of Scythian.

    He thinks he's made Latin
more his own thing
than the Germans have
Persian or Egyptian.

    He handles the Tuscan
with such elegance
listeners say he must have
been born in Coimbra;

    as for his Portuguese
when he speaks it you'd think he
was suckled in Logroño
by a she-donkey.

    He never went far
in cosmography, though
he's read the "Seven
Divisions" of King Alfonso.

    Of maps and their measurements
he knows as much
as maps understand
of urinary infections.

    He knows that in the Alps
the snow is cold
and that fire is hot
in the Philippines;

    that Zamora grew up
on the banks of the Duero
and that Burgos is
a native of Castille,

    and that from La Mancha
men take longer
to reach Medina

que las golondrinas.
    Es hombre que gasta
en Astrología
toda su pobreza
con su picardía.
    Tiene su astrolabio
con sus baratijas,
su compás y globos
que pesan diez libras.
    Conoce muy bien
las siete Cabrillas,
la Bocina, el Carro
y las tres Marías.
    Sabe alzar figura,
si halla por dicha
o rey, o caballo,
o sota caída.
    Es fiero poeta,
si lo hay en la Libia,
y cuando lo toma
su mal de poesía,
    hace verso suelto
con Alejandría,
y con algarrobas
hace redondillas;
    compone romances
que cantan y estiman
los que cardan paños
y ovejas desquilan,
    y hace canciones
para su enemiga,
que de todo el mundo
son bien recibidas,
    pues en sus rebatos
todo el mundo limpia
con ellas de ingleses
a Fuenterrabía.
    Finalmente, él es,
señorazas mías,
el que dos mil veces

than the swallows.
    He's one who spends
more on astrology
than he can afford
plus all his astuteness.

    He has his astrolabe,
and the other baubles,
his compass and globes,
weighing ten pounds.

    He's pretty familiar
with the Pleiades,
the big Bear and the little one,
and Orion's belt.

    He'll show his hand
if he happens to pick up
a discarded king
or a queen or a jack.

    He's a ferocious poet,
if there's any in Libya,
and when he's seized by
the poetry mania

    he'll produce you loose verse
as if he's been purged,
while with carob seeds
he makes little round ones.

    He composes ballads
that are sung and admired
by the carders of cloth
and shearers of sheep,

    and he makes songs
to his sweet enemy
that people in general
seem to appreciate,

    for in time of need
they use them for wiping
Fuenterrabía
clean of the English.

    Finally he is,
great ladies, one who
two thousand times

os pide y suplica,
   que con los gorrones
de las plumas rizas
os hagáis gorronas
y os mostréis arpías;
   que no os sepultéis
el gusto en campillas,
y que a los bonetes
queráis las bonitas.

15. Soneto (1588)

Duélete de esa puente, Manzanares;
mira que dice por ahí la gente
que no eres río para media puente,
y que ella es puente para muchos mares.

Hoy, arrogante, te ha brotado a pares
húmedas crestas tu soberbia frente,
y ayer me dijo humilde tu corriente
que eran en marzo los caniculares.

Por el alma de aquel que ha pretendido
con cuatro onzas de agua de chicoria
purgar la villa y darte lo purgado,

me dí ¿cómo has menguado y has crecido?
¿cómo ayer te vi en pena y hoy en gloria?
—Bebióme un asno ayer, y hoy me ha meado.

16. Soneto (1588)

Grandes más que elefantes y que abadas,
títulos liberales como rocas,
gentiles hombres, sólo de sus bocas,
illustri cavaglier, llaves doradas;

begs and implores you
    that with regard to
the curly-haired whoremongers
you squeeze them dry,
use them like harpies;
    just don't hide your talents
under a bushel,
and as for the clergy,
let the pretty ones love them.

15. [The Bridge of Segovia]

That bridge of yours, Manzanares, it's a laugh;
listen to what the people round here say:
it's a bridge that ought to span a mighty sea,
and you're not river enough to merit half.

Today you're swollen with pride because you've grown
watery crests to grace your haughty brow,
but yesterday your meager flow said how
already in March the dog days had begun.

By the spirit of him who lately had a plan
to give Madrid a purgative and bestow
on you the filthy product of this deed,

tell me, I beg, how did you wax and wane,
in glory today, when yesterday so low?
"A donkey drank me—and today he peed."

16. [Elephant or rhinoceros]

Dukes weightier than elephant or rhinoceros,
noblemen as generous as a stone,
mouthpieces serving no mouth but their own,
court servants, *cavalieri* most illustrious;

hábitos, capas digo remendadas,
damas de haz y envés, viudas sin tocas,
carrozas de ocho bestias, y aun son pocas
con las que tiran y que son tiradas;

catarriberas, ánimas en pena,
con Bártulos y Abades la milicia,
y los derechos con espada y daga;

casas y pechos, todo a la malicia;
lodos con perejil y yerbabuena:
esto es la Corte. ¡Buena pro les haga!

17. Romance (1590)

Lloraba la niña
(y tenía razón)
la prolija ausencia
de su ingrato amor.
   Dejóla tan niña,
que apenas creo yo
que tenía los años
que ha que la dejó.
   Llorando la ausencia
del galán traidor,
la halla la luna
y la deja el sol,
   añadiendo siempre
pasión a pasión,
memoria a memoria,
dolor a dolor.
   Llorad corazón,
   que tenéis razón.

   Dícele su madre:
"Hija, por mi amor,
que se acabe el llanto,
o me acabe yo."

uniforms, patched capes with rank sewn on them,
two-faced females, widows done with mourning,
eight-horse coaches—an understatement, counting
the beasts that are pulled as well as those that pull them;

investigating officers, souls in torment,
militia armed with oath and affidavit,
laws that rely on swordsmen to construe them,

houses and hearts of malice, as they term it,
all wallowing in mud that's spiced with shit:
this is their court. And much good may it do them!

17. [The girl was mourning]

The girl was mourning
(and she had reason)
the prolonged absence
of her cruel lover.
So young he left her
I scarcely believe
she had then lived the years
that have passed since his leaving.
Mourning the absence
of the handsome cheat,
the moon finds her
as the sun leaves her,
adding forever
passion to passion,
memory to memory,
pain to pain.
Weep, heart,
for you have reason,

"Daughter, I beg you,"
her mother says,
"unless you would kill me,
let the tears cease."

Ella le responde:
"No podrá ser, no:
las causas son muchas,
los ojos son dos.

　"Satisfagan, madre,
tanta sinrazón,
y lágrimas lloren
en esta ocasión

　"tantas, como dellos
un tiempo tiró
flechas amorosas
el arquero diós.

　"Ya no canto, madre,
y si canto yo,
muy tristes endechas
mis canciones son;

　"porque el que se fue,
con lo que llevó,
se dejó el silencio,
y llevó la voz."

　Llorad corazón,
　que tenéis razón.

18. *Letrilla (1590)*

Ya que rompí las cadenas
de mis grillos y mis penas,
de extender con mucho error
la jurisdición de Amor,
que ahora me da por libre,
　Dios me libre.
Y de andar más por escrito
publicando mi delito,
sabiendo de ajenas vidas
tantas culpas cometidas
de que puedo hacer alarde,
　Dios me guarde.

De dama que se atribula
de comer huevos sin bula,

But she replies:
"That will not do:
the causes are many,
the eyes only two.

For so much injustice
let them atone,
as many tears weeping
for this situation

as in other days
from them were fired
amorous arrows
by the archer god.

I sing no more, Mother;
or if I do,
my song is only
a tale of woe,

since he who departed
making off with the spoils,
left only the silence,
the voice he stole."

Weep, heart,
for you have reason.

18. [Since I have broken free]

Since I have broken free
of every bond that bound me,
from the idiocy of renewing
Love's authority now when
he has no power over me,
Lord, deliver me.
And from appearing in print
to publicize my follies,
when in the lives of others
I see such faults committed,
so many examples to serve me,
Lord, preserve me.

From ladies who suffer torments
of conscience from eating an egg,

sabiendo que de su fama
un escrúpulo ni dragma
no podrá lavar el Tibre,
    Dios me libre.
Y del mercader devoto,
de conciencia manirroto,
que, acrecentando sus rentas,
pasa a menudo sus cuentas,
y a las ajenas tarde,
    Dios me guarde.

De doncella con maleta,
ordinario y estafeta,
que quiere contra derecho,
pasando por el estrecho,
llegar entera a Colibre,
    Dios me libre.
Y del galán perfumado,
para holocaustos guardado,
que hace cara a los afeites
para dar a sus deleites
espaldas, como cobarde,
    Dios me guarde.

De dama que de un ratón
huye al postrero rincón,
desmayada de mirallo,
y no temerá a caballo
que Ruger su lanza vibre,
    Dios me libre.
Y del galán que en la plaza
acuchilla y amenaza,
y si sale sin terceros,
hará como Don Gaiferos,
aunque Melisendra aguarde.
    Dios me guarde.

De doncella que entra en casa,
porque guisa y porque amasa,
y hace mejor un guisado

when even the river Tiber
would not suffice to cleanse
their tarnished reputations,
    Lord, deliver me.
And from the pious merchant
with a liberal conscience,
busily telling his beads
and presenting his accounts,
who never pays other people's,
    Lord, preserve me.

From the virgin with two couriers,
one regular, one express,
who defying natural law
plans to reach Collioure intact
by using the back door,
    Lord, deliver me.
And from the dandy perfumed
like a sacrificial victim,
who faces up to makeup,
but like a coward presents
his back to his delights,
    Lord, preserve me.

From the lady who sees a mouse
and fleeing to the furthest corner,
swoons at the sight, yet has,
when Roger's astride, no aversion
to seeing his lance quiver,
    Lord, deliver me.
From the buck who in the square
makes great play with his blade,
but if challenged on his own
exits like Don Gaiferos
when he made Melisandre wait,
    Lord, preserve me.

From the maid who comes to the house
to take charge in the kitchen
and cooks up a spicier stew

con la mujer del honrado
que con clavos y gengibre,
   Dios me libre.
Y de amigo cortesano
con las insignias de Jano,
desvelado en la cautela,
cuyo soplo a veces hiela,
y a veces abrasa y arde,
   Dios me guarde.

19. *Soneto* (*1594*)

De un caminante enfermo que se enamoró donde fue hospedado

Descaminado, enfermo, peregrino,
en tenebrosa noche, con pie incierto
la confusión pisando del desierto,
voces en vano dio, pasos sin tino.

Repetido latir, si no vecino,
distincto oyó de can siempre despierto,
y en pastoral albergue mal cubierto
piedad halló, si no halló camino.

Salió el Sol, y entre armiños escondida,
soñolienta beldad con dulce saña
salteó al no bien sano pasajero.

Pagará el hospedaje con la vida;
más le valiera errar en la montaña
que morir de la suerte que yo muero.

20. *Romance* (*1599*)

   Las aguas de Carrïón,
que a los muros de Palencia,
o son grillos de cristal,

with the injured citizen's wife
than she can with cloves and ginger,
    Lord, deliver me.
From the courtier friend,
with the insignia of Janus,
always looking behind him,
whose breath will sometimes freeze one,
and sometimes scald and burn one,
    Lord, preserve me.

19. [The sick traveler]

On a sick traveler, who fell in love in the place where he lodged

Directionless and sick, a pilgrim mired
in deepest night, with faltering foot advancing,
treading the incoherence of the desert,
all bearings lost, his cries remained unheard.

He heard the persistent barking, far away
yet quite distinct, of an unsleeping watchdog,
and in a rustic refuge, poorly roofed,
compassion found, but surely not his way.

The sun appeared and with it, nestled in ermine,
a beauty slowly waking, who with sweet strife
waylaid this traveler, still not well but ailing.

This lodging he must pay for with his life.
Was it not better wandering on the mountain,
than to die in the manner that I'm dying?

20. [Waters of the Carrión]

    A fisherman, a stranger,
with tears was augmenting
the Carrión's waters,

o espejos de sus almenas,
   un pescador extranjero
en un barquillo acrecienta,
llorando su libertad,
mal perdida en sus riberas.
   ¡Oh, qué bien llora!
   ¡Oh, cómo se lamenta!

Vio la ninfa más hermosa
que dio al aire rubias trenzas
que en el coro de Dïana,
que bajaba de las selvas
   tras un corcillo herido,
que, de bien flechado, vuela,
porque in la fuga son alas,
las que en la muerte son flechas.
   ¡Oh, qué bien llora!
   ¡Oh, cómo se lamenta!

Las redes al sol tendía
sobre la caliente arena,
cuando se vio salteado
de la cazadora bella.
   Más despedían sus ojos,
que trae su aljaba saetas,
y tanto más ponzoñosas,
cuanto es más desdén que hierba.
   ¡Oh, qué bien llora!
   ¡Oh, cómo se lamenta!

   "!Oh fiera para los hombres
perseguidora de fieras!"
—decía al son de los remos,
que gimen cuando él se queja—
"De ti murmuran las aguas,
por disimular mis quejas,
que no alcanzas lo que sigues,
y matas lo que te espera."
   ¡Oh, qué bien llora!
   ¡Oh, cómo se lamenta!

those crystal fetters
   of Palencia's walls
or their imaging mirrors,
mourning the freedom
he lost on these shores.
   Oh, how he weeps!
   How he complains!

   The fairest nymph ever
to let loose her gold hair
he'd seen with Diana
coming down from the hills
   in pursuit of a deer
which flees from its hurt,
for the arrows of death
are the feathers of flight.
   Oh, how he weeps!
   How he complains!

   On the burning sand
he was spreading his nets
when he felt the assault
of the beautiful huntress.
   Her eyes shot more arrows
than there were in her quiver:
for disdain is a poison
more deadly than herbs.
   Oh, how he weeps!
   How he complains!

   "O proud one," he sings,
"O slayer of beasts,"
to the creak of the oars
that endorse his lament,
   "these waters are whispering,
to hide my complaints,
that you miss what you chase
and kill only what waits."
   Oh, how he weeps!
   How he complains!

21. Soneto (1600)

Al nacimiento de Cristo, Nuestro Señor

Pender de un leño, traspasado el pecho,
y de espinas clavadas ambas sienes,
dar tus mortales penas en rehenes
de nuestra gloria, bien fue heroico hecho;

pero más fue nacer en tanto estrecho,
donde, para mostrar en nuestros bienes
a donde bajas y de donde vienes,
no quiere un portalillo tener techo.

No fue ésta más hazaña, oh gran Dios mío,
del tiempo por haber la helada ofensa
vencido en flaca edad con pecho fuerte

(que más fue sudar sangre que haber frío),
sino porque hay distancia más inmensa
de Dios a hombre, que de hombre a muerte.

22. Romance (1602)

En un pastoral albergue,
que la guerra entre unos robres
lo dejó por escondido,
o la perdonó por pobre,
　do la paz viste pellico,
y conduce, entre pastores,
ovejas del monte al llano,
y cabras del llano al monte,
　mal herido y bien curado,
se alberga un dichoso joven,
que, sin clavarle Amor flecha,
le coronó de favores.
　Las venas con poca sangre,
los ojos con mucha noche,

21. [Hung from the Cross]

On the Nativity of Christ our Lord

Hung from the Cross, pierced by a lance in the side,
both temples punctured with a crown of thorns,
to offer such mortal suffering in exchange
for our salvation, that was indeed a deed;

yet greater still to be born in want, as proof
how far for us you'll stoop, how far you'll travel,
born where there's no lodging but a stable,
where a simple porch must serve, without a roof.

It was not the greater deed, O my great Lord,
to overcome time's brutal, chill offensive,
opposing it in weakness with a strong breast

(as to sweat blood is more than suffering cold),
because there is a distance more immense
between God and man than between man and death.

22. [Angelica and Medoro]

In a simple shepherd's cabin,
which, because well hidden, war
passed by, or perhaps pardoned
simply because too poor,
    where peace goes clad in sheepskin,
and helps shepherds drive the flocks,
sheep from the mountain to the plain,
goats from the plain to the mountain,
    gravely wounded, well attended,
lies a fortunate young man
Love's arrows did not target,
yet whom Love's favors crown.
    With little blood in his veins,
and a deal of night in his eyes,

le halló en el campo aquella,
vida y muerte de los hombres.
   Del palafrén se derriba,
no porque al moro conoce,
sino por ver que la hierba
tanta sangre paga en flores.
   Límpiale el rostro, y la mano
siente el Amor que se esconde
tras las rosas, que la muerte
va violando sus colores
   (escondióse tras las rosas
por que labren sus harpones
el diamante del Catay
con aquella sangre noble).
   Ya le regala los ojos,
ya le entra, sin ver por donde,
una piedad mal nacida
entre dulces escorpiones;
   ya es herido el pedernal,
ya despide el primer golpe
centellas de agua. ¡Oh, piedad,
hija de padres traidores!
   Hierbas aplica a sus llagas,
que, si no sanan entonces,
en virtud de tales manos
lisonjean los dolores.
   Amor le ofrece su venda,
mas ella sus velos rompe
para ligar sus heridas;
los rayos del sol perdonen.
   Los últimos nudos daba,
cuando el cielo la socorre
de un villano en una yegua,
que iba penetrando el bosque.
   Enfrénanlo de la bella
las tristes piadosas voces,
que los firmes troncos mueven,
y las sordas piedras oyen,
   y la que mejor se halla
en las selvas que en la corte,

he was found in a field by the one
for whom a man lives and dies.

Down she flew from her mount
—not that she knew the Moor, but
she could see in a pool of flowers
how the grass was replacing his blood.

She wipes his face, and her hand
discovers Love's touch, Love hiding
among those roses, whose color
Death is silently stealing.

(Love hid in the roses so that
his darts could work to transfigure
this diamond of Cathay,
with that noble blood's power.)

Love fills her eyes with delight,
and she feels, without comprehension,
a pity fatally bred
among the scorpions of passion.

Now the heart of flint is wounded,
and at the first blow discharges
watery sparks. Wretched pity,
child of a traitorous family!

She applies sweet herbs to his wounds,
which may not cure him forthwith,
yet by virtue of those soft hands
the pain is at once relieved.

Love offers to lend his blindfold
but she starts tearing her veil
to use for binding those wounds;
may the sun spare her complexion!

She was tying the final knots
when heaven sent to assist her
a peasant riding a mare
who trotted into the clearing.

He comes to a sudden halt
on hearing her piteous cries,
which could move the sturdiest trunks
or make dumb stones arise;

and that which it's easier to find
in the wilderness than at court,

simple bondad, al pío ruego
cortésmente corresponde.

Humilde se apea el villano,
y sobre la yegua pone
un cuerpo con poca sangre,
pero con dos corazones.

A su cabaña los guía,
que el sol deja su horizonte,
y el humo de su cabaña
les va sirviendo de norte.

Llegaron temprano a ella,
do una labradora acoge
un mal vivo con dos almas,
y una ciega con dos soles.

Blando heno, en vez de pluma,
para lecho les compone,
que será tálamo luego,
do el garzón sus dichas logre.

Las manos, pues, cuyos dedos
de esta vida fueron dioses,
restituyen a Medoro
salud nueva, fuerzas dobles;

y le entregan, cuando menos,
su beldad, y un reino en dote,
segunda invidia de Marte,
primera dicha de Adonis.

Corona un lascivo enjambre
de cupidillos menores
la choza, bien como abejas,
hueco tronco de alcornoque.

¡Qué de nudos le está dando
a un aspid la Invidia torpe,
contando de las palomas
los arrullos gemidores!

¡Qué bien la destierra Amor,
haciendo la cuerda azote,
porque el caso no se infame,
y el lugar no se inficione!

Todo es gala el africano,
su vestido espira olores,

natural kindness, responds
to her compassionate suit.
    Submissive, the man dismounts,
and onto the mare he hoists
a body with little blood
but with two hearts beating at once;
    to his simple hut he guides them,
as the sun nears the horizon
and smoke from his cabin rising
is the compass to direct them.
    It's not long before they reach it,
and a countrywoman welcomes
one scarcely alive, with two souls,
and a beauty, blind with two suns.
    Soft hay does service for feathers
in the bed she improvises,
the couch that is destined to be
seat of the young man's pleasures.
    Meanwhile those delicate fingers,
to Medoro, lords of his life,
were gently restoring to him
renewed vigor and strength,
    entrusting to him as dowry
her beauty and lands, no less,
to make him the envy of Mars
with the fortune that fell to Adonis.
    A mischievous swarm of Cupids
delightedly hover at work
above the roof of the cabin
like bees round a hollow oak.
    How many knots dull Envy
ties in the length of a snake,
recording each deep-throated moan
that the lovebirds make!
    How right for Love to expel her,
with the knotted cord for a lash,
silencing Envy's slander,
redeeming the place from taint!
    The African's all perfection:
his clothes breathe out sweet perfumes,

el lunado arco suspende,
y el corvo alfanje depone.

Tórtolas enamoradas
son sus roncos atambores,
y los volantes de Venus,
sus bien seguidos pendones.

Desnuda el pecho anda ella,
vuela el cabello sin orden;
si le abrocha, es con claveles,
con jazmines, si lo coge.

El pie calza en lazos de oro,
porque la nieve se goce,
y no se vaya por pies
la hermosura del orbe.

Todo sirve a los amantes,
plumas les baten, veloces,
airecillos lisonjeros,
si no son murmuradores.

Los campos les dan alfombras,
los arboles, pabellones,
la apacible fuente, sueño,
música, los ruiseñores.

Los troncos les dan cortezas
en que se guarden sus nombres,
mejor que en tablas de mármol
o que in láminas de bronce.

No hay verde fresno sin letra,
ni blanco chopo sin mote,
si un valle "Angelica" suena,
otro "Angelica" responde.

Cuevas, do el silencio apenas
deja que sombras las moren,
profanan con sus abrazos,
a pesar de sus horrores.

Choza, pues, tálamo y lecho,
cortesanos labradores,
aires, campos, fuentes, vegas,
cuevas, troncos, aves, flores,

fresnos, chopos, montes, valles,
contestes de estos amores,

he's laid aside his arched bow,
put by his curving scimitar.
    The muffled drum that leads him
is the cooing of turtledoves,
the pennants he loyally follows
are the floating veils of Venus.
    The lady goes bare-breasted
her hair in flying disorder,
pinned back with carnations only,
or clasped with sprays of jasmine.
    A gold noose circles each ankle,
to enhance its snow and also
to hold the world's beauty down,
lest it take to its heels and run.
    All things are to serve the lovers:
feathers lightly promote
swift little breezes to cool them,
flattering but not indiscreet.
    The fields provide them with carpets,
the trees a sheltering arch,
the gentle stream gives them sleep,
the nightingales soft music.
    The tree trunks have plenty of bark,
more apt for recording their names
than weighty tablets of marble,
tedious panels of bronze.
    No ash tree remains uninscribed,
no poplar lacks a device;
"Angelica" sounds in one vale,
"Angelica" the next replies.
    Caves where there's silence so thick
shadows can scarcely breathe,
they profane with their embraces,
paying the horrors no heed.
    Hut then, marriage chamber, couch,
simple courteous country folk,
breezes, fields, fountains, plains,
caves and trees and birds and flowers,
    ash trees, poplars, hills and valleys,
each complicit in this love,

el cielo os guarde, si puede,
de las locuras del Conde.

23. *Soneto (1603)*

Llegué a Valladolid; registré luego
desde el bonete al clavo de la mula;
guardo el registro, que será mi bula
contra el cuidado del señor Don Diego.

Busqué la Corte en él, y yo estoy ciego,
o en la ciudad no está, o se disimula.
Celebrando dïetas vi a la gula,
que Platón para todos está en griego.

La lisonja hallé y la ceremonia
con luto, idolatrados los caciques,
amor sin fe, interés con sus virotes.

Todo se halla en esta Babilonia,
como en botica, grandes alambiques,
y más en ella títulos que botes.

24. *Romance (1603)*

En los pinares de Júcar
vi bailar unas serranas,
al son del agua en las piedras
y al son del viento en las ramas.
No es blanco coro de ninfas
de las que aposenta el agua,
o las que venera el bosque,
seguidoras de Dïana:
serranas eran de Cuenca,
honor de aquella montaña,
cuyo pie besan dos ríos,

may heaven guard you if it can
from the mad ravings of the count.

23. [Valladolid]

Arriving in Valladolid, I had to go
and register, from my hat to my mule's shoes.
I kept the receipt, which I may need to use
as warrant against the attentions of Don Diego.

And then to court. I must surely have gone blind!
Either it's away or it's in hiding.
Gluttony I saw, enjoying dieting,
but great Plato, big plates? None to be found!

I saw flattery there and ceremony
down on their luck, nabobs adored like idols,
and Love bankrupt—self-interest stole his arrows.

This Babylon resembles an apothecary's:
great alembics slowly dripping favors,
more labels to stick on than there are bottles.

24. [In the pinewoods of the Júcar]

In the pinewoods of the Júcar
I saw some girls dancing
to the sound of the running brook,
to the sound of wind in the branches.
This was no troop of nymphs,
those who live in the waters,
or those whom the woods revere,
followers of Diana:
these were country girls of Cuenca,
famous on that mountain,
whose foot two rivers kiss

por besar de ella las plantas.
Alegres corros tejían,
dándose las manos blancas
de amistad, quizá temiendo
no la truequen las mudanzas.
¡Qué bien bailan las serranas!
¡Qué bien bailan!

El cabello en crespos nudos
luz da al sol, oro a la Arabia,
cúal de flores impedido,
cúal de cordones de plata.
Del color visten del cielo,
si no son de la esperanza,
palmillas que menosprecian
al zafiro y la esmeralda.
El pie (cuando lo permite
la brújula de la falda)
lazos calza, y mirar deja
pedazos de nieve y nácar.
Ellas, cuyo movimiento
honestamente levanta
el cristal de la columna
sobre la pequeña basa—
¡Qué bien bailan las serranas!
¡Qué bien bailan!

Una entre los blancos dedos
hiriendo negras pizarras,
instrumento de marfil
que las musas le invidiaran,
las aves enmudeció,
y enfrenó el curso del agua;
no se movieron las hojas,
por no impedir lo que canta:
"Serranas de Cuenca
iban al pinar,
unas, por piñones,
otras, por bailar.
Bailando y partiendo

doing service to its plants.
   They weave spirited figures,
and give each other white hands
in friendship, as fearing perhaps
to lose touch in the changes.
      How those country girls can dance!
      How they can dance!

   Their hair in twining knots
lends the sun light, Arabia gold,
sometimes fastened with flowers,
sometimes with a silver braid.
   The color they wear is the sky's,
though not the color of hope,
fine Cuenca cloth that outshines
the fire of emeralds and sapphires.
   See their ankles (when the skirt's
brief aperture permits)
bound with laces that reveal
glimpses of mother-of-pearl.
   Look how the swirling movement
delicately defines
the stately crystal column
on its much smaller base,
      How those country girls can dance!
      How they can dance!

   One between her white fingers
beating black pebbles together,
(an ivory instrument
the Muses surely envy)
   made the birds fall silent
and halted the water's flow;
and even the leaves were still,
lest they disturb her song:
      "The girls of Cuenca
      went to the pinewood,
      some for pine nuts,
         others for the dance.
      Dancing and breaking

las serranas bellas
un piñon con otro,
si ya no es con perlas,
    de Amor las saetas
huelgan de trocar,
unas, por piñones,
    otras, por bailar.
    Entre rama y rama,
cuando el ciego dios
pide al Sol los ojos
por verlas mejor,
    los ojos del sol
las veréis pisar,
unas, por piñones,
    otras, por bailar."

25. *Romance (1608)*

Las flores del romero,
    niña Isabel,
hoy son flores azules,
mañana serán miel.

    Celosa estás, la niña,
celosa estás de aqúel,
dichoso, pues le buscas,
ciego, pues no te ve,
    ingrato, pues te enoja,
y confiado, pues
no se disculpa hoy
de lo que hizo ayer.
    Enjuguen esperanzas
lo que lloras por él;
que celos entre aquellos
que se han querido bien,
hoy son flores azules,
    mañana serán miel.

    Aurora de ti misma,
que cuando a amanecer

—those dazzling girls—
the cones with each other
or with their white fingers,
    while the arrows of love
they gaily exchange,
some for pine nuts,
    others for the dance.
    Between branch and branch,
when the blind god
begs the sun for his eyes
to see them better,
    you'll observe them treading
the eyes of the sun,
some for pine nuts,
    others for the dance."

25. [Flowers of the rosemary]

Flowers of the rosemary,
Isabel, Isabel,
although today they're blue,
tomorrow they'll be honey.

You're jealous, child, suspicious,
suspicious of a man
who since you choose him's lucky,
not seeing you is blind,
    hurts you because unfeeling
and so arrogantly unkind
he won't apologize
for the wrongs of yesterday.
    But let hope wipe away
the tears you weep for him,
for suspicions between those
who've had a love that's true
    although today they're blue,
    tomorrow they'll be honey.

Your own dawn, you seem to be,
for when light begins to break

a tu placer empiezas,
te eclipsan tu placer,
   serénense tus ojos,
y más perlas no des,
porque al sol le está mal
lo que a la aurora bien.
   Desata como nieblas
todo lo que no ves;
que sospechas de amantes
y querellas después,
   hoy son flores azules,
   mañana serán miel.

26. Letrilla (1609)

No son todos ruiseñores
los que cantan entre las flores,
sino campanitas de plata,
que tocan a la alba;
sino trompeticas de oro,
que hacen la salva
a los soles que adoro.

No todas las voces ledas
son de sirenas con plumas,
cuyas húmedas espumas
son las verdes alamedas.
Si suspendido te quedas
a los süaves clamores,
   no son todos ruiseñores
   los que cantan entre las flores,
   sino campanitas de plata,
   que tocan a la alba;
   sino trompeticas de oro,
   que hacen la salva
   a los soles que adoro.

Lo artificioso que admira,
y lo dulce que consuela,

on your pleasure, your own eyes
eclipse you with this dew,
    so teach your eyes more calm
and shed these pearls no more,
because what's right for dawn
does not suit the midday sun.
    Make vanish like the mists
all things you cannot see;
for suspicions lovers have
and the quarrels that ensue,
    although today they're blue,
    tomorrow they'll be honey.

26. [Not just nightingales]

It's not just nightingales
that sing among the flowers;
there are little silver bells
that ring in the dawn,
and little golden trumpets
sounding to salute
the two suns I adore.

Not all the joyful voices
are from feathered sirens
who frolic in the foam
of the leafy groves.
If you stop and listen well
to the gentle hubbub,
    it's not just nightingales
    that sing among the flowers;
    there are little silver bells
    that ring in the dawn,
    and little golden trumpets
    sounding to salute
    the two suns I adore.

The art that so impresses,
the sweetness that consoles,

no es de aquel violín que vuela
ni de esotra inquieta lira;
otro instrumento es quien tira
de los sentidos mejores:
    No son todos ruiseñores
    los que cantan entre las flores,
    sino campanitas de plata,
    que tocan a la alba;
    sino trompeticas de oro,
    que hacen la salva
    a los soles que adoro.

Las campanitas lucientes,
y los dorados clarines
en coronados jazmines,
los dos hermosos corrientes
no sólo recuerdan gentes
sino convocan amores.
    No son todos ruiseñores
    los que cantan entre las flores,
    sino campanitas de plata,
    que tocan a la alba;
    sino trompeticas de oro,
    que hacen la salva
    a los soles que adoro.

27. *Soneto (1611)*

Del túmulo que hizo Córdoba en las honras
de la Señora Reina Doña Margarita

A la que España toda humilde estrado
y su horizonte fue dosel apenas,
el Betis esta urna en sus arenas
majestüosamente ha levantado.

¡Oh peligroso, oh lisonjero estado,
golfo de escollos, playa de sirenas!

comes not from that winged violin
or this wandering lyre;
there is another instrument
that sounds our deepest feeling:
it's not just nightingales
that sing among the flowers;
there are little silver bells
that ring in the dawn,
and little golden trumpets
sounding to salute
the two suns I adore.

The little shining bells
and the golden bugles
floating above the jasmine,
two lovely streams of sound,
call to us and rouse us,
and awaken love.
It's not just nightingales
that sing among the flowers;
there are little silver bells
that ring in the dawn,
and little golden trumpets
sounding to salute
the two suns I adore.

27. [Queen Margaret's Monument, 1]

On the monument that Córdoba erected in honor
of Her Majesty the Queen, Doña Margarita

For her to whom all Spain was but a plank
in her world's stage, scarce wide enough its skies
for a fitting canopy, Betis supplies
this glorious tomb erected on its bank.

O perilous, o flattering estate,
o gulf of reefs and sandbanks home to sirens,

Trofeos son del agua mil entenas,
que aun rompidas, no sé si han recordado.

La Margarita, pues, luciente gloria
del sol de Austria, y la concha de Baviera,
más coronas ceñida que vio años,

en polvo ya el clarín final espera:
siempre sonante a aquel, cuya memoria
antes peinó que canas, desengaños.

28. Soneto (1611)

En la misma ocasión

Máquina funeral, que desta vida
nos decís la mudanza, estando queda;
pira, no de aromática arboleda,
si a más gloriosa Fénix construida;

bajel en cuya gavia esclarecida
estrellas, hijas de otra mejor Leda,
serenan la Fortuna, de su rueda
la volubilidad reconocida,

farol luciente sois, que solicita
la razón, entre escollos naufragante,
al puerto; y a pesar de lo luciente,

obscura concha de una Margarita
que, rubí en caridad, en fe diamante,
renace a nuevo Sol en nuevo Oriente.

29. Soneto (1612)

Despidióse el francés con grasa buena,
(con buena gracia, digo, señor Momo),

a thousand masts have foundered in such waters,
who knows if the mariners didn't recall too late!

This Margaret, this pearl, fruit of the union
of Austria's sun, and the Bavarian shell,
who wore more earthly crowns than she saw years,

now, as dust, awaits the final call,
the sound that is ever present to the one
who acquires wisdom earlier than white hairs.

28. [Queen Margaret's Monument, 2]

For the same

You blaze, great monument, that in your stillness
remind us of the world's continual changes,
like a pyre, a pyramid of fragrant branches,
built to commemorate this greater Phoenix;

or like a ship upon whose maintop glow
two stars, the offspring of a greater Leda,
to mark the end of storms, of Fortune's anger,
as her unstable wheel begins to slow;

your light shines out, a beacon to the mind
to bring it safely through the reef-filled sea
to harbor, and yet you also are, though bright,

the dark shell within which this Margaret's confined,
whence (love's ruby and faith's diamond) she
shall rise to a new Sun in a new Orient.

29. [The French Duke's visit]

Most greasily the Frenchman bade farewell,
("with grace" is what I mean, of course, Sir Momus!)

hizo España el deber con el Vandomo,
y al pagar le hará con el de Pena.

Reales fiestas le impidió al de Humena
la ya engastada Margarita en plomo,
aunque no hay toros para Francia como
los de Guisando, su comida y cena.

Estrellóse la gala de diamantes
tan al tope, que alguno fue topacio,
y aun Don Cristalïán mintió finezas.

Partióse al fin, y tan brindadas antes
nos dejó las saludes de Palacio,
que otro día enfermaron Sus Altezas.

30. *Soneto (1614)*

Inscripción para el sepulcro de Domínico Greco

Esta en forma elegante, oh peregrino,
de pórfido luciente dura llave
el pincel niega al mundo más suave,
que dio espíritu a leño, vida a lino.

Su nombre, aun de mayor aliento digno
que en los clarines de la Fama cabe,
el campo ilustra de ese mármol grave.
Venérale, y prosigue tu camino.

Yace el Griego. Heredó Naturaleza
arte, y el Arte, estudio; Iris, colores;
Febo, luces—si no sombras, Morfeo.—

Tanta urna, a pesar de su dureza,
lágrimas beba y cuantos suda olores
corteza funeral de árbol sabeo.

Spain for Monsieur has done what it was supposed to.
Later we will have to foot the bill.

Festivities were rendered somewhat thinner
by Margaret, the pearl now set in lead,
although in France of bulls there's little said
—unless bulls of Guisando (think lunch and dinner).

The diamond-studded gala came a cropper
—the brillants so abundant some were topaz,
while even Sir Crystal had a go at chic.

Well, now he's gone. But as was only proper
the Palace health was toasted many times over.
The following day their Majesties were sick.

30. [El Greco's tomb]

Inscription for the tomb of Dominico Greco

Pilgrim, behold this cold slab's elegance,
this pediment of gleaming porphyry,
that to the world denies the sweetest brush
ever to give wood spirit, canvas life.

The name, worthy to be bruited with more breath
than Fame's trumpets could ever exercise,
makes this grave marble's face illustrious.
Pay tribute, and proceed along your path.

Here lies the Greek. Nature has thus acquired
Art, while Art acquires example, Iris
color, Phoebus light, and Morpheus shade.

May this great tomb, though in hard stone attired,
soak up wet tears and fragrances exhaled
by the costly bark that's from the East conveyed.

31. Soneto 1614

A Don Pedro de Cárdenas, en un encierro de toros

Salí, señor Don Pedro, esta mañana
a ver un toro que en un Nacimiento
con mi mula estuviera más contento
que alborotando a Córdoba la llana.

Romper la tierra he visto en su abesana
mis prójimos con paso menos lento,
que él se entró en la ciudad tan sin aliento,
y aun más, que me dejó en la barbacana.

No desherréis vuestro Zagal, que un clavo
no ha de valer la causa, si no miente
quien de la cuerda apela para el rabo.

Perdonadme el hablar tan cortésmente
de quien, ya que no alcalde por lo Bravo,
podrá ser, por lo Manso, presidente.

32. Romance (1620)

Al Nacimiento de Cristo Nuestro Señor

¡Cuántos silbos, cuántas voces
tus campos, Belén, oyeron,
sentidas bien de sus valles,
guardadas mal de sus ecos!
Pastores las dan, buscando
el que celestial Cordero
nos abrió piadoso el libro,
que negaban tantos sellos.
¿Qué buscáis, los ganaderos?
—Uno, ay, niño, que su cuna
los brazos son de la luna,
si duermen sus dos luceros.

31. [Viewing a bull]

To Don Pedro de Cárdenas at an encierro

This morning, my friend Don Pedro, I went to see
a bull that would have looked better with my mule
meekly attending in a Nativity
than on the plain of Córdoba raising hell.

I have seen my bovine friends, tied to the yoke,
ploughing a furrow with less measured tread
than he who entered the city with hung head
so listlessly one could hardly bear to look.

Don't bother to unshoe your Hero for a nail:
no need to employ a stop, if we're to go by
the fellow who dropped the rope to pull the tail.

Forgive me now for speaking so politely
of one who couldn't stand for mayor as Bravo,
but might well serve for president as Manso.

32. [The Nativity]

For the birth of Christ our Lord

What whistling and what shouting,
O Bethlehem, your pastures heard,
ringing out among your valleys,
by their echoes spread abroad!
    It's the shepherds who are searching
for that celestial Lamb
whose love has opened up the book
so many seals had sealed.
Shepherds, what do you seek?
—A child, a boy, and he's cradled
in the arms of the moon,
although the two stars sleep.

No pastor, no abrigó fiera
frágil choza, albergue ciego,
que no penetre el cuidado,
que no escudriñe el deseo.
    La diligencia, calzada,
en vez de abarcas, el viento,
cumbres pisa coronadas
de paraninfos del cielo.
    ¡Qué buscáis, los ganaderos!
    —Uno, ay, niño, que su cuna
    los brazos son de la luna,
    si duermen sus dos luceros.
            —Pediros albricias puedo.
Pastores   *¿De qué, Gil?*
Gil   *No déis más paso;*
            que dormir vi al niño.
Pastores   *¡Paso!*
            quedo, ¡ay, queditico, quedo!

    Tanto he visto celestial,
tan luminoso, tan raro,
que, a pesar, hallarás claro,
de la noche, este portal.
    Enfrena el paso, Pascual,
deja a la puerta el denuedo.
            —Pediros albricias puedo.
Pastores   *¿De qué, Gil?*
Gil   *No déis más paso;*
            que dormir vi al niño.
Pastores   *¡Paso,*
            quedo, ¡ay, queditico, quedo!

33. Soneto (1620)

Al padre Maestro Hortensio, de una audiencia
del padre Maestro Fray Luis de
Aliaga, confesor del señor Rey Don Felipe III

No home of shepherd or wild beast
in flimsy hut or hidden lair
that's not visited by their love,
explored by their desire.
  Diligence, shod in wind,
not sandals, combs the hills,
and finds them with a host
of heavenly messengers filled.

Shepherds, what do you seek?
—A child, a boy, and he's cradled
in the arms of the moon,
although the two stars sleep.
                    —give me thanks for the good news!
Shepherds   *What news, Gil?*
Gil   *Go no further;*
                    I have seen the child, asleep.
Shepherds   *Let's go,*
                    hush now, take care or you'll wake him!

Such a celestial event I've seen,
so luminous and rare,
that the night notwithstanding
you'll easily see where.
  Slow down, Pascual,
leave your bravado at the door.
                    —give me thanks for the good news!
Shepherds   *What news, Gil?*
Gil   *Go no further;*
                    I have seen the child, asleep.
Shepherds   *Let's go,*
                    hush now, take care or you'll wake him!

33. [The King's confessor]

To Father Hortensio, on an audience given
by the Learned Friar, Father
Luis de Aliaga, confessor to His Majesty King Philip III

Al que de la consciencia es del Tercero
Filipo digno oráculo prudente,
de una y otra saeta impertinente
si mártir no le vi, le vi terrero.

Tanto, pues, le ceñía ballestero,
cuanta le estaba coronando gente,
dejándole el concurso el despidiente
hecho pedazos, pero siempre entero.

Hortensio mío, si ésta llamo audiencia,
¿cuál llamaré robusta montería,
donde cient flechas cosen un venado?

Ponderé en nuestro dueño una paciencia,
que en la atención modesta fue alegría,
y en la resolución, sucinto agrado.

34. *Letrilla (1621)*

Al Nacimiento de Cristo Nuestro Señor

Caído se le ha un Clavel
hoy a la Aurora del seno:
¡qué glorioso que está el heno,
porque ha caído sobre él!

Cuando el silencio tenía
todas las cosas del suelo,
y, coronada del yelo,
reinaba la noche fría,
en medio la monarquía
de tiniebla tan crüel,
caído se le ha un Clavel
hoy a la Aurora del seno:
¡qué glorioso que está el heno,
porque ha caído sobre él!

I saw that wise and worthy oracle,
keeper of the conscience of the king,
targeted by much uncalled-sniping,
survive a storm of shots ballistical.

A mob of suitors seemed to have him backed
into a corner where they hemmed him in
and through their savage importuning left him
shattered, but with integrity intact,

Hortensio, my dear, if this is an audience,
what shall I call the deer hunt when
a hundred huntsmen go in for the kill?

Watching our friend, I had to admire the patience
that sponsored quiet listening and then
manifested in the verdict plain goodwill.

34. [A carnation has fallen]

For the birth of Christ Our Lord

A carnation has fallen
from the bosom of dawn.
How blessed the hay is,
for that's where it's fallen.

While silence possesses
all things on earth
and cold night's enthroned
with its crown of ice,
into the dominion
of the cruel dark,
a carnation has fallen
from the bosom of dawn.
How blessed the hay is,
for that's where it's fallen.

De un solo Clavel ceñida,
la Virgen, Aurora bella,
al mundo se lo dio, y ella
quedó cual antes florida;
a la púrpura caída
solo fue el heno fiel.
Caído se le ha un Clavel
hoy a la Aurora del seno:
¡qué glorioso que está el heno,
porque ha caído sobre él!

El heno, pues, que fue dino,
a pesar de tantas nieves,
de ver en sus brazos leves
este rosicler divino,
para su lecho fue lino,
oro para su dosel.
Caído se le ha un Clavel
hoy a la Aurora del seno:
¡qué glorioso que está el heno,
porque ha caído sobre él!

35. *Soneto* (1622)

De las muertes de Don Rodrigo Calderón,
del Conde de Villamediana y Conde de Lemos

Al tronco descansaba de una encina
que invidia de los bosques fue lozana,
cuando segur legal una mañana
alto horror me dejó con su rüina.

Laurel que de sus ramas hizo digna
mi lira, ruda si, mas castellana,
hierro luego fatal su pompa vana
(culpa tuya, Calíope) fulmina.

En verdes hojas cano el de Minerva
árbol culto, del Sol yace abrasado,
aljófar, sus cenizas, de la yerba.

Just the one flower she bore,
the Virgin, dawn's beauty,
and to the world gave it,
and still remained pure.
With the glory that's fallen
only hay will keep faith.
A carnation has fallen
from the bosom of dawn.
How blessed the hay is,
for that's where it's fallen.

That hay was deemed worthy
in spite of the snow,
lightly to cradle
dawn's holy bloom,
to be the bed linen
and gold for the throne.
A carnation has fallen
from the bosom of dawn.
How blessed the hay is,
for that's where it's fallen.

35. [I leaned against the trunk]

On the deaths of Don Rodrigo Calderón, the Count
of Villamediana, and the Count of Lemos

I leaned against the trunk of a sturdy oak tree
that was the vigorous envy of all the wood,
until one morning the law's stern reaper called
and left me trembling, bereft of sanctuary.

A laurel whose branches bestowed dignity
on my poor lyre, unpolished but Castilian,
received one fatal blow whereby its vain
pomp was blasted (your fault, Calliope).

Green-leaved and white with wisdom Minerva's tree
the sun destroys as soon as his favors cease;
its ashes then like dew on the grass you'll see.

¡Cuánta esperanza miente a un desdichado!
¿A qué más engaños me reserva,
a qué escarmientos me vincula el hado?

36. Soneto (1623)

Infiere, de los achaques de la vejez, cercano
el fin a que católico se alienta

En este occidental, en este, oh Licio,
climatérico lustro de tu vida,
todo mal afirmado pie es caída,
toda fácil caída es precipicio.

¿Caduca el paso? Ilústrese el juicio.
Desatándose va la tierra unida.
¿Qué prudencia, del polvo prevenida,
la rüina aguardó del edificio?

La piel no sólo, sierpe venenosa,
mas con la piel los años se desnuda,
y el hombre, no. ¡Ciego discurso humano!

¡Oh aquel dichoso, que la ponderosa
porción depuesta en una piedra muda,
la leve da al zafiro soberano!

37. Soneto (1623)

De la brevedad engañosa de la vida

Menos solicitó veloz saeta
destinada señal, que mordió aguda;
agonal carro por la arena muda
no coronó con más silencio meta,

How false is hope to one whose fate's adverse!
What disappointments are in store for me?
What further punishments, what new reverse?

36. [During this westering hour]

From the afflictions of age, he infers the approach
of the end, and takes comfort from his faith

During this westering hour, my friend, in this
climacteric, these last five years of all,
every ill-placed step denotes a fall,
and every minor fall's a precipice.

The body withers? Then let judgement flower!
Articulated clay is coming apart.
What wise man, seeing dust announce the start,
awaits the final crumbling of the tower?

Venomous snakes not only put off skin
but with the skin divest themselves of years.
Not man, however! How blind is human reason!

Happy is he who to a silent stone
commits the weighty portion, then confers
the lighter to the azure vault of heaven!

37. [Less eagerly did the swift arrow seek]

On the deceptive brevity of life

Less eagerly did the swift arrow seek
the appointed target that it flew to bite,
not more quietly did the chariot
gliding across the sand attain the mark,

que presurosa corre, que secreta
a su fin nuestra edad. A quien lo duda,
(fiera que sea de razón desnuda,)
cada sol repetido es un cometa.

¿Confiésalo Cartago, y tu lo ignoras?
Peligro corres, Licio, si porfiás
en seguir sombras y abrazar engaños.

Mal te perdonarán a ti las horas;
las horas que limando están los días,
los días que royendo están los años.

38. Soneto (1623)

De la ambición humana

Mariposa, no sólo no cobarde,
mas temeraria, fatalmente ciega,
lo que la llama al Fénix aun le niega,
quiere obstinada que a sus alas guarde,

pues en su daño arrepentida tarde,
del esplandor solicitada, llega
a lo que luce, y ambiciosa entrega
su mal vestida pluma a lo que arde.

Yace gloriosa en la que dulcemente
huesa le ha prevenido abeja breve,
¡suma felicidad a yerro sumo!

No a mi ambición contrario tan luciente,
menos activo sí, cuanto más leve,
cenizas la hará, si abrasa el humo.

than hastens ever forward, speeds unseen
our life towards its end. For you who doubt,
bereft though you be of reason like a beast,
each time the sun repeats there is a sign.

Carthage proclaims it, yet you, you're unaware?
Danger, my friend, if you don't change your ways,
chasing shadows and embracing errors;

don't tell me that you think the hours will spare
just you, the hours that are grinding down the days,
the days forever gnawing at the years?

38. [On human ambition]

Far from being a coward, the moth chooses
—rashly bold, endowed with fatal blindness—
obstinately to claim for its wings a kindness
which even to the phoenix flame refuses;

too late aware to save itself, it turns
toward a splendor, enchanted by the blaze
of that which shines; ambition thus betrays
the ill-assembled plumes to that which burns.

In glory now it lies in the tomb most sweetly
which in advance a little bee had fashioned.
The greatest bliss rewards a fault that's great!

But my ambition does not need this enemy:
it can by smoke alone be turned to ashes,
which has no burning power, no shine, no weight.

"... a famous ship set off ... its name, Victoria" (*First Solitude*).
Orthelius's famous map of the Pacific shows Magellan's ship
(referred to in line 480 of the *First Solitude*) in miniature.
Ortelius, *Maris Pacifici* (1589), available at http://www.orteliusmaps.com.

II

FIRST SOLITUDE

Introduction

The *Solitudes* and the *Fable of Polyphemus and Galatea* are the two great works of Góngora's middle period on which he staked his reputation and that earned him both fame and notoriety by their complex style and, in the case of the former, the obscurity of the subject matter. They circulated among friends and rivals and were attacked and defended in a fierce literary war that must surely have added to the bitterness of Góngora's final years. Paradoxically, however, the subject of the *Solitudes* is simplicity, and they were mainly written in Córdoba, where he had rented a house in the Plazuela de la Trinidad and a country place outside, the Huerta de Don Marcos, which bordered on a stream and had, as we know from contracts, a variety of fruit trees. He had returned there in 1609 from an unsuccessful trip to Madrid, where he failed to get justice for his sister, whose eldest son had been killed in a street incident. His weariness with court life is expressed in the *tercetos* he wrote at the time:

> ¡Mal haya quien en señores idolatra
> y en Madrid desperdicia sus dineros,
> si ha de hacer al salir una mohatra!

> [What a fool is he who idolizes gentry
> and fritters away his fortune in Madrid,
> when all he'll do is end up in the red!]

He goes on to say how he misses the flattering stream of his orchard: "but no, not flattering, you are clear and honest!"—unlike courtiers, in other words. In 1611 he transferred his post at Córdoba Cathedral to a nephew and was free for the first time to devote himself entirely to poetry.

It is thought that Góngora intended there to be four solitudes, but he only completed the first and the greater part of the second. The *First Solitude* follows "the steps of a pilgrim," an unhappy lover shipwrecked in a storm, who finds refuge with some shepherds in the mountains and is invited to join a village wedding down on the plain. The *Second Solitude* finds him on the shore of an estuary with fishermen, where he later observes a group of noblemen on horseback out hunting with hawks. The action thus moves away from the sea into the mountains and then back down to the sea again. But such an outline would not prepare anyone for the manner in which the narrative is presented. Readers unused to Góngora's style may have the feeling of struggling through a verbal landscape in which the signposts of subjects, verbs, and objects have been carefully hidden. Their plight is similar to that of the shipwrecked pilgrim the poem describes.

It may be more profitable to look just at one short passage, for example the richly metaphorical lines 481–490 [493–504], which refer to the "immobile fleet of firm islands in that Dawn sea." Jammes, in the notes to his edition (p. 296), speaks of how this image evokes those islands of the Pacific or the South China Sea in the white light of dawn, and how suggestive it is of the joy of discovery. The word Góngora uses here for dawn is *Alba,* with its root meaning of white, but dawn is also the beginning of something new, and in a physical sense it means the East. In the same sentence Góngora compares the islands, in their beauty and variety, to the sight of Diana and her nymphs when Actaeon surprised them bathing: these islands could cause, he says, the same "sweet confusion." He describes the limbs of the goddess and nymphs as "reefs of Parian marble or smooth ivory" (which are also white) and adds that it is no surprise if Actaeon lost himself among them. At this point we seem to have completed a circle: the islands in the sea metaphorically are nymphs and the nymphs metaphorically are reefs, pieces of solid land in the sea like islands. And reefs are not only a danger to mariners but also, as in the first sonnet on Queen Margaret's monument (no. 31), represent the dangers of court life. But as agents of a "sweet confusion," these islands, nymphs, or reefs amount to a seductive danger. The next chunk of verse, again a single sentence, will describe the spread of luxuries resulting from the voyages of discovery and illustrate their human cost: the loss at sea of the old man's son and his fortune, as well as the loss of the world's innocence. But the pain does not cancel the beauty of the images. The comparison with the Actaeon myth brings to mind the Renaissance discovery (or rediscovery, or invention?) of the classical world, with the nude in painting and sculpture and the intellectual excitement of humanism. The verb *perderse*, to lose oneself, seems to express ambiguities. Actaeon could not but lose himself: he was lost in contemplation of beauty and he lost his identity because he was metamorphosed into a stag. Similarly the sailor is confused among a multitude of exotic islands and a maze of channels, or loses his life when his ship goes aground and sinks. And the sailor is reminiscent of the courtiers who lose sight of the truth as they pursue ephemeral worldly advantage. If we want to condemn Góngora (as some have) for being obsessed by an aesthetic vision and concentrating on style at the expense of substance, I do not think we can accuse him of being blind to the dangers of such an obsession.

If we disregard its complex style and images, the *First Solitude* seems quite simple. Its message seems to be that changes to modern life, in particular the opening up of trade routes providing access to wealth and luxuries, have destroyed the austere ideals of the past, its Golden Age simplicity. Yet, in the work as a whole, there are several mysteries. Firstly, the pilgrim himself: is he Góngora or just a conventional unrequited lover? Why is he forced to wander the world this way, what is the sin he speaks of in the *Second Solitude*, the presumption that makes him another Icarus? To whom is the song in praise of the simple life, near the beginning of the first part, addressed? And by whom? (we are not told that it represents the pilgrim's thoughts, though this is often assumed to be the case). Who is the man with the goatherds who was apparently once a soldier, and what is the significance of those dilapidated signs of a glorious past now vanished? Who exactly is the old man who delivers the attack on Greed? Was Góngora seriously intending to write four solitudes, and what would the others have contained? Most of these are open questions and they provoke one more: did Góngora intend them to be so?

I have translated quite freely, eliminating or replacing a few of the classical or mythological references and sometimes making substantial changes to the order in which ideas and images are presented. I have not tried to reproduce Góngora's hyperbaton (unusual word order) because I believe Latinate word order is awkward in English and is too much associated with "poetic" style. Instead, I have pushed the branching and embedding potential of English to its limit, to produce something like an English equivalent for Góngora's complexity. I have followed Góngora's predilection for long sentences, but I have tried to compensate for the difficulties by a change in layout: originally Góngora's text was not broken or indented, but I have used both spaces and indentation, in some places to try to clarify the syntax and elsewhere to indicate stages in the narrative. The aim was not to replace a reading of the original but to provide orientation by making the outline of the narrative recognizable and maintaining its flow. This has led to the English being slightly longer than the original.

There is some further justification for all this in the fact that the poem's verse form, the *silva*, is much freer than, say, a sonnet or the rhyming stanzas of *Polyphemus and Galatea*. Góngora himself knew that to critics his poem appeared both obscure and formally haphazard. He says in the attributed sonnet no. 21 that "the *Solitude*" came out in Madrid "with little light and even less discipline": he is expressing the viewpoint of an unfriendly critic, assumed to be Quevedo. In terms of versification, the poem is a random mix of seven- and eleven-syllable lines, each line provided with an end rhyme somewhere, but not according to a regular rhyme scheme: there may be up to fourteen lines between rhyming words. What is remarkable is the way this flexible instrument enables Góngora to develop an image or collection of images in a single sentence covering many lines of verse and still maintain a forward movement. Presumably this narrative skill has much to do with his experience of writing ballads.

I have not tried to match Góngora's rhyming but encouraged end rhyme and internal rhyme to crop up occasionally. I have also tried to approximate Góngora's line length with my own lines of predominantly 6–7 and 10–11 syllables.

Dedication to the Duke of Béjar

The dedication is important, far more than an exercise in flattery: it provides an introduction to the theme and manner of the poem and perhaps, too, genuine insight into the reasons for writing it. Apart from the four-verse opening and the five-verse conclusion, the dedication consists of a single sentence extending over twenty-eight lines!

It was not surprising that Góngora should dedicate the *Solitudes* to the Duke of Béjar, a nobleman who had withdrawn from the court to live on his country estate and occupy himself with country pursuits like hunting. He was one of several such people for whom Góngora expressed admiration: others were the Marqués de Ayamonte, who had at the last minute turned down a prestigious appointment as viceroy of Mexico, probably for family reasons (his wife feared the journey and his brother had recently died at sea), and the Conde de Niebla (see my introduction to *The Fable of Polyphemus and Galatea* in part 3), who appears in the *Second Solitude* as the ideal of a hunting nobleman. As Jammes has pointed out, nobles like this complemented rather than contradicted Góngora's idealization of simple country life and people because they preferred country pursuits to life at court (*Soledades,*

p. 80). In a sense theirs was a rather conservative life style, particularly at this time when Philip III's court was attracting more of the nobility, gentry, and hangers-on than in the reign of his father.

Of course Góngora also wanted help from these aristocrats. Anyone with literary ambition needed support from the rich and famous, and Góngora was undoubtedly ambitious for his two longer works, however careless he might be about preserving his shorter poems. The attributed sonnet 21 describes the *First Solitude* going forth in Madrid like a penitent in a Holy Week procession, passing various convents as it proceeds towards its goal, the Royal Palace, despite the hostility of other writers like Quevedo. Góngora wanted to be known in the highest circles, and he wanted to defeat his critics. Also, by the time he was writing the *Solitudes* his fortunes were already in decline. Later in 1617, when he moved to Madrid to try to revive them, he hoped that friends with influence would help him obtain a lucrative position at court.

The Duke of Béjar also had Pedro Espinosa's famous anthology, *Flores de poetas ilustres* dedicated to him as well as part 1 of *Don Quijote*. Pedro Espinosa was his chaplain and painted a verbal picture of him which could be by Góngora: "when his son-in-law the Duke of Lerma was in charge, deaf to his entreaties and promises, he decided to retire to the solitude of Huelva, saying: 'A spring, sir, is as satisfying as a river. The Court, where all life is short, is best seen from a distance, like a painting by El Greco'" (see *Soledades*, ed. Jammes, p. 81).

◈ ◈ ◈

Al Duque de Béjar

Pasos de un peregrino son errante   1
cuantos me dictó versos dulce Musa:
    en soledad confusa
perdidos unos, otros inspirados.

¡Oh tú, que, de venablos impedido   ·   5
—muros de abeto, almenas de diamante—,
bates los montes, que, de nieve armados,
gigantes de cristal los teme el cielo;
donde el cuerno, del eco repetido,
fieras te expone, que—al teñido suelo,   10
muertas, pidiendo términos disformes—
espumoso coral le dan al Tormes!:
arrima a un fresno el fresno—cuyo acero,
sangre sudando, en tiempo hará breve
    purpurear la nieve—   15
y, en cuanto da el solícito montero
al duro robre, al pino levantado
—émulos vividores de las peñas—
    las formidables señas
del oso que aun besaba, atravesado,   20
la asta de tu luciente jabalina,
—o lo sagrado supla de la encina
lo augusto del dosel; o de la fuente

To the Duke of Béjar

Steps of a pilgrim straying   1
   in the wilderness alone,
such are the verses that a gentle muse
   dictated to me: those lost and these inspired.

So then, O Duke, do you—   5
   with javelins encumbered, combing the
tree-lined ramparts, diamond battlements
of snow-clad peaks, rebellious crystal Titans,
for game the echoing horn delivers to you,
   monsters no ordinary words describe   10
that dye the ground with blood,
   painting the Tormes red like foaming coral!—
lean your ashen shaft against an ash tree,
   where its dripping blade at once
     stains the snow purple,   15
while on some doughty oak or upreared pine,
   trees rivalling the cliffs in their endurance,
the faithful huntsman nails
   your awe-inspiring trophy,
     the bear that had seemed to kiss   20
      humbly the glinting spear transfixing it
and, taking the sacred oak as substitute
   for the solemn canopy,

la alta zanefa, lo majestuoso
del sitïal a tu deidad debido—,   25
   ¡oh Duque esclarecido!,
templa en sus ondas tu fatiga ardiente,
y, entregados tus miembros al reposo
sobre el de grama césped no desnudo,
déjate un rato hallar del pie acertado   30
que sus errantes pasos ha votado
a la real cadena de tu escudo.

Honre süave, generoso nudo
libertad, de Fortuna perseguida:
que, a tu piedad Euterpe agradecida,   35
su canoro dará dulce instrumento,
cuando la Fama no su trompa al viento.

Soledad Primera

Era del año la estación florida   1
en que el mentido robador de Europa
—media luna las armas de su frente,
y el Sol todos los rayos de su pelo—,
   luciente honor del cielo,   5
en campos de zafiro pace estrellas;
cuando el que ministrar podía la copa
a Júpiter mejor que el garzón de Ida,
—náufrago y desdeñado, sobre ausente—
lagrimosas de amor dulces querellas   10
   da al mar; que condolido,
   fue a las ondas, fue al viento
   el mísero gemido,
segundo de Arïón dulce instrumento.

Del siempre en la montaña opuesto pino   15
   al enemigo Noto,
   piadoso miembro roto
—breve tabla—delfín no fue pequeño
al inconsiderado peregrino

the source's upraised verge
    for the loftier seat your birth and state deserve,   25
in its waters finding
    relief for your heated brow
    and for your limbs repose
        on the bare turf with grass just pointing through,
allow the fortunate words to reach you   30
    of one who craves to bind his wayward steps
    with the royal chain depicted on your shield.

And may this welcome servitude confirm
    the liberty of one threatened, at bay,
while Euterpe lends her sweet airs in return,   35
    rather than Fame her trumpet,
    to proclaim your virtue.

First Solitude

It was in the season of the year's flowering   1
    when Europa's masked abductor
        his brow armed with the shape of a half moon,
        the whole sun figured in his stiff hide's sheen,
    Grand Master of the skies,   5
        comes to the azure pastures grazing stars
that one more qualified
    than Ida's bright-eyed boy
    to keep Jove's cup supplied
(shipwrecked, forlorn, and banished from love's presence)   10
sang out his grieving to an audience of waves
    and had them on his side
    to win from the storm the same relief that once
        Arion's lyre obtained.

The sympathetic broken   15
    limb of a pine that many years resisted
        the south wind on the mountain,
the merest plank, stood in
    as substantial dolphin

que a una Libia de ondas su camino   20
    fio, y su vida a un leño.

Del Océano pues antes sorbido,
    y luego vomitado
no lejos de un escollo coronado
de secos juncos, de calientes plumas,   25
    —alga todo y espumas—
halló hospitalidad donde halló nido
    de Júpiter el ave.

Besa la arena, y de la rota nave
    aquella parte poca   30
que le expuso en la playa dio a la roca;
    que aun se dejan las peñas
lisonjear de agradecidas señas.

Desnudo el joven, cuanto ya el vestido
    Océano ha bebido,   35
restituir le hace a las arenas;
    y al sol lo extiende luego,
    que, lamiéndolo apenas
su dulce lengua de templado fuego,
lento lo embiste, y con süave estilo   40
la menor onda chupa al menor hilo.

No bien pues de su luz los horizontes
—que hacían desigual, confusamente
montes de agua y piélagos de montes—
    desdorados los siente,   45
cuando—entregado el mísero extranjero
en lo que ya del mar redimió fiero—
entre espinas crepúsculos pisando,
riscos que aun igualara mal volando
    veloz, intrépida ala,   50
—menos cansado que confuso—escala.

Vencida al fin la cumbre
—del mar siempre sonante,

to the rash pilgrim who'd entrusted   20
          his way to a desert of waves,
          his life to a wooden hull.
By the ocean, that had
      sucked him in, vomited up
              beside a reef with a crown   25
                  of dry reeds and warm feathers,
              all ocean wrack and spume,
he found hospitality
      where Jove's bird had lodged its nest.

He kisses the sand and makes of that small part   30
                  of the broken ship
              that delivered him on shore
          an offering to the reef:
gratitude, they say, can even soften rocks.

He strips and makes his clothing   35
          restore to the sands all
      the ocean it had drunk,
then spreads it to the sun,
          who licking it lightly
              with the delicate fire of his sweet tongue,   40
          assaults it gently and, with languid tread,
              each last wave sucks from each least thread.

Hardly of the sun's golden
      light had the horizons
              (made ragged and confused   45
                  by liquid mountains, oceans of peaks)
          appeared bereft,
when this poor alien, dressed
          in what he had redeemed from the sea's rage,
through thorns and shadows treading twilights picks   50
      his way, and cliffs a challenge even to
          the swiftest boldest wing
begins, uncertain more than tired, to climb.

Conquered at last the heights that stand between
      the ever-sounding sea   55

de la muda campaña
árbitro igual e inexpugnable muro—,   55
   con pie ya más seguro
   declina al vacilante
breve esplendor de mal distinta lumbre:
   farol de una cabaña
que sobre el ferro está, en aquel incierto   60
golfo de sombras anunciando el puerto.
'Rayos—les dice—ya que no de Leda
trémulos hijos, sed de mi fortuna
término luminoso.' Y—recelando
de invidïosa bárbara arboleda   65
   interposición, cuando
de vientos no conjuración alguna—
   cual, haciendo el villano
la fragosa montaña fácil llano,
   atento sigue aquella   70
—aun a pesar de las tinieblas bella,
aun a pesar de las estrellas clara—
   piedra, indigna tiara
—si tradición apócrifa no miente—
de animal tenebroso, cuya frente   75
carro es brillante de nocturno día:
   tal, diligente, el paso
   el joven apresura,
   midiendo la espesura
   con igual pie que el raso,   80
fijo—a despecho de la niebla fría—
en el carbunclo, norte de su aguja,
o el Austro brame o la arboleda cruja.

   El can ya, vigilante,
convoca, despidiendo al caminante;   85
   y la que desvïada
luz poca pareció, tanta es vecina,
que yace en ella la robusta encina,
mariposa en cenizas desatada.

Llegó pues el mancebo, y saludado,   90
sin ambición, sin pompa de palabras,

and silent countryside
    as demarcation line, defensive screen,
his footsteps, become firmer, now start to sink
    toward the tremulous glimmer
        of a light that's barely seen,   60
    mark of some local cabin
        at anchor there in that vague gulf of shadows
    signaling haven.
"If not a sign from heaven," he declares,
    "may this beam mean at least   65
an end to my misfortunes." And fearing
    the hostile intervention
    of some jealous screen of trees or the light's
    assassination by a sudden gust,
like the countryman who makes   70
    of the rugged mountain an easy plain
    by fixing his eyes on
    the gleam of that famed gem
        —beauty blazing through the dark,
        beauty brighter than the stars—   75
    improbable tiara,
        if what they say is true,
    of the mysterious animal whose brow
        bears it like a nighttime sun,
so now, pressing on   80
        over smooth, over rough,
the young man holds his pace
despite the chill, despite the murk, intent
        on that jewel, lodestone of his compass,
            roar how it will the south wind or groan the wood.   85

The watchdog, roused, gives voice,
    but the warning guides instead of putting off,
and what from far had seemed
        no more than a dot of light is now at hand
revealed as a holm oak burning,   90
        great moth resolved to ashes.

Approaching, he is greeted
    unpretentiously, with simple words, by

de los conducidores fue de cabras,
que a Vulcano tenían coronado.

"¡Oh bienaventurado
albergue a cualquier hora,   95
templo de Pales, alquería de Flora!
No moderno artificio
borró designios, bosquejó modelos,
al cóncavo ajustando de los cielos
el sublime edificio;   100
retamas sobre robre
tu fábrica son pobre,
do guarda en vez de acero
la inocencia al cabrero,
más que el silbo al ganado.   105
¡Oh bienaventurado
albergue a cualquier hora!

No en ti la Ambición mora
hidrópica de viento,
ni la que su alimento   110
el áspid es gitano;
no la que, en vulto comenzando humano,
acaba en mortal fiera,
esfinge bachillera,
que hace hoy a Narciso   115
Ecos solicitar, desdeñar fuentes;
ni la que en salvas gasta impertinentes
la pólvora del tiempo más preciso:
Ceremonia profana
que la sinceridad burla villana   120
sobre el corvo cayado.
¡Oh bienaventurado
albergue a cualquier hora!

Tus umbrales ignora
la Adulación, sirena   125
de Reales Palacios, cuya arena
besó ya tanto leño:

the goatherds sitting in a circle round
    their blessed fire.   95

"What a sanctuary
for all seasons!
Green chapel, sacred grange:
no architect
on modern lines   100
scribbled sketches, tried designs
to copy heaven in a dome;
oak and broom
furnish your room,
the shepherd's defence   105
not steel but innocence,
clean as the whistle by which he guides the flock.
What a sanctuary
for all seasons!

Swollen ambition   110
doesn't dwell here, stuffing wind,
nor does calumny
gorging on poison
nor the garrulous sphinx,
flattery, with her human face   115
mounted on a deadly beast,
who now has Narcissus
trading reflection for an echo,
nor the busy wastrel
court ceremony   120
murdering time
 while the honest shepherd
leans on his crook to mock.
What a sanctuary
for all seasons!   125

Adulation
shuns your portals,
palace siren on whose shoals
so many courtiers' ships have foundered,
victims of slumbering self-deceit.   130

trofeos dulces de un canoro sueño.
No a la Soberbia está aquí la Mentira
dorándole los pies, en cuanto gira   130
   la esfera de sus plumas,
ni de los rayos baja a las espumas
   Favor de cera alado.
   ¡Oh bienaventurado
   albergue a cualquier hora!"   135

No pues de aquella sierra—engendradora
más de fierezas que de cortesía—
   la gente parecía
   que hospedó al forastero
con pecho igual de aquel Candor primero,   140
   que, en las selvas contento,
tienda el fresno le dio, el robre alimento.

Limpio sayal, en vez de blanco lino,
   cubrió el cuadrado pino;
y en boj, aunque rebelde, a quien el torno   145
forma elegante dio sin culto adorno,
leche que exprimir vio la Alba aquel día
   —mientras perdían con ella
los blancos lilios de su frente bella—,
   gruesa le dan y fría,   150
impenetrable casi a la cuchara,
del viejo Alcimedón invención rara.
El que de cabras fue dos veces ciento
esposo casi un lustro—cuyo diente
no perdonó a racimo aun en la frente   155
de Baco, cuanto más en su sarmiento—
(triunfador siempre de celosas lides,
lo coronó el Amor; mas rival tierno,
breve de barba y duro no de cuerno,
redimió con su muerte tantas vides)   160
   servido ya en cecina,
purpúreos hilos es de grana fina.
Sobre corchos después, más regalado

Falsehood's not seen
gilding the feet
of peacock Pride who flaunts his feathers
nor the favorite's plunge
from firmament to waves   135
as the wings' wax fails.
What a sanctuary
for all seasons!"

It seemed a wilderness
        more apt to spawn coarse manners   140
    than the courtesy these locals showed,
welcoming the foreigner
    with the simplicity of that noble age
    when people were content with what the forest
    gave: food from the oak, the ash tree's shelter.   145

Damask dinner napkins there were not,
    but the homespun cloth was clean,
    spread over rough-hewn pine;
and in a bowl that needed
    no antique decoration to enhance   150
        the beauty of its form, hard won from boxwood,
they gave him milk that Dawn had seen that day
    drawn from the udder, so white the lilies
    of her own fair brow might blush, cold and thick
    enough to stand the spoon up.   155
The old billy goat, nearly
    five years lord of two hundred wives, from whose
        sharp tooth no grape (even on Bacchus's brow)
        was ever safe,
    crowned victor by Cupid   160
        in many an amorous dispute
        till recently when a younger rival,
            short in the beard and still unhard of horn,
            redeemed with his death so many ruined vines,
is now dried meat, served up   165
    in slivers of crimson flesh.
After this the wanderer slept
    on fleeces spread on cork

sueño le solicitan pieles blandas,
que al Príncipe entre holandas,   165
púrpura tiria o milanés brocado.
No de humosos vinos agravado
es Sísifo en la cuesta, si en la cumbre
de ponderosa vana pesadumbre,
es, cuanto más despierto, más burlado.   170
De trompa militar no, o destemplado
son de cajas, fue el sueño interrumpido;
    de can sí, embravecido
    contra la seca hoja
que el viento repeló a alguna coscoja.   175

Durmió, y recuerda al fin, cuando las aves
—esquilas dulces de sonora pluma—
    señas dieron süaves
del alba al Sol, que el pabellón de espuma
    dejó, y en su carroza   180
rayó el verde obelisco de la choza.

Agradecido, pues, el peregrino,
deja el albergue y sale acompañado
de quien lo lleva donde, levantado,
distante pocos pasos del camino,   185
imperïoso mira la campaña
un escollo, apacible galería,
que festivo teatro fue algún día
de cuantos pisan faunos la montaña.
    Llegó, y, a vista tanta   190
obedeciendo la dudosa planta,
inmóvil se quedó sobre un lentisco,
verde balcón del agradable risco.

Si mucho poco mapa les despliega,
mucho es más lo que, nieblas desatando,   195
confunde el Sol y la distancia niega.
Muda la admiración habla callando,
y, ciega un río sigue, que—luciente
    de aquellos montes hijo—

a sweeter sleep than princes have between
   crisp sheets with Tyrian purple   170
   covers, Milanese brocade.
He'd drunk no heady wine
   to make him sweat like Sisyphus up the slope
     of ambition's weary dream and at the top
   wake to see himself the dupe.   175
No harsh sounds disturbed his rest
   no martial trump, cacophony of drums,
only the bark of a dog
   outraged at the scurrying of a leaf
     the wind has snatched from some dry oak tree.   180

He slept and was recalled when the tongues of birds,
   soft bells of ringing feathers,
gently signaled dawn to the sun who quits
   his couch amid the foam
   and leaning from his car   185
strikes the tip of the hut's green obelisk.

Gratefully the pilgrim
   leaves the refuge and goes with
one who leads him to a knoll
   which rises to survey the countryside   190
   no great distance from the road,
a tranquil gallery
   that in its time has served as
     theater to all the fauns who haunt this district.
As he gains the crest the view   195
   arrests his steps: he stands
   motionless above a terebinth perched
     as a green balcony on that friendly cliff.

Like a small map encompassing a world
much is unfolded to him while much more's   200
   obscured by the sun undressing mists, denied
     by distance. Admiration
speechless speaks volumes while his gaze
   follows blindly the gleaming
   river of these mountains born   205
   that with meandering though fluent discourse

con torcido discurso, aunque prolijo,   200
tiraniza los campos útilmente;
orladas sus orillas de frutales,
quiere la Copia que su cuerno sea
—si al animal armaron de Amaltea
    diáfanos cristales—;   205
engazando edificios en su plata,
    de muros se corona,
rocas abraza, islas aprisiona,
de la alta gruta donde se desata
hasta los jaspes líquidos, adonde   210
su orgullo pierde y su memoria esconde.

'Aquéllas que los árboles apenas
dejan ser torres hoy—dijo el cabrero
con muestras de dolor extraordinarias—
las estrellas nocturnas luminarias   215
    eran de sus almenas,
cuando el que ves sayal fue limpio acero.
Yacen ahora, y sus desnudas piedras
    visten piadosas yedras:
    que a rüinas y a estragos,   220
sabe el tiempo hacer verdes halagos.'

Con gusto el joven y atención le oía,
cuando torrente de armas y de perros,
que si precipitados no los cerros,
las personas tras de un lobo traía,   225
tierno discurso y dulce compañía
    dejar hizo al serrano,
que—del sublime espacïoso llano
al huésped al camino reduciendo—
    al venatorio estruendo,   230
    pasos dando veloces,
número crece y multiplica voces.

Bajaba entre sí el joven admirando,
armado a Pan o semicapro a Marte,
en el pastor mentidos, que con arte   235
culto principio dio al discurso, cuando
rémora de sus pasos fue su oído,

practises on fields fruitful tyranny:
its banks are fringed with orchards and could serve
for Plenty's cornucopia
if one envisaged Amalthea's goat armed   210
with limpid crystal horns;
it wears buildings strung on its silver chain,
surrounds itself with walls,
embraces boulders and lassoes islands,
right the way down from the high   215
grotto of its unleashing
to the liquid jasper where
its pride is swallowed, memory interred.

Looking like someone overwhelmed by loss
the goatherd speaks: 220
"Those towers, which scarce the undergrowth reveals
    as towers, on their battlements, before,
    the stars of the night sky seemed poised,
    when this rough cloth of mine was burnished steel.
Now they are brought low and their stripped stones   225
    wear charitable coats of ivy,
for time knows how to give green consolations
    to ruins and the wounds of war."

The voyager was listening spellbound when
    an avalanche of dogs and huntsmen,   230
    which left the slopes intact
    but hurled men headlong in pursuit of a wolf,
caused his informant to break off,
return him from the lookout to the path
and rush to join the hunt,   235
    increasing its numbers by only one
        but doubling the shouts.

As the stranger went on down the path alone
    he wondered, what was he,
this goatherd with the cultivated style: 240
    a Pan in armor or a Mars half goat?
till he was pulled up short,

    dulcemente impedido
de canoro instrumento, que pulsado
era de una serrana junto a un tronco,   240
sobre un arroyo, de quejarse ronco,
mudo sus ondas, cuando no enfrenado.
Otra con ella montaraz zagala
juntaba el cristal líquido al humano
por el arcaduz bello de una mano   245
que al uno menosprecia, al otro iguala.
Del verde margen otra las mejores
rosas traslada y lilios al cabello,
o por lo matizado o por lo bello,
si Aurora no con rayos, Sol con flores.   250
Negras pizarras entre blancos dedos
ingenïosa hiere otra, que dudo
que aun los peñascos la escucharan quedos.
    Al son pues deste rudo
    sonoroso instrumento   255
    —lasciva el movimiento,
    mas los ojos honesta—
altera otra, bailando, la floresta.
Tantas al fin el arroyuelo, y tantas
montañesas da el prado, que dirías   260
ser menos las que verdes Hamadrías
    abortaron las plantas:
    inundación hermosa
que la montaña hizo populosa
    de sus aldeas todas   265
    a pastorales bodas.

    De una encina embebido
en lo cóncavo, el joven mantenía
la vista de hermosura, y el oído
    de métrica armonía.   270
    El Sileno buscaba
de aquellas que la sierra dio Bacantes
—ya que Ninfas las niega ser errantes
    el hombro sin aljaba—;
    o si—del Termodonte   275

apprehended by sweet sound:
next to a tree that overhung a brook
   hoarse with the tumult of its descent and   245
   voiceless now, though flowing swiftly onward,
a girl was playing. A second girl, from
   the stream joined liquid to human crystal
   with an arm's translucent arc
   equal to her face in whiteness, brighter   250
   than water she poured on it.
A third was filching the green bank's best
   roses, irises, adding them to her hair;
      call her you might—such beauty and such color!—
      Aurora blazing bright or Sun with flowers.   255
One girl was using stones as castanets
   —black stones between white fingers—
setting up such a cunning beat, the cliffs
   themselves, for sure, must struggle to be still,
   while to this impromptu music   260
another rolled her hips and danced
   provocatively
   but with innocence in her eyes.
There were so many of them, about the brook
   and over the meadow, if   265
   the green hamadryads stood forth, expelled
      from every tree, they'd be
      outnumbered you'd suppose:
this flux of beauty that rose
   to flood the mountain, emptying   270
   all its villages, was heading
      for a country wedding.

He hid, watching, in a hollow oak,
   his eyes and ears overwhelmed
   by beauty and the rhythmic beat.   275
He sought in vain the master
   of these who seemed Bacchantes,
   no hunting party since
   none carried bow and arrows—
or could one take perhaps   280
      this modest burn, loosed from the craggy upland,
      for another Thermidon,

émulo el arroyuelo desatado
    de aquel fragoso monte—
escuadrón de Amazonas, desarmado,
    tremola en sus riberas
    pacíficas banderas.   280
    Vulgo lascivo erraba
    al voto del mancebo,
(el yugo de ambos sexos sacudido)
al tiempo que—de flores impedido
    el que ya serenaba   285
la región de su frente rayo nuevo—
purpúrea terneruela, conducida
de su madre, no menos enramada,
entre albogues se ofrece, acompañada
    de juventud florida.   290
Cuál dellos las pendientes sumas graves
de negras baja, de crestadas aves,
cuyo lascivo esposo vigilante
doméstico es del Sol nuncio canoro,
y—de coral barbado—no de oro   295
ciñe, sino de púrpura, turbante.
    Quién la cerviz oprime
    con la manchada copia
de los cabritos más retozadores,
    tan golosos, que gime   300
el que menos peinar puede las flores
    de su guirnalda propia.
    No el sitio, no, fragoso,
no el torcido taladro de la tierra,
    privilegió en la sierra   305
la paz del conejuelo temeroso;
trofeo ya su número es a un hombro,
    si carga no y asombro.
    Tú, ave peregrina,
arrogante esplendor—ya que no bello—   310
    del último Occidente:
penda el rugoso nácar de tu frente
sobre el crespo zafiro de tu cuello,

and these on its banks a troop
of Amazons who'd downed their arms
to wave pacific banners?   285
Finally he concludes they're just young women
on a carefree outing
taking no direction from either sex,
for at that moment to the sound of flutes
appears a group of gilded youths escorting   290
a fine new calf upon
whose brow the bright horns dawning
are garlanded with flowers,
preceded by his mother
no less adorned than he.   295
There are some weighed down by strings
of black and crested chickens,
birds whose vigilant lascivious spouse
is lyric domestic herald to the sun
and like some coral-bearded sultan bears   300
a turban on his head
—a scarlet not a gold one.
Across his shoulders one man
carries a speckled pair
of frisky kids so greedy   305
one bleats in desperation
at not managing to curl his tongue round
the flowers with which he's crowned.
The burden another's hung about with is
an amazing quantity of rabbits: 310
poor things, the siting and the labyrinthine
architecture of their home
earned them on that mountain
no privilege of peace.
And now, what's this? The weird exotic fowl,   315
arrogant prize albeit not for beauty
of the far West, who lowers his nacreous
corrugated brow over the ragged
sapphire of his neck, as well
he may, for he too is destined for the feast!   320

que Himeneo a sus mesas te destina.
Sobre dos hombros larga vara ostenta   315
en cien aves cien picos de rubíes,
tafiletes calzadas carmesíes,
    emulación y afrenta
    aun de los Berberiscos,
en la inculta región de aquellos riscos.   320
    Lo que lloró la Aurora
    —si es néctar lo que llora—,
    y, antes que el Sol, enjuga
    la abeja que madruga
a libar flores y a chupar cristales,   325
en celdas de oro líquido, en panales
    la orza contenía
    que un montañés traía.
    No excedía la oreja
    el pululante ramo   330
    del ternezuelo gamo,
    que mal llevar se deja,
y con razón: que el tálamo desdeña
la sombra aun de lisonja tan pequeña.

El arco del camino pues torcido,   335
    —que habían con trabajo
por la fragosa cuerda del atajo
las gallardas serranas desmentido—
de la cansada juventud vencido,
    —los fuertes hombros con las cargas graves,   340
    treguas hechas süaves—
sueño le ofrece a quien buscó descanso
el ya sañudo arroyo, ahora manso:
merced de la hermosura que ha hospedado,
efectos si no dulces, del concento   345
que, en las lucientes de marfil clavijas,
las duras cuerdas de las negras guijas
hicieron a su curso acelerado,
en cuanto a su furor perdonó el viento.

Menos en renunciar tardó la encina   350
    el extranjero errante,

Two men carrying a long pole display
    a hundred red-beaked birds
    sporting crimson slippers
    as handsome as the ones
        imported from Morocco   325
—rare ornament in a backwater like this.
The product of Dawn's weeping—
    if what she weeps be tears of nectar wiped
    before sunup by the bee
        rising early to sip   330
    flowers, suck on crystal, and
        turned now into liquid gold—
is held in cells, in combs,
    within a plain earthen jar
    one of the young men carries.   335
Also a young deer
whose budding antlers
    don't exceed his ears in length
is dragged protesting, and with reason, for
    the marriage bed resents   340
    the merest shadow of such endowments.

When the bent bow of the road
    (which with some effort the girls,
    by taking the abrupter way
    that mimicks the bowstring, abbreviated)   345
was completed by the tired young men,
they first, to ease their shoulders, concluded
    with their burdens a truce,
and then sought rest, finding in adddition
    sleep, lulled by the boisterous stream, now tamed,   350
    either through harboring so much beauty
    or from hearing the sweet harmonies
    with which hard black strings of slate,
        pegged as they seem to be
        by ivory trunks of trees,   355
    responded to its swift flow
        once the wind's bluster had relented.

The outsider from his hollow tree emerged
    in less time than it took the least

que en reclinarse el menos fatigado
sobre la grana que se viste fina
su bella amada, deponiendo amante
en las vestidas rosas su cuidado.   355

Saludólos a todos cortésmente,
    y—admirado no menos
de los serranos que correspondido—
las sombras solicita de unas peñas.
De lágrimas los tiernos ojos llenos,   360
reconociendo el mar en el vestido
—que beberse no pudo el Sol ardiente
las que siempre dará cerúleas señas—,
    político serrano,
de canas grave, habló desta manera: 365

    "¿Cuál tigre, la más fiera
    que clima infamó hircano,
    dio el primer alimento
al que—ya deste o aquel mar—primero
    surcó, labrador fiero,   370
el campo undoso en mal nacido pino,
    vaga Clicie del viento,
en telas hecho—antes que en flor—el lino?
Más armas introdujo este marino
monstro, escamado de robustas hayas,   375
a las que tanto mar divide playas,
    que confusión y fuego
al frigio muro el otro leño griego.
Náutica industria investigó tal piedra,
    que, cual abraza yedra   380
escollo, el metal ella fulminante
de que Marte se viste, y, lisonjera,
solicita el que más brilla diamante
en la nocturna capa de la esfera,
estrella a nuestro polo más vecina;   385
    y, con virtud no poca,
    distante la revoca,
    elevada la inclina
    ya de la Aurora bella
al rosado balcón, ya a la que sella   390

exhausted of the men to lay his head   360
    gratefully in his lover's lap,
    clad in her flowery best,
confiding to her his care.

He greeted them politely
and when they'd replied in kind,   365
    as pleased to see him as they were surprised,
he sought the shade of a rock.
With tears of emotion
    from recognizing on the stranger's clothing
    the sea's mark, which even the blazing sun   370
        could not erase entirely,
a white-haired man who seemed
a refugee from court held forth as follows:

"How savagely he sinned
who first presumed to open furrows   375
    on wave-tossed fields of one sea or the other
        in his accursed craft
    employing flax, transformed
    not like Clytie into a sunflower
    but canvas sails turning to seek the wind!   380
These monsters of the deep with planks for scales,
    more treacherous than Greece's wooden gift
    that brought fire and confusion to Troy's walls,
have transported so much pain
    to worlds so many seas apart!   385
Marine endeavor explored
    the stone which close as ivy on a ruin
    clings to the shining metal Mars is clad in
    and with flattery courts the steadiest jewel
        in the globe's nocturnal cap,   390
        the star that sits closest to our Pole
        and has the art
        to seek it out from afar,
        but takes when it's overhead
        deflection either toward   395
        Dawn's rosy balcony

cerúlea tumba fría
las cenizas del día.
En esta, pues, fiándose atractiva
del Norte amante dura, alado roble,
no hay tormentoso cabo que no doble,   395
ni isla hoy a su vuelo fugitiva.
Tifis el primer leño mal seguro
condujo, muchos luego Palinuro;
si bien por un mar ambos, que la tierra
estanque dejó hecho,   400
cuyo famoso estrecho
una y otra de Alcides llave cierra.
Piloto hoy la Codicia, no de errantes
árboles, mas de selvas inconstantes,
al padre de las aguas Ocëano   405
—de cuya monarquía
el Sol, que cada día
nace en sus ondas y en sus ondas muere,
los términos saber todos no quiere—
dejó primero de su espuma cano,   410
sin admitir segundo
en inculcar sus límites al mundo.
Abetos suyos tres aquel tridente
violaron a Neptuno,
conculcado hasta allí de otro ninguno,   415
besando las que al Sol el Occidente
le corre, en lecho azul de aguas marinas,
turquesadas cortinas.
A pesar luego de áspides volantes
—sombra del sol y tósigo del viento—   420
de Caribes flechados, sus banderas
siempre gloriosas, siempre tremolantes,
rompieron los que armó de plumas ciento
Lestrigones el istmo, aladas fieras:
el istmo que al Océano divide,   425
y—sierpe de cristal—juntar le impide
la cabeza, del Norte coronada,
con la que ilustra el Sur cola escamada

or the cold blue tomb that seals
the ashes of the day.
And now by virtue of this
sympathetic stone lover of the North,   400
no cape's too stormy for ships to round it
or isle remote enough
to be beyond their reach.
The first uncertain voyages as we know
—the Argonauts, the fleet that bore Aeneas—   405
traversed a sea the land has made a pond
whose famous straights are closed
by Hercules' twin gates.
Today Greed is at the helm
not of single ships alone   410
but of whole restless fleets,
and Greed leads the attack
on the father of all waters, Ocean,
of whose vast realm
the Sun himself though born   415
and dying in its waves each day
does not desire to visit all the regions,
and Greed turns Ocean's hair white with his own foam
and will admit no rival
in rehearsing to the world   420
just how far its boundaries stretch.
First they were three, the ships
that sailed under Greed's flag
and plundered Neptune's trident
—his kingdom that till then   425
no other foot infringed—
touching the turquoise curtains
the West draws to behind the Sun when he sinks
to his aquamarine bed.
Unabashed when flying clouds   430
of Caribs' poisoned arrows
dimmed the sun, tainted the wind
Greed marched on with flying banners and smashed
the plumed cannibals, bird-beasts
of the isthmus: that isthmus that bisects   435
the crystal snake, Ocean,
preventing his head crowned by the Pole Star

de antárticas estrellas.
Segundos leños dio a segundo Polo   430
en nuevo mar, que le rindió no sólo
las blancas hijas de sus conchas bellas,
mas los que lograr bien no supo Midas
    metales homicidas.
No le bastó después a este elemento   435
conducir orcas, alistar ballenas,
murarse de montañas espumosas,
infamar blanqueando sus arenas
con tantas del primer atrevimiento
señas—aun a los buitres lastimosas—,   440
para con estas lastimosas señas
temeridades enfrenar segundas.
Tú, Codicia, tú, pues, de las profundas
estigias aguas torpe marinero,
cuantos abre sepulcros el mar fiero   445
    a tus huesos, desdeñas.
El promontorio que Éolo sus rocas
candados hizo de otras nuevas grutas
para el Austro de alas nunca enjutas,
para el Cierzo espirante por cien bocas,   450
doblaste alegre, y tu obstinada entena
cabo le hizo de esperanza buena.
Tantos luego astronómicos presagios
frustrados, tanta náutica doctrina,
debajo aun de la zona más vecina   455
al Sol, calmas vencidas y naufragios,
los reinos de la Aurora al fin besaste,
cuyos purpúreos senos perlas netas,
    cuyas minas secretas
hoy te guardan su más precioso engaste.   460
La aromática selva penetraste,
que al pájaro de Arabia—cuyo vuelo
    arco alado es del cielo,
    no corvo, mas tendido—
pira le erige y le construye nido.   465
Zodíaco después fue cristalino
    a glorïoso pino,
émulo vago del ardiente coche
    del Sol, este elemento,

                    from joining the scaly tail
                that the South illustrates with
                    Antarctic constellations.   440
When Greed assigned a new fleet to the other
    Pole, a further sea gave up her treasures
    the white daughters of her glistening shells
    as well as what Midas failed to profit from:
    the homicidal metals.   445
In vain did Ocean seek
    to hold back this second reckless onslaught
        —mustering sharks, conscripting whales,
        compiling mounds of foam like city walls
        or cruelly whitening his beaches   450
        with first adventurers' bones,
            so many even vultures pitied them,—
    all was to no avail.
Vile Greed that will navigate
        the murkiest waters cares   455
    not a whit how many graves the fierce sea
        inaugurs for the dead.
The cape upon whose rocky coasts the winds
    are once more serving out their term—Auster,
    whose wings are never dry,   460
    Boreas who breathes through a hundred mouths—
she gleefully rounded, her stubborn bowsprit
    converting it to an emblem of good hope.
Later, confounding so
    many astronomical predictions   465
    so much nautical dogma,
overcoming calms, shipwreck,
    below those latitudes closest to the sun,
she touched at last the kingdoms of Dawn,
    whose purple bosom held fine pearls for her   470
    and secret mines surrender still
        the richest element for their setting.
She invaded the aromatic forest
    which for the Arabian bird whose transit leaves
        a rainbow trace drawn flat across the sky   475
    furnishes both pyre and nest.
Then it was sea supplied the crystal track
    round which like a rival to Sun's flaming car

que cuatro veces había sido ciento   470
dosel al día y tálamo a la noche,
cuando halló de fugitiva plata
la bisagra, aunque estrecha, abrazadora
de un Océano y otro, siempre uno,
o las columnas bese o la escarlata,   475
  tapete de la Aurora.
  Esta pues nave, ahora,
en el húmido templo de Neptuno
varada pende a la inmortal Memoria
  con nombre de Victoria.   480
De firmes islas no la inmóvil flota
en aquel mar del Alba te describo,
cuyo número—ya que no lascivo—
por lo bello, agradable y por lo vario
la dulce confusión hacer podía   485
que en los blancos estanques del Eurota
la virginal desnuda montería,
haciendo escollos o de mármol pario
o de terso marfil sus miembros bellos,
que pudo bien Acteón perderse en ellos.   490
El bosque dividido en islas pocas,
fragrante productor de aquel aroma
—que, traducido mal por el Egito,
tarde le encomendó el Nilo a sus bocas,
y ellas más tarde a la gulosa Grecia—,   495
clavo no, espuela sí del apetito
—que cuanto en conocello tardó Roma
fué templado Catón, casta Lucrecia—,
quédese, amigo, en tan inciertos mares,
  donde con mi hacienda   500
del alma se quedó la mejor prenda,
cuya memoria es buitre de pesares.'

  En suspiros, con esto,
y en más anegó lágrimas el resto
de su discurso el montañés prolijo,   505
que el viento su caudal, el mar su hijo.

a famous ship set off
and—after sea had served four hundred times 480
    as backdrop to the day, night's couch—
discovered the narrow liquid silver hinge
coupling one part of Ocean to the other,
        meaning it's one and the same
        whether it kisses Hercules' pillars 485
        or laps dawn's scarlet carpet—
the ship which, beached, now hangs
    to eternal memory in Neptune's
    humid temple; its name: Victoria.
Of the immobile fleet of islands lying 490
    at anchor in that dawn sea
I say nothing, a multitude, though not
    licentious, that through its beauty and delight
        and variety might arouse
the same sweet perturbation 495
as did in the white pools of the Eurotas
the naked virginal troop
whose ravishing limbs formed reefs
as if of marble or smooth ivory
among which Actaeon 500
could not but lose his way.
As for that fragrant forest
    divided among small islands,
source of the spice that, dragged the length of Egypt
    to reach the many mouths of Nile, 505
comes with yet more delays to expectant Greece
    —cloves we call it (like clover),
    that makes men into pigs, stirring their senses,
        for only before the Romans knew its use
        could there be temperate Cato, chaste Lucrece— 510
all that, my friend, let it remain in those
    perilous seas where with my sunken fortune
the greatest treasure of my life lies buried,
    whose memory gnaws, a vulture, at my entrails."

This extensive speech foundered in sighs 515
    and in more tempestuous tears than the wind
    that took the old man's wealth,
    the seas that took his son.

Consolallo pudiera el peregrino
con las de su edad corta historias largas,
si—vinculados todos a sus cargas,
cual próvidas hormigas a sus mieses—   510
no comenzaran ya los montañeses
a esconder con el número el camino,
y el cielo con el polvo. Enjugó el viejo
del tierno humor las venerables canas,
y levantando al forastero, dijo: 515
        'Cabo me han hecho, hijo,
deste hermoso tercio de serranas;
si tu neutralidad sufre consejo,
y no te fuerza obligación precisa,
la piedad que en mi alma ya te hospeda   520
hoy te convida al que nos guarda sueño
        política alameda,
verde muro de aquel lugar pequeño
que, a pesar de esos fresnos, se divisa;
sigue la femenil tropa conmigo: 525
verás curioso y honrarás testigo
el tálamo de nuestros labradores,
que de tu calidad señas mayores
me dan que del Océano tus paños,
o razón falta donde sobran años.'   530

Mal pudo el extranjero, agradecido,
en tercio tal negar tal compañía
y en tan noble ocasión tal hospedaje.
Alegres pisan la que, si no era
de chopos calle y de álamos carrera,   535
el fresco de los céfiros rüido,
el denso de los árboles celaje,
en duda ponen cuál mayor hacía
guerra al calor o resistencia al día.

Coros tejiendo, voces alternando,   540
sigue la dulce escuadra montañesa
del perezoso arroyo el paso lento,

The pilgrim might have sought to divert him
    with the long history of his own short life,   520
had not just then the mountain lads set off,
    reunited to their various loads like
        provident ants bearing away their harvest,
    their number sufficient to hide the road,
    the dust they raised to veil the sky.   525
The old man wiped away his tears
    and pulling the stranger to his feet, said:
"They have put me in command, young friend, of this
    fair company of ladies;
and if you will listen to my proposal,   530
    and have no previous plan,
the sympathy that I feel towards you
    urges this invitation: come with us
and share the rest that waits
    in that well-sited grove   535
    making a green precinct to
    the village you can glimpse beyond the ash trees.
Come to our country wedding;
it may amuse you and I'm sure will honor us,
    for your clothes give evidence   540
        as much of quality as of the sea,
or else my understanding
    is as lacking as my years are in excess."

The foreigner was grateful and in no
    position to reject the company   545
    of such a troop, or turn down
    the lodging their big event provided.
They proceeded joyfully along a road
    which though no stately highway offered freely
    the refreshing sound of breezes   550
    and thick foliage of trees, making a doubt
    which service it best performs: war on heat
    or opposition to the sunlight.

Dancing, singing, the gallant mountain platoon
    advances with the stream,   555
        which lazily flows along

en cuanto él hurta blando,
entre los olmos que robustos besa,
pedazos de cristal, que el movimiento   545
libra en la falda, en el coturno ella,
    de la coluna bella,
    ya que celosa basa,
dispensadora del cristal no escasa.

Sirenas de los montes su concento,   550
a la que menos del sañudo viento
    pudiera antigua planta
temer rüina o recelar fracaso,
pasos hiciera dar el menor paso
    de su pie o su garganta.   555
Pintadas aves—cítaras de pluma—
coronaban la bárbara capilla,
mientras el arroyuelo para oílla
    hace de blanca espuma
tantas orejas cuantas guijas lava,   560
de donde es fuente adonde arroyo acaba.

Vencedores se arrogan los serranos
los consignados premios otro día,
ya al formidable salto, ya a la ardiente
lucha, ya a la carrera polvorosa.   565
El menos ágil, cuantos comarcanos
convoca el caso, él solo desafía,
consagrando los palios a su esposa,
    que a mucha fresca rosa
beber el sudor hace de su frente,   570
    mayor aún del que espera
en la lucha, en el salto, en la carrera.

Centro apacible un círculo espacioso
a más caminos que una estrella rayos,
hacía, bien de pobos, bien de alisos,   575
    donde la Primavera,
—calzada abriles y vestida mayos—
centellas saca de cristal undoso

between strong elms it kisses
and smoothly robs white treasure
by movement released from skirts and thence transferred
to more revealing sandals   560
which, though they may seem jealous
bases to fair columns,
of their capital are generous lenders.

Such a chorus, like sirens of the mountain,
could with the lightest lilt   565
    of foot or throat set dancing
    the most stately tree, the one
    that least fears ruin or
    catastrophe from raging winds.
Colored birds like feathered harps   570
    augment the rustic harmony,
while better to hear the stream
    shapes ears of foam with every
    pebble it washes over
from where it springs to where as stream it ceases.   575

The men meanwhile are boasting
    of victories yet to come,
claiming tomorrow's prizes, whether it be
    for prodigious leaping, might in wrestling,
    or speed on the dusty track.   580
Even the least athletic thinks to take on
    all comers single-handed
and already makes a gift of the unwon crown
    to his lady who approaches
            the red roses of her cheeks   585
to his, soaked in more perspiration now
    than the coming games will raise.

There was a broad and tranquil circle,
    on which more ways converged
    than a star has rays,   590
of alders and white poplars
where Spring with Aprils shod and dressed in Mays
    strikes liquid crystal sparks from

a un pedernal orlado de narcisos.
   Este, pues, centro era   580
meta umbrosa al vaquero convecino,
y delicioso término al distante,
donde, aún cansado más que el caminante,
   concurría el camino.

Al concento se abaten cristalino   585
   sedientas las serranas,
cual simples codornices al reclamo
que les miente la voz, y verde cela,
entre la no espigada mies, la tela.

Músicas hojas viste el menor ramo   590
del álamo que peina verdes canas;
no céfiros en él, no ruiseñores
lisonjear pudieron breve rato
   al montañés, que—ingrato
al fresco, a la armonía y a las flores—   595
   del sitio pisa ameno
la fresca hierba, cual la arena ardiente
de la Libia, y a cuantas da la fuente
sierpes de aljófar, aún mayor veneno
que a las del Ponto, tímido, atribuye,   600
según el pie, según los labios huye.

Pasaron todos pues, y regulados
cual en los Equinocios surcar vemos
los piélagos del aire libre algunas
   volantes no galeras,   605
   sino grullas veleras,
tal vez creciendo, tal menguando lunas
   sus distantes extremos,
caracteres tal vez formando alados
en el papel diáfano del cielo   610
   las plumas de su vuelo.

Ellas en tanto en bóvedas de sombras,
   pintadas siempre al fresco,
cubren las que Sidón telar turquesco

the flint of a boulder fringed
with narcissus. This was the center, shady   595
    goal of local cowherds and a welcome
    terminus to those from further off;
for here the road, exhausted
    more truly than the traveler, meets its end.

The thirsty girls swoop down   600
    to drink from the tinkling source
as the innocent quail to the hunter's call,
    who mimics its voice, hiding
    the traitor net in the still earless corn.

The aspen wears musical leaves   605
    on every branch, combed into white-haired green;
but neither this breeze, nor the nightingale,
    could for a moment please
the old man, who disdains
    all the freshness, the harmony, the flowers   610
    of the delightful place, treading the grass
    as if it were the burning sands of Libya,
and seems fearful of the source's pearly rills,
    deeming them serpents more
        deadly than those of Pontus   615
to judge by the way his foot, his lips flee them.

The men went on their way, loosely disposed
as during the equinoxes we observe
ploughing the oceans of the empty air
    the sailing cranes,   620
        those airborne galleys
            the separate extremes of whose formation
    wax and wane continually
        like moons, sometimes writing winged characters
            on the diaphanous page of the sky   625
        with their feathered quills.

The girls meanwhile, under their cupola
    of shade, painted *al fresco*,
stretch out on the green carpet

no ha sabido imitar verdes alfombras.   615
Apenas reclinaron la cabeza,
cuando, en número iguales y en belleza,
los márgenes matiza de las fuentes
segunda primavera de villanas,
que—parientas del novio aun más cercanas   620
que vecinos sus pueblos—de presentes
prevenidas, concurren a las bodas.
    Mezcladas hacen todas
teatro dulce—no de escena muda—
el apacible sitio: espacio breve   625
en que, a pesar del sol, cuajada nieve,
y nieve de colores mil vestida,
    la sombra vio florida
    en la hierba menuda.

Viendo, pues, que igualmente les quedaba   630
para el lugar a ellas de camino
lo que al Sol para el lóbrego Occidente,
cual de aves se caló turba canora
a robusto nogal que acequia lava
    en cercado vecino,   635
cuando a nuestros Antípodas la Aurora
las rosas gozar deja de su frente:
tal sale aquella que sin alas vuela
hermosa escuadra con ligero paso,
haciéndole atalayas del Ocaso   640
cuantos humeros cuenta la aldehuela.
    El lento escuadrón luego
    alcanzan de serranos,
y—disolviendo allí la compañía—
al pueblo llegan con la luz que el día   645
cedió al sacro volcán de errante fuego,
a la torre, de luces coronada,
que el templo ilustra, y a los aires vanos
artificiosamente da exhalada
luminosas de pólvora saetas,   650
    purpúreos no cometas.

Los fuegos, pues, el joven solemniza,
mientras el viejo tanta acusa tea

that Sidon's Turkish art can never copy.   630
Barely have they laid down their heads before
    (equal in number and in
    charms) a second spring of country beauties
        paints the margins of the source,
    these being the groom's close kin,   635
        who living near at hand have come provided
        each with her wedding gift.
As they mingle, the two groups
    make in the quiet spot amusing theater
but not in pantomime!   640
and for a little time despite the sun
    with coagulate snow,
        snow in myriad colors clad,
the short grass blooms in the shade.

Seeing they have about as long to travel   645
    to reach their destination
        as the sun to the gloomy West,
like a noisy flock of birds
    gathering at some robust walnut tree
        in a well-watered neighboring garden   650
    when Dawn submits the roses of her fair brow
        to be enjoyed in the antipodes,
the lovely squadron rises
    in wingless flight and with light step departs,
the smoke starting from chimneys of the village   655
    their harbinger of sunset.
They quickly overtake
    the slower men's company,
whereupon all dividing
    enter the village just as day cedes its light   660
    to the church tower, which
    —sacred volcano scattering brightness—
exhales to the vacuous air
    what we'll not call ill-omened comets but
        blazing swarms of arrows,   665
    masterworks of fire.

The stranger celebrates this rich display
but the old man scolds the god of weddings

al de las bodas dios, no alguna sea
de nocturno Faetón carroza ardiente,   655
    y miserablemente
campo amanezca estéril de ceniza
    la que anocheció aldea.

De Alcides lo llevó luego a las plantas,
    que estaban, no muy lejos,   660
trenzándose el cabello verde a cuantas
da el fuego luces y el arroyo espejos.
    Tanto garzón robusto,
tanta ofrecen los álamos zagala,
que abrevïara el Sol en una estrella,   665
    por ver la menos bella,
cuantos saluda rayos el Bengala,
    del Ganges cisne adusto.

La gaita al baile solicita el gusto,
    a la voz el salterio;   670
cruza el Trión más fijo el Hemisferio,
y el tronco mayor danza en la ribera;
    el eco, voz ya entera,
no hay silencio a que pronto no responda;
fanal es del arroyo cada onda,   675
luz el reflejo, la agua vidrïera.

Términos le da el sueño al regocijo,
mas al cansancio no: que el movimiento
verdugo de las fuerzas es prolijo.
Los fuegos—cuyas lenguas, ciento a ciento,   680
desmintieron la noche algunas horas,
cuyas luces, del Sol competidoras,
fingieron día en la tiniebla oscura—
murieron, y en sí mismos sepultados,
sus miembros, en cenizas desatados,   685
piedras son de su misma sepultura.

Vence la noche al fin, y triunfa mudo
el silencio, aunque breve, del rüido:
    sólo gime ofendido

for his profligacy,
fearing some nocturnal imitation   670
    of Phaeton's incendiary chariot
so that disastrously
what went to bed a village
will wake a waste of ashes.

Next the old man leads him to some poplars,   675
the trees of Heracles, that stand hard by
plaiting their green locks, aided
    by firelight and the looking glass of the stream.
Here many fine young men
are gathered and village girls,   680
the least of whom so bonny that for a glimpse
the Sun would be prepared to trade his rays,
    which now by Bengal's sons are greeted (dark
swans of Ganges), and shrink to a star's compass.

The bagpipe now invites to dancing, the   685
    psaltery to song; even
the sky's most steadfast star
    cuts loose, the stoutest tree
starts jigging; Echo, and not
    with half words, fills in all silences at once.   690
Each ripple of the stream's a lamp fuelled by
    reflections, glassed with water.

Sleep puts an end to the merrymaking,
    not weariness, for dancing
goes on till the dancer drops.   695
The fires whose hundred tongues
    kept night at bay for hours, their
light competing with the sun's
    to fashion day from darkness,
die and are in themselves interred, their limbs   700
    transformed to graying embers
    becoming their own tombstones.

Night conquers in the end
and silence triumphs mutely
    over noise for a brief spell.   705

el sagrado laurel del hierro agudo;   690
deja de su esplendor, deja desnudo
de su frondosa pompa al verde aliso
    el golpe no remiso
    del villano membrudo;
    el que resistir pudo   695
al animoso Austro, al Euro ronco,
chopo gallardo—cuyo liso tronco
papel fue de pastores, aunque rudo—
a revelar secretos va a la aldea,
que impide Amor que aun otro chopo lea.   700

Estos árboles, pues, ve la mañana
mentir florestas, y emular viales
cuantos muró de líquidos cristales
    agricultura urbana.

Recordó al Sol, no, de su espuma cana,   705
la dulce de las aves armonía,
sino los dos topacios que batía
—orientales aldabas—Himeneo.

    Del carro, pues, febeo
    el luminoso tiro,   710
mordiendo oro, el eclíptico zafiro
pisar quería, cuando el populoso
    lugarillo, el serrano
con su huésped, que admira cortesano
—a pesar del estambre y de la seda—   715
    el que tapiz frondoso
tejió de verdes hojas la arboleda,
y los que por las calles espaciosas
    fabrican arcos, rosas:
oblicuos nuevos pénsiles jardines,   720
de tantos como víolas jazmines.

Al galán novio el montañés presenta
su forastero; luego al venerable

One sound continues: the sob
   of laurels wounded by the woodsman's axe.
Shorn of their splendor, stripped
   of their leafy pomp are the green alders
by the unrelenting blows   710
   of strong-armed countrymen.
The tree, that had withstood
   the blustering south wind, the hoarse easterly,
a game poplar whose smooth trunk
   had served the shepherds for a makeshift book,   715
is off to the village to reveal secrets
   Love forbade even other trees to read.

Morning finds these trees, then,
   as imitation woods, emulating
those walks devised by urban agriculture   720
   set in bounds of crystal.

Not by birds' sweet music
   is the Sun roused from his white foam today
but two topaz doorknockers
   with which Hymen hammers on the eastern gate.   725

Champing at their golden bits,
   the shining train of Phoebus' car
   are ready for launching
   into their azure orbit
when the old man reaches   730
   the crowded village with his guest,
who politely praises
(though more accustomed to fine cloth or silk)
   the leafy tapestry
trees weave with their branches   735
and in the broader streets
   roses forming arches, new
      hanging gardens, swagged and spilling over
         with violets and jasmines.

First to the handsome groom the old man presents   740
   his stranger, then to the respected father
of one who, gently solemn, hides inside

padre de la que en sí bella se esconde
con ceño dulce, y, con silencio afable, 725
beldad parlera, gracia muda ostenta:
cual del rizado verde botón donde
abrevia su hermosura virgen rosa,
 las cisuras cairela
un color que la púrpura que cela 730
por brújula concede vergonzosa.
 Digna la juzga esposa
de un héroe, si no augusto, esclarecido,
el joven, al instante arrebatado
a la que, naufragante y desterrado, 735
 lo condenó a su olvido.
Este, pues, Sol que a olvido lo condena,
cenizas hizo las que su memoria
negras plumas vistió, que infelizmente
sordo engendran gusano, cuyo diente, 740
minador antes lento de su gloria,
inmortal arador fue de su pena.
Y en la sombra no más de la azucena,
que del clavel procura acompañada
imitar en la bella labradora 745
el templado color de la que adora,
víbora pisa tal el pensamiento,
que el alma, por los ojos desatada,
señas diera de su arrebatamiento,
 si de zampoñas ciento 750
y de otros, aunque bárbaros, sonoros
instrumentos, no, en dos festivos coros,
vírgenes bellas, jóvenes lucidos,
 llegaran conducidos.

El numeroso al fin de labradores 755
 concurso impacïente
los novios saca: él, de años floreciente,
y de caudal más floreciente que ellos;
ella, la misma pompa de las flores,
la esfera misma de los rayos bellos. 760
 El lazo de ambos cuellos
entre un lascivo enjambre iba de amores

her beauty, whose cheerful silences express
    speaking charms and wordless grace,
like the virgin rose whose green bud's puckered folds,   745
    where beauty waits condensed,
shyly betray the glory they conceal,
    as if through a pinhole glimpsed.
He judges her a catch
    for any but the highest in the realm   750
and is at once seized by the memory
of her who sentenced him,
this castaway, this exile,
to oblivion. His thoughts approaching
    too close to that Sun who to   755
    oblivion condemned him,
the black plumes that the memory had donned
ignite and burn to ashes,
    from which like the phoenix yet unhappily
    a silent worm is born,   760
    which working first underground
saps his well-being slowly,
and then as ploughman turns up all his grief;
so that among the ghosts of lilies mixed
    with pink carnations   765
that seek in the country girl to counterfeit
    the finer complexion of her he dotes on,
his mind treads such a viper
that the soul leaking through his eyes
    would have signaled his despair,   770
but for the opportune arrival
of two festive choirs, one female and one
    male, led by a piper
and others with cheerful, if crude, instruments.

Now the impatient company assembled   775
fetch out the bride and groom:
he in the flower of youth,
and, as a farmer, better-off than most,
she the essence of spring flowers,
sunlight's epitome.   780
Yoking their necks the god
    of marriage commences tying the knot,

Himeneo añudando,
mientras invocan su deidad la alterna
de zagalejas cándidas voz tierna   765
y de garzones este acento blando:

Coro I

Ven, Himeneo, ven donde te espera
con ojos y sin alas un Cupido,
cuyo cabello intonso dulcemente
niega el vello que el vulto ha colorido: 770
el vello, flores de su primavera,
y rayos el cabello de su frente.

Niño amó la que adora adolescente,
villana Psiques, ninfa labradora
de la tostada Ceres. Esta, ahora,   775
en los inciertos de su edad segunda
crepúsculos, vincule tu coyunda
    a su ardiente deseo.
Ven, Himeneo, ven; ven, Himeneo.

Coro II

Ven, Himeneo, donde, entre arreboles   780
de honesto rosicler, previene el día
—aurora de sus ojos soberanos—
virgen tan bella, que hacer podría
tórrida la Noruega con dos soles,
y blanca la Etiopia con dos manos.   785
Claveles del abril, rubíes tempranos,
cuantos engasta el oro del cabello,
cuantas—del uno ya y del otro cuello
cadenas—la concordia engarza rosas,
de sus mejillas, siempre vergonzosas,   790
    purpúreo son trofeo.
Ven, Himeneo, ven; ven, Himeneo.

surrounded by a swarm of playful Cupids,
whilst the alternating song invokes him
    now in the candid voices of young girls,   785
    now in the men's smooth tones:

First Chorus

    Come, Hymen, to one who awaits you:
    a clear-eyed Love who'll never fly,
    whose unshorn locks sweetly gainsay
    the down that softly shades his face,   790
    this down sprung like flowers in May,
    these locks that flaunt his summer grace;
    she in childhood was his sweetheart,
    whom now he loves at higher rate,
    a village Psyche, nymph laboring   795
    for Ceres under the sun's fire;
    at her new age's dawn find her
    trembling, and with your yoke bind her
    to his amorous desire.
    Come, Hymen; Hymen, come.   800

Second Chorus

    Come, Hymen, see how her blushes
    announce like roseate clouds the day,
    two sovereign eyes that dawning say,
    twin suns are here that could conspire
    to change the North from ice to fire   805,
    two hands to make Ethiopia white;
    while all those early April blooms,
    like rubies set in the gold hair,
    and all the roses wreathed to form
    the linking garland both necks bear   810
    as sign of union, these are the palm
    she'll shyly wear.
    Come, Hymen; Hymen, come.

Coro I

Ven, Himeneo, y plumas no vulgares
al aire los hijuelos den alados
de las que el bosque bellas Ninfas cela;   795
de sus carcajes, éstos, argentados,
flechen mosquetas, nieven azahares;
vigilantes aquéllos, la aldehuela
rediman del que más o tardo vuela,
o infausto gime pájaro nocturno;   800
mudos coronen otros por su turno
el dulce lecho conjugal, en cuanto
lasciva abeja al virginal acanto
    néctar le chupa hibleo.
Ven, Himeneo, ven; ven, Himeneo.   805

Coro II

Ven, Himeneo, y las volantes pías
que azules ojos con pestañas de oro
sus plumas son, conduzgan alta diosa,
gloria mayor del soberano coro.
Fíe tus nudos ella, que los días   810
disuelvan tarde en senectud dichosa;
y la que Juno es hoy a nuestra esposa,
casta Lucina—en lunas desiguales—
tantas veces repita sus umbrales,
que Níobe inmortal la admire el mundo,   815
no en blanco mármol, por su mal fecundo,
    escollo hoy del Leteo.
Ven, Himeneo, ven; ven, Himeneo.

Coro I

Ven, Himeneo, y nuestra agricultura
de copia tal a estrellas deba amigas   820
progenie tan robusta, que su mano

First Chorus

Come, Hymen, and let the winged loves
—not cupids these, but wood nymphs' brood,   815
Love's commoners—boldly take wing;
let some from the silver quiver's store
roses and orange blossom fling;
and some patrol the place all night
to ban the bird of slowest flight   820
that utters most ill-omened cries;
while others silently take turn
to guard the marriage bed wherein
the sensual bee sips nectar from
the virginal acanthus.   825
Come, Hymen; Hymen, come.

Second Chorus

Come, Hymen, and let the bright birds
whose plumes are eyed with blue and gold
draw hither the goddess, the pride
of the supreme Olympian stage;   830
let her confirm the knots you've tied
so they hold good till ripe old age;
and chaste Lucina too attend
when the moon's new and when it's old
to make like Niobe the bride   835
equally mother of boys and girls,
though with a kinder fate than hers,
transformed to marble, doomed to stand
on Lethe's strand.
Come, Hymen; Hymen, come.   840

First Chorus

Come, Hymen, that from this couple
our agriculture may receive
sturdy offspring who with strong hands

toros dome, y de un rubio mar de espigas
inunde liberal la tierra dura;
y al verde, joven, floreciente llano
blancas ovejas suyas hagan, cano,   825
en breves horas caducar la hierba;
oro le expriman líquido a Minerva,
y—los olmos casando con las vides—
mientras coronan pámpanos a Alcides
    clava empuñe Liëo.   830
Ven, Himeneo, ven; ven, Himeneo.

Coro II

Ven, Himeneo, y tantas le dé a Pales
cuantas a Palas dulces prendas ésta
apenas hija hoy, madre mañana.
De errantes lilios unas la floresta   835
cubran: corderos mil, que los cristales
vistan del río en breve undosa lana;
de Aracnes otras la arrogancia vana
modestas acusando en blancas telas,
no los hurtos de amor, no las cautelas   840
de Júpiter compulsen: que, aun en lino,
ni a la pluvia luciente de oro fino,
    ni al blanco cisne creo.
Ven, Himeneo, ven; ven, Himeneo.

El dulce alterno canto   845
a sus umbrales revocó felices
los novios, del vecino templo santo.
Del yugo aún no domadas las cervices,
novillos—breve término surcado—
restituyen así el pendiente arado   850
al que pajizo albergue los aguarda.
Llegaron todos pues, y, con gallarda
civil magnificencia, el suegro anciano,
cuantos la sierra dio, cuantos dio el llano
    labradores convida   855
a la prolija rústica comida

will master bulls and flood our lands
with rippling yellow seas of grain,   845
turn the wide flourishing, green plain
white with woolly tides of sheep,
press smooth gold from olives, marry
vines to elms till we think to see
Hercules with the vine-leaves crowned,   850
Bacchus with the club.
Come, Hymen; Hymen, come.

Second Chorus

Come, Hymen, let her offspring serve
both husbandry and the homely arts,
who's scarcely born yet nearly mother: 855
one half adorn the mead with lambs,
wandering lilies that at the ford
dress the river in waves of wool;
the rest by weaving plain designs,
rather than painting Love's assaults,   860
rebuke Arachne's arrogance,
for even pictured such deceits
as golden rain or Leda's swan,
we ought to shun.
Come, Hymen; Hymen, come.   865

The alternating song accompanies them
    the short way from the temple to their doorstep.
So do novice oxen
    new to the yoke, return
after their brief labor   870
        to the thatched shelter, the plough
    still dangling from their necks.
The others follow and the father of the bride
    with courtly hospitality
invites all from mountain or from plain   875
        to the abundant local fare
    with which long tables have quietly been spread.

que sin rumor previno en mesas grandes.
Ostente crespas blancas esculturas
artífice gentil de dobladuras
en los que damascó manteles Flandes,   860
mientras casero lino Ceres tanta
ofrece ahora, cuantos guardó el heno
dulces pomos, que al curso de Atalanta
    fueran dorado freno.
    Manjares que el veneno   865
y el apetito ignoran igualmente
les sirvieron, y en oro, no, luciente,
confuso Baco, ni en bruñida plata
    su néctar les desata,
sino en vidrio topacios carmesíes   870
    y pálidos rubíes.
Sellar del fuego quiso regalado
los gulosos estómagos el rubio,
imitador süave de la cera,
quesillo—dulcemente apremïado   875
    de rústica, vaquera,
blanca, hermosa mano, cuyas venas
la distinguieron de la leche apenas—;
mas ni la encarcelada nuez esquiva,
ni el membrillo pudieran anudado,   880
    si la sabrosa oliva
no serenara el bacanal diluvio.

Levantadas las mesas, al canoro
son de la Ninfa un tiempo, ahora caña,
seis de los montes, seis de la campaña,   885
—sus espaldas rayando el sutil oro
que negó al viento el nácar bien tejido—
terno de Gracias bello, repetido
cuatro veces en doce labradoras,
entró bailando numerosamente;   890
y dulce Musa entre ellas—si consiente
bárbaras el Parnaso moradoras—

    'Vivid felices,' dijo,
'largo curso de edad nunca prolijo;

Well, let court masters of deft folds concoct
on Flanders' finest damask if they wish
        their convolute white sculptures—   880
here plain household linen is the setting
        for quantities of bread
and apples from the hayloft
that to Atalanta's race
        might supply the golden brake.   885
Innocent, the food that's served,
        of fatal draughts and stimulants alike,
while white wine mixed with red's decanted not
        into gleaming gold or polished silver
but plain glass that highlights what we'll call its   890
        blushing topaz, timid rubies.
To seal the eager stomachs
        there was lightly roasted cheese
        that blond soft imitator
of wax, formed by the gentle pressure of   895
        the dairymaid's fair hand, so similar,
        but for blue veins, to milk.
But not this, nor the shy imprisoned walnut
        would suffice, nor jellied quince,
had the piquant olive lacked,   900
        to announce to that bacchanalian flood
        the peace of a conclusion.

When the tables are cleared a flute (erstwhile
        nymph now reed) strikes up.
Enter a dozen girls dancing in step,   905
        six from the mountain, six from the plain,
        trio of Graces four times repeated—
supple gold lies shining on their shoulders,
        secured by a spangled loop.
One of them (a gentle muse   910
        if villagers are allowed
        as dwellers on Parnassus) makes this speech:

"May you both be happy and may your years
be many but not tedious

y si prolijo, en nudos amorosos   895
    siempre vivid, esposos.
Venza no solo en su candor la nieve
mas plata en su esplendor sea cardada
cuanto estambre vital Cloto os traslada
de la alta fatal rueca al huso breve.   900
    Sean de la Fortuna
    aplausos la respuesta
    de vuestras granjerías.
    A la reja importuna,
    a la azada molesta   905
fecundo os rinda—en desiguales días—
    el campo agradecido
oro trillado y néctar exprimido.
Sus morados cantuesos, sus copadas
encinas la montaña contar antes   910
deje que vuestras cabras, siempre errantes,
que vuestras vacas, tarde o nunca herradas.
Corderillos os brote la ribera,
    que la hierba menuda
y las perlas exceda del rocío   915
    su número, y del río
la blanca espuma, cuantos la tijera
    vellones les desnuda.
Tantos de breve fábrica, aunque ruda,
albergues vuestros las abejas moren,   920
y Primaveras tantas os desfloren,
que—cual la Arabia madre ve de aromas
sacros troncos sudar fragrantes gomas—
vuestros corchos por uno y otro poro
en dulce se desaten líquido oro.   925
Próspera, al fin, mas no espumosa tanto,
    vuestra fortuna sea,
que alimenten la Invidia en nuestra aldea
áspides más que en la región del llanto.
Entre opulencias y necesidades,   930
medianías vinculen competentes
    a vuestros descendientes
—previniendo ambos daños—las edades.
Ilustren obeliscos las ciudades,
a los rayos de Júpiter expuesta   935

and for whatsoever span may love's bond 915
ever unite you, let the thread of life
that Clotho spins you from her distaff be
whiter than the snow and like
combed silver in its shining.
May Fortune greet with applause 920
the outcome of your farming;
to the importunate ploughshare,
the vexing spade, may grateful fields give
in due turn, in days of decreasing length,
threshed gold and then pressed nectar. 925
May your ever-wandering goats,
your cattle, be late or never branded,
being hard to number as the mountain's
purple boulders, the thick-crowned mountain oaks.
May the river banks engender lambs for you 930
more numerous than dew's pearls
and fleeces cut by the shears
surpass in quantity the river's foam.
By the bees may so many of your hives,
basic but neatly made, be colonized 935
and so many springs deflowered by them
that as Arabia, mother of perfumes, sees
sacred trunks sweat fragrant gum,
so may these cork houses render every cell
into sweet liquid gold. 940
May your fortune be truly prosperous
but not so spectacular that envy
find more snakes to breed from in our village
than the place of perpetual weeping.
May time entail on your 945
descendants a middling
serviceable state, neither
opulence nor need, avoiding each one's pain.
Cities, for sure, will raise great towers to heaven
their tops exposed no less 950
to Fortune's thunderbolts than the sun's rays:
but the shepherd's hut is spared
while trees around are blasted.
May your last hour find you
when your heads are white as swans 955

—aún más que a los de Febo—su corona,
cuando a la choza pastoral perdona
el cielo, fulminando la floresta.
Cisnes pues una y otra pluma, en esta
tranquilidad os halle labradora   940
    la postrimera hora:
cuya lámina cifre desengaños,
que en letras pocas lean muchos años.'

Del himno culto dio el último acento
fin mudo al baile, al tiempo que seguida   945
la novia sale de villanas ciento
a la verde florida palizada,
cual nueva Fénix en flamantes plumas
matutinos del sol rayos vestida,
de cuanta surca el aire acompañada   950
    monarquía canora;
y, vadeando nubes, las espumas
del Rey corona de los otros ríos:
en cuya orilla el viento hereda ahora
    pequeños no vacíos   955
de funerales bárbaros trofeos
que el Egipto erigió a sus Ptolomeos.

Los árboles que el bosque habían fingido,
umbroso coliseo ya formando,
    despejan el ejido,   960
    olímpica palestra
de valientes desnudos labradores.
Llegó la desposada apenas, cuando
    feroz ardiente muestra
hicieron dos robustos luchadores   965
de sus músculos, menos defendidos
del blanco lino que del vello obscuro.
Abrazáronse, pues, los dos, y luego
—humo anhelando el que no suda fuego—
de recíprocos nudos impedidos   970
cual duros olmos de implicantes vides,
yedra el uno es tenaz del otro muro.
Mañosos, al fin, hijos de la tierra,
    cuando fuertes no Alcides,

in the same tranquil productivity
and your tomb's motto speak to the beholder
enduring wisdom though the legend's brief."

Her eloquent conclusion brought to the dance
    a silent end, just as   960
the bride with a hundred village girls in tow
    entered the leafy green enclosure, like
the reborn phoenix with its brave new plumes,
    dressed in Sun's first morning rays, escorted
    by all the songful citizens of air,   965
when it breasts the clouds and soars
    above the King of Rivers, on whose banks
    the wind inherits vast
spaces by the barbarous tombs Egypt
    erected for its pharaohs   970
long since vacated.

The artificial groves are now arranged
    to form a well-shaded colosseum,
the common has become
    an Olympic stadium   975
    to the sturdy farmers stripped for action.
Scarcely had the bride arrived
when two stout wrestlers began
    furiously showing off their muscles,
dressed in white shorts that hide their bodies less   980
    than the dark pelt that shades them.
They come to grips and each
    (breathing smoke, sweating fire)
is equally impeded by the other,
    like two stout elms fastened by winding vines   985
    or ivy, one of them, gripping the other's wall;
at last, resourceful sons of earth that they are
(if not quite Hercules) they contrive to throw

procuran derribarse, y, derribados,   975
cual pinos se levantan arraigados
en los profundos senos de la sierra.
Premio los honra igual. Y de otros cuatro
ciñe las sienes glorïosa rama,
con que se puso término a la lucha.   980

Las dos partes rayaba del teatro
el Sol, cuando arrogante joven llama
    al expedido salto
la bárbara corona que le escucha.
Arras del animoso desafío   985
un pardo gabán fue en el verde suelo,
a quien se abaten ocho o diez soberbios
montañeses, cual suele de lo alto
calarse turba de invidiosas aves
a los ojos de Ascálafo, vestido   990
de perezosas plumas. Quién, de graves
piedras las duras manos impedido,
su agilidad pondera; quién sus nervios
desata estremeciéndose gallardo.
Besó la raya pues el pie desnudo   995
del suelto mozo, y con airoso vuelo
pisó del viento lo que del ejido
tres veces ocupar pudiera un dardo.
La admiración, vestida un mármol frío,
apenas arquear las cejas pudo;   1000
la emulación, calzada un duro hielo,
torpe se arraiga. Bien que impulso noble
de gloria, aunque villano, solicita
a un vaquero de aquellos montes, grueso,
    membrudo, fuerte roble,   1005
que, ágil a pesar de lo robusto,
al aire se arrebata, violentando
lo grave tanto, que lo precipita
—Ícaro montañés—su mismo peso,
de la menuda hierba el seno blando   1010
piélago duro hecho a su rüina.
Si no tan corpulento, más adusto
    serrano le sucede,

each other. No sooner down
   than up again, being rooted   990
   like pine trees in the earth's deep core.
They share the prize, and then another four
   are likewise crowned with laurels.
And thus the wrestling ended.

The sun had invaded two-thirds   995
   of the arena when
an arrogant young man
challenged to the long jump
   all who were there to hear him;
a brown overcoat thrown down on the green turf   1000
   serving as gage, around it flocked a dozen
proud young mountain men, like
   the envious mob of birds
   darting at the eyes of owl Ascalaphus,
   bunched in his drowsy feathers.   1005
Some weighting their hands with heavy stones test
   their agility. Others
relax their sinews ostentatiously
   making the muscles quiver.
Now the challenger's bare foot kisses the line   1010
   and with buoyant flight he treads
that length of air which over the common
   a javelin might fill thrice.
Admiration become cold marble scarce
knows how to raise an eyebrow;   1015
dumb emulation shod in boots of ice
is rooted to the ground.
But thirst for glory, even in peasants
   noble, goads one local,
a cowherd strong and heavy   1020
   as a thick-limbed mountain oak,
to hurl himself (agile despite his build)
   into the air, his assault on gravity
so violent that like a village Icarus
   he's undone by his own weight   1025
   and the soft greensward becomes hard sea to him.
Another, less solid but more wiry,

que iguala y aun excede
al ayuno leopardo,   1015
al corcillo travieso, al muflón sardo
que de las rocas trepa a la marina
sin dejar ni aun pequeña
del pie ligero bipartida seña.
Con más felicidad que el precedente,   1020
pisó las huellas casi del primero
el adusto vaquero.
Pasos otro dio al aire, al suelo coces.
Y premïados graduadamente,
advocaron a sí toda la gente   1025
—Cierzos del llano y Austros de la sierra—
mancebos tan veloces,
que cuando Ceres más dora la tierra,
y argenta el mar desde sus grutas hondas
Neptuno, sin fatiga   1030
su vago pie de pluma
surcar pudiera mieses, pisar ondas,
sin inclinar espiga,
sin vïolar espuma.
Dos veces eran diez, y dirigidos   1035
a dos olmos que quieren, abrazados,
ser palios verdes, ser frondosas metas,
salen cual de torcidos
arcos, o nervïosos o acerados,
con silbo igual, dos veces diez saetas.   1040
No el polvo desparece
el campo, que no pisan alas hierba;
es el más torpe una herida cierva,
el más tardo la vista desvanece,
y, siguiendo al más lento,   1045
cojea el pensamiento.
El tercio casi de una milla era
la prolija carrera
que los hercúleos troncos hace breves;
pero las plantas leves   1050
de tres sueltos zagales
la distancia sincopan tan iguales,
que la atención confunden judiciosa.
De la Peneida virgen desdeñosa,

follows on, as lithe, or more,
    as a hungry leopard fasting, a leaping
    deer or the Sardinian ram,   1030
    which plunges from cliff to seashore leaving
    no trace of cloven hoof.
This third contestant, happier than the last,
    and almost in the footprints of the first,
kicks the ground and continues taking steps   1035
    as he flies through the air.
When in turn each had received a medal
others from plain or mountain
draw all eyes towards them,
    like the north or the south wind,   1040
    moving so swiftly that where
    Ceres most gilds the land
    or Neptune from his deep caves
    whips the sea to silver
they could sail on feet as light   1045
    as feathers through the corn
or pace the waves, without
    bending a single ear,
    raising a speck of foam.
There were twenty of them, the leafy goal,   1050
their race's green objective,
    two elms they must embrace:
like twenty arrows with a single twang
    of the taut bowstring's gut
    or steel they're off! No dust   1055
    conjures the field away,
    for arrows tread no ground;
the dullest of them's like
    a wounded deer the hindmost
    quicker than eye can follow   1060
the slowest outstrips thought;
the course close to a third part
    of a mile, the end so far tall trees
    looked small, but the light feet
of three outstanding runners   1065
    reduced the distance with such equal pace
        the judges were confounded.
Not more tightly, closely,

los dulces fugitivos miembros bellos   1055
en la corteza no abrazó, reciente,
más firme Apolo, más estrechamente,
que de una y otra meta glorïosa
las duras basas abrazaron ellos
   con triplicado nudo.   1060
Árbitro Alcides en sus ramas, dudo
   que el caso decidiera,
bien que su menor hoja un ojo fuera
   del lince más agudo.

En tanto pues que el palio neutro pende   1065
y la carroza de la luz desciende
a templarse en las ondas, Himeneo
—por templar, en los brazos, el deseo
del galán novio, de la esposa bella—
los rayos anticipa de la estrella,   1070
cerúlea ahora, ya purpúrea guía
de los dudosos términos del día.
El jüicio—al de todos, indeciso—
   del concurso ligero,
el padrino con tres de limpio acero   1075
cuchillos corvos absolvello quiso.
Solícita Junón, Amor no omiso,
al son de otra zampoña que conduce
Ninfas bellas y Sátiros lascivos,
los desposados a su casa vuelven,   1080
   que coronada luce
de estrellas fijas, de astros fugitivos
que en sonoroso humo se resuelven.
Llegó todo el lugar, y, despedido,
casta Venus—que el lecho ha prevenido   1085
de las plumas que baten más süaves
en su volante carro blancas aves—
los novios entra en dura no estacada:
que, siendo Amor una deidad alada,
bien previno la hija de la espuma   1090
a batallas de amor campo de pluma.

did Apollo clutch the sweet fleeing limbs
of the disdainful virgin   1070
in their fast hardening bark than
these three in a triple knot
embraced the sturdy trunks
of their triumphant goal.
Had Hercules sat judging in the branches   1075
I doubt he could have called it,
even were every individual leaf
the sharpest recording eye.

While the contest hangs thus
in the balance, and as the blazing chariot   1080
goes down to cool in the waves,
Hymen to temper in love's arms desire
of groom and bride, of each for each, advances
the shining of that star
one time day's bright herald, now   1085
pale guide to spreading darkness.
Since all agreed the outcome
impossible to decide,
the umpire settles it presenting
three equal bright steel knives.   1090
Now Juno, solicitous, Cupid no less
attentive, with music of another flute
heading a troop of girls and raucous males,
return the couple home
to a house made gay with lights,   1095
some fixed in place, some that like shooting stars
dissolve in sound and smoke.
The whole village assisted and when they left
chaste Venus, who had prepared the nuptial bed
with soft feathers from the white wings that pull   1100
her flying chariot,
leads the pair into the mild stockade:
for since Love is a winged god,
rightly had the foam born one assigned
Love's skirmishes a battlefield of swan's down.   1105

". . . resounding vault of Vulcan's forge maybe, / or sealing the rash Titan's bones, a tomb . . ." (*Polyphemus and Galatea*, 4). Velázquez, like Góngora, used classical mythology not as an appeal to authority but as a pretext for more intense observation. Diego Rodríguez de Silva y Velázquez, *The Forge of Vulcan* (1630). Museo del Prado, Madrid, Spain. Photograph © Alinari / Art Resource, New York.

III

THE FABLE OF POLYPHEMUS AND GALATEA

Introduction

Góngora's *Fable of Polyphemus and Galatea* is based on Ovid's *Metamorphoses*, with some important differences. In Góngora there is as at least as much emphasis on the love of Acis and Galatea as on the jealousy of Polyphemus. The development of this love is subtly described, with telling details. There is a delicate balance between sensuality and courtliness, which has led some readers to detect a pagan, animal element, while others see only an elegant intellectual exercise. The character of Polyphemus is by no means simple: he is not just the monster we might expect. To anyone who has read Góngora's ballads, it will not be surprising that Polyphemus can be both lyrical and absurd or that his address to Galatea contains pathos as well as menace. His boasting and lack of self-knowledge are dangerous, but they are also comic.

Polyphemus and Galatea differs from the *First Solitude* by including elements of ugliness and violence. It is of course possible that if Góngora had completed all four of the *Solitudes* they would have constituted a more inclusive view of the world. There is some indication in the *First Solitude* and even more in the second that Góngora is moving toward a less purely idyllic vision. But *Polyphemus*, starting with its reference to Vulcan's forge and the Titan's tomb, is immediately concerned with darker matters. Most readers, however, have not found the ending tragic, despite the death of Acis. The lovers are destroyed by a force of nature, but in compensation Acis becomes himself an embodiment of natural forces.

The fable has a clear structure. After a few introductory stanzas addressed to the Conde de Niebla at dawn, there is a description of the setting, Sicily. Following this, the three characters, Polyphemus, Galatea, and Acis are introduced one after the other. The encounter of the lovers takes place at midday, the hottest time. The action then switches abruptly to Polyphemus at sunset. His song, adddressing Galatea, lasts for thirteen stanzas. Then the lovers are discovered, and the conclusion is very rapid.

Compared with the *Solitudes*, the poem is written in the much tighter form of the *octava real*, stanzas of eight lines, rhyming *abababcc*. In my translation I have tried to give an approximation of this form, and I have sometimes sacrificed some of the content in order to maintain the shape of the stanza. The poem's sound quality is of special importance and so is Góngora's habitual delight in wordplay. There is no formula for transferring either of these to English, and inevitably much is lost.

The first stanza is a dedication and consists of the usual praise of a patron and plea for his attention. The similarity to the opening of the *First Solitude* is obvious. The address is to another nobleman who has retired from court to enjoy the country pursuits of hunting and falconry and who may in fact be out hunting at this moment. The Conde de Niebla, who also makes an appearance in the *Second Solitude*, was a relative of the Duke of Béjar (to whom the *First Solitude* was dedicated), and in 1616 was to become Duke of Medina-Sidonia on the death of his father, who had been the reluctant commander of the Spanish Armada.

Fábula de Polifemo y Galatea (1612)

1

Estas que me dictó rimas sonoras,
culta sí, aunque bucólica, Talía
—¡oh excelso conde!—, en las purpúreas horas
que es rosas la alba y rosicler el día,
ahora que de luz tu Niebla doras,
escucha, al son de la zampoña mía,
si ya los muros no te ven, de Huelva,
peinar el viento, fatigar la selva.

2

Templado, pula en la maestra mano
el generoso pájaro su pluma,
o tan mudo en la alcándara, que en vano
aun desmentir al cascabel presuma;
tascando haga el freno de oro, cano,
del caballo andaluz la ociosa espuma;
gima el lebrel en el cordón de seda.
Y al cuerno, al fin, la cítara suceda.

3

Treguas al ejercicio sean robusto,
ocio atento, silencio dulce, en cuanto
debajo escuchas de dosel augusto,

The Fable of Polyphemus and Galatea

1

To the music of these verses, which Thalia,
the pastoral but not less cultured muse,
dictated to me, now during this bright hour
that decorates the sky with dawn's rich hues
give ear, O worthy count, in Niebla's halls,
the seat your gracious sun with light endues
—unless the moment finds you from your home,
combing the wind, beating the woods, for game.

2

Now let the noble bird, hungry for prey,
sit quietly preening on the mastering arm,
or silent on his perch, as if to deny
the enslaving bell has any hold on him;
while the Andalusian steed is made to stay
coating the golden bit with idle foam,
and the hound is left on its silken leash to pine:
in brief, let the milder lute replace the horn.

3

Thus manly exercise will concede the day
to gentle silence and attentive ease,
that beneath your stately canopy you may

del músico jayán el fiero canto.
Alterna con las Musas hoy el gusto;
que si la mía puede ofrecer tanto
clarín (y de la Fama no segundo),
tu nombre oirán los términos del mundo.

4
Donde espumoso el mar sicilïano
el pie argenta de plata al Lilibeo
(bóveda o de las fraguas de Vulcano,
o tumba de los huesos de Tifeo),
pálidas señas cenizoso un llano
—cuando no del sacrílego deseo—
del duro oficio da. Allí una alta roca
mordaza es a una gruta, de su boca.

5
Guarnición tosca de este escollo duro
troncos robustos son, a cuya greña
menos luz debe, menos aire puro
la caverna profunda, que a la peña;
caliginoso lecho, el seno obscuro
ser de la negra noche nos lo enseña
infame turba de nocturnas aves,
gimiendo tristes y volando graves.

6
De este, pues, formidable de la tierra
bostezo, el melancólico vacío
a Polifemo, horror de aquella sierra,
bárbara choza es, albergue umbrío
y redil espacioso donde encierra
cuanto las cumbres ásperas cabrío,
de los montes, esconde: copia bella
que un silbo junta y un peñasco sella.

7
Un monte era de miembros eminente
este (que, de Neptuno hijo fiero,
de un ojo ilustra el orbe de su frente,

hear the singing giant's fierce pleas.
Permit the Muses now to have their say,
for mine, if able to find sufficient breath
to blow her trumpet not less loud than Fame,
to the world's utmost limits will sound your name.

4

Where the rich foam of the broad Sicilian sea
plates with silver the foot of Lilibaeum
(resounding vault of Vulcan's forge maybe,
or, sealing the rash Titan's bones, a tomb)
there is a plain whose cinders one may see
as sign of either the sacrilegious aim
or of the workshop. There a high crag
thrusts across a cave's mouth like a gag.

5

Coarse garnish to this rough stopper are some trees
with sturdy limbs, forming a matted pelf
which more denies the light, the cleansing breeze,
to the cave within than does the rock itself.
In this lightless refuge black night has
her tenebrous couch—the observer sees the proof
in vile nocturnal flocks that issue out
with chilling cries, in a dense foreboding rout.

6

Know that the melancholy void of this,
earth's awful yawn, this dark and dank retreat,
for Polyphemus, terror of these hills
serves as his rustic cabin, shadowy seat,
and also as a spacious pen he fills
with the horde of goats that overruns the steep
and rugged mountain peaks; a living fortune
that a whistle gathers and a rock seals in.

7

Himself a mountain, massive, thickset, high,
the Cyclops is a belligerent son of Neptune,
his forehead's orb adorned by a single eye,

émulo casi del mayor lucero)
cíclope, a quien el pino más valiente,
bastón, le obedecía, tan ligero,
y al grave peso junco tan delgado,
que un día era bastón y otro cayado.

8

Negro el cabello, imitador undoso
de las obscuras aguas del Leteo,
al viento que lo peina proceloso,
vuela sin orden, pende sin aseo;
un torrente es su barba impetüoso,
que (adusto hijo de este Pirineo)
su pecho inunda, o tarde, o mal, o en vano
surcada aun de los dedos de su mano.

9

No la Trinacria en sus montañas, fiera
armó de crüeldad, calzó de viento,
que redima feroz, salve ligera,
su piel manchada de colores ciento:
pellico es ya la que en los bosques era
mortal horror al que con paso lento
los bueyes a su albergue reducía,
pisando la dudosa luz del día.

10

Cercado es (cuanto más capaz, más lleno)
de la fruta, el zurrón, casi abortada,
que el tardo otoño deja al blando seno
de la piadosa hierba, encomendada:
la serba, a quien le da rugas el heno;
la pera, de quien fue cuna dorada
la rubia paja, y—pálida tutora—
la niega avara, y pródiga la dora.

11

Erizo es el zurrón, de la castaña,
y (entre el membrillo o verde o datilado)
de la manzana hipócrita, que engaña,

which glares not much less fiercely than the sun;
the monster to assist him on his way
has plucked for his convenience a whole pine,
which, like a reed beneath his weight deformed,
from prop to shepherd's crook can be transformed.

8

His hair that's black, a rippling imitation
of Lethe's turbid waters, flies on the storming
blast that combs it without regard for fashion,
or hangs unkempt, disordered, rank and tangling;
his impetuous beard's an arid inundation,
which from this fire-formed Pyrenee depending
engulfs his chest in hair either uncombed,
or roughly, or to no purpose, by his hand.

9

In all its mountains the three-cornered isle
holds no animal fierce or swift enough
to redeem by fighting or to save by guile
the coat it boasts like a multicolored stuff:
the beast now serves as his garment, which erstwhile
struck fear to the peasants' hearts, who slow and loath
lead their oxen homeward toward their rest,
treading in terror the doubtful light of dusk.

10

His bag is like a walled garden, wide but stuffed
so full with fruit it seems about to burst,
and spill those goods autumn's last days entrust
to the soft embrace of charitable grass;
the sorb with patterns by the hay impressed,
the pear, to which straw, its golden palliasse,
plays the pallid tutor, who his ward's
estate both richly gilds and closely guards.

11

It bristles too with chestnuts and with quince,
green or mature, and that feigning hypocrite,
the apple, that belies with rosy tints

a lo pálido no, a lo arrebolado,
y, de la encina (honor de la montaña,
que pabellón al siglo fue dorado)
el tributo, alimento, aunque grosero,
del mejor mundo, del candor primero.

12

Cera y cáñamo unió (que no debiera)
cien cañas, cuyo bárbaro rüído,
de más ecos que unió cáñamo y cera
albogues, duramente es repetido.
La selva se confunde, el mar se altera,
rompe Tritón su caracol torcido,
sordo huye el bajel a vela y remo:
¡tal la música es de Polifemo!

13

Ninfa, de Doris hija, la más bella,
adora, que vio el reino de la espuma.
Galatea es su nombre, y dulce en ella
el terno Venus de sus Gracias suma.
Son una y otra luminosa estrella
lucientes ojos de su blanca pluma:
si roca de cristal no es de Neptuno,
pavón de Venus es, cisne de Juno.

14

Purpúreas rosas sobre Galatea
la Alba entre lilios cándidos deshoja:
duda el Amor cuál más su color sea,
o púrpura nevada, o nieve roja.
De su frente la perla es, eritrea,
émula vana. El ciego dios se enoja,
y, condenado su esplendor, la deja
pender en oro al nácar de su oreja.

15

Invidia de las ninfas y cuidado
de cuantas honra el mar deidades era;
pompa del marinero niño alado

its pale inside (like, in reverse, a whited
sepulchre), and the sheltering oak's fruits
—the tree that in the golden age provided
such simple nourishment as for the time
sufficed a world still in its innocent prime.

12

With wax and hemp he binds—disastrously!—
a set of hollow canes, whose barbarous sound
is multiplied by echoes endlessly
to spread the sound of piping all around:
there's uproar in the forests, storms at sea,
the Triton casts his conch upon the ground,
the stunned ship's crew, fleeing, wish they were earless,
such is the music made by Polyphemus!

13

He loves a nymph, Doris's daughter, fairer
than any the waves' kingdom yet has seen.
Galatea she's called, and in her perfect features
Venus makes her trio of Graces one;
radiant as the stars are her two eyes:
bright eyes, soft pallor, thus united mean
she's Aphrodite's peacock, Juno's swan,
as well as crystal from the realm of Neptune.

14

On Galatea Dawn scattered bright-hued roses
with pure white lilies intermingled, so
Love's uncertain what term he proposes
for her color: rosy snowfall, blushing snow?
The finest pearl from Eritrea loses
a contest with the whiteness of her brow,
and hothead Cupid banishes it to where
it hangs in gold from the seashell of her ear.

15

Envy of all the nymphs is Galatea,
pursued by every deity the ocean
bows to, and glory of the winged boy sailor

que sin fanal conduce su venera.
Verde el cabello, el pecho no escamado,
ronco sí, escucha a Glauco la ribera
inducir a pisar la bella ingrata,
en carro de cristal, campos de plata.

16
Marino joven, las cerúleas sienes,
del más tierno coral ciñe Palemo,
rico de cuantos la agua engendra bienes,
del Faro odioso al promontorio extremo;
mas en la gracia igual, si en los desdenes
perdonado algo más que Polifemo,
de la que, aún no le oyó, y, calzada plumas,
tantas flores pisó como él espumas.

17
Huye la ninfa bella; y el marino
amante nadador, ser bien quisiera,
ya que no áspid a su pie divino,
dorado pomo a su veloz carrera;
mas, ¿cuál diente mortal, cuál metal fino
la fuga suspender podrá ligera
que el desdén solicita? ¡Oh cuánto yerra
delfín que sigue en agua corza en tierra!

18
Sicilia, en cuanto oculta, en cuanto ofrece,
copa es de Baco, huerto de Pomona:
tanto de frutas ésta la enriquece,
cuanto aquél de racimos la corona.
En carro que estival trillo parece,
a sus campañas Ceres no perdona,
de cuyas siempre fértiles espigas
las provincias de Europa son hormigas.

19
A Pales su viciosa cumbre debe
lo que a Ceres, y aún más, su vega llana;
pues si en la una granos de oro llueve,

who sails his cockle without illumination.
Everyone hears Glaucus, green-haired, scaleless
from the waist up, now hoarse from exhortation,
as he begs the haughty beauty (but in vain)
to ride with him over the silver plain.

16

Youthful Palemon like a bold buccaneer
binding his sea-blue brow with a coral band,
is rich in every gift the seas can bear
between the dread lighthouse and furthest headland.
But he, like Polyphemus, can't get near,
although a touch less haughtily disdained:
she no sooner hears his voice than she runs and hides,
treading flowers, while he on the seafoam rides.

17

The beauty still speeds on; and the aquatic
lover, if he could, would lie in the way,
either as asp to bite her hallowed foot,
or golden apple to cause her some delay.
But how can mortal tooth or noble metal
a flight inspired by scorn have power to stay?
Foolish dolphin, to think the chase can end
pursuing in water, when the doe's on land!

18

Sicily in what it holds, in what it offers,
is Bacchus' cup and orchard of Pomona;
the latter loads it down with fruit as richly
as the former crowns its sunny hills with vine leaves.
Ceres drives her chariot like a thresher
and gives no respite to the cultured levels
with their rolling fields of wheat, whose heavy ears
like ants to its stores the whole of Europe bears.

19

The heights to Pales owe as much and more
as to Ceres does the undulating plain;
for if on the latter golden cereals pour,

copos nieva en la otra mil de lana.
De cuantos siegan oro, esquilan nieve,
o en pipas guardan la exprimida grana,
bien sea religión, bien amor sea,
deidad, aunque sin templo, es Galatea.

20
Sin aras, no: que el margen donde para
del espumoso mar su pie ligero,
al labrador, de sus primicias ara,
de sus esquilmos es al ganadero;
de la Copia a la tierra poco avara
el cuerno vierte el hortelano, entero,
sobre la mimbre que tejió, prolija,
si artificiosa no, su honesta hija.

21
Arde la juventud, y los arados
peinan las tierras que surcaron antes,
mal conducidos, cuando no arrastrados
de tardos bueyes, cual su dueño errantes;
sin pastor que los silbe, los ganados
los crujidos ignoran resonantes
de las hondas, si, en vez del pastor pobre,
el céfiro no silba, o cruje el robre.

22
Mudo la noche el can, el día, dormido,
de cerro en cerro y sombra en sombra yace.
Bala el ganado; al mísero balido,
nocturno el lobo de las sombras nace.
Cébase; y fiero, deja humedecido
en sangre de una lo que la otra pace.
¡Revoca, Amor, los silbos, o a su dueño
el silencio del can siga, y el sueño!

23
La fugitiva ninfa, en tanto, donde
hurta un laurel su tronco al sol ardiente,
tantos jazmines cuanta hierba esconde

on the former a thousand snowy fleeces rain.
Galatea, for all with snow to shear
or who reap gold or store the purple wine
—whether it be religion or just simple
love—is a goddess, though without a temple.

20

But not without her altars; for the foaming
shore where her lightfooted running ceases
is where the farmer offers his first fruits
and where the herdsman dedicates his fleeces,
where plenty's horn, as tribute to the unstinting
earth, the cultivator upturns to heap
the mats his daughter weaves, she on whose part
industriousness makes up for lack of art.

21

But now youth is on fire: ploughs barely break
the surface of the earth they used to open,
ill handled, roughly hauled by oxen that lack
will and direction, aberrant as their masters;
no shepherd whistles, summoning the flock;
they hear no crack of slingshots from their pastors,
nor other sound, unless the wind calling,
or through the branches of the oak trees rustling.

22

Silent by night, the dog just sleeps all day,
drifts from rise to rise and lolls in the shade.
A sheep bleats; to its pathetic cry
comes the nocturnal wolf, from shadows bred.
He gorges himself; and where his victim lay
blood soaks the grass on which other sheep must feed.
Bring order back, Oh Love, or abandon here
dog and master, both mute, both unaware.

23

The fleeing nymph, meanwhile, throws herself down
where the laurel hides its trunk from the burning sun:
jasmine gazing back from the spring's glass

la nieve de sus miembros, da a una fuente.
Dulce se queja, dulce le responde
un ruiseñor a otro, y dulcemente
al sueño da sus ojos la armonía,
por no abrasar con tres soles el día.

24
Salamandria del Sol, vestido estrellas,
latiendo el Can del cielo estaba, cuando
(polvo el cabello, húmidas centellas,
si no ardientes aljófares, sudando)
llegó Acis; y, de ambas luces bellas
dulce Occidente viendo al sueño blando,
su boca dio, y sus ojos cuanto pudo,
al sonoro cristal, al cristal mudo.

25
Era Acis un venablo de Cupido,
de un fauno, medio hombre, medio fiera,
en Simetis, hermosa ninfa, habido;
gloria del mar, honor de su ribera.
El bello imán, el ídolo dormido,
que acero sigue, idólatra venera,
rico de cuanto el huerto ofrece pobre,
rinden las vacas y fomenta el robre.

26
El celestial humor recién cuajado
que la almendra guardó entre verde y seca,
en blanca mimbre se lo puso al lado,
y un copo, en verdes juncos, de manteca;
en breve corcho, pero bien labrado,
un rubio hijo de una encina hueca,
dulcísimo panal, a cuya cera
su néctar vinculó la primavera.

27
Caluroso, al arroyo da las manos,
y con ellas las ondas a su frente,
entre dos mirtos que, de espuma canos,

matches the limbs of snow that press the grass;
sweetly, above, the nightingale complains
and sweetly to the song its mate replies;
such music lulls the nymph to close her eyes
and keep three suns from blazing in the skies.

24
Salamander in the sun, the Dog of Heaven,
pricked out in stars, just then was in full cry
as, hair all dust, Acis burst on the scene,
sweating wet sparks or dewdrops hot and dry;
who, when he'd seen those two lights set in sleep,
like the sun gone down behind the western sky,
fastened his mouth to the sounding crystal stream
and eyes, where he could, to the silent crystal form.

25
Acis was a true straight arrow of Cupid,
begotten of a faun, half man, half beast,
upon Simetis, a most alluring nymph,
glory of all the sea, pride of its shores.
Like steel he's drawn, like an idolater prays
to that fair magnet, sleeping idol, but
he's only rich in what the orchard and fields
render, what cows produce, or the oak yields.

26
He laid beside her in a plaited creel
freshly peeled almonds, between green and dry,
barely formed and set from celestial dew,
with a pat of butter reposing on green reeds,
and a small box, skilfully made from cork,
containing that blonde child of the hollow oak,
the honeycomb, where in each compact sector
spring has bound to wax her sweetest nectar.

27
To cool himself, he gave his hands to the stream,
and with them water to his heated brow,
between two myrtles, that, white with foam, became

dos verdes garzas son de la corriente.
Vagas cortinas de volantes vanos
corrió Favonio lisonjeramente
a la (de viento cuando no sea) cama
de frescas sombras, de menuda grama.

28
La ninfa, pues, la sonorosa plata
bullir sintió del arroyuelo apenas,
cuando, a los verdes márgenes ingrata,
segur se hizo de sus azucenas.
Huyera; mas tan frío se desata
un temor perezoso por sus venas,
que a la precisa fuga, al presto vuelo,
grillos de nieve fue, plumas de hielo.

29
Fruta en mimbres halló, leche exprimida
en juncos, miel en corcho, mas sin dueño;
si bien al dueño debe, agradecida,
su deidad culta, venerado el sueño.
A la ausencia mil veces ofrecida,
este de cortesía no pequeño
indicio la dejó—aunque estatua helada—
más discursiva y menos alterada.

30
No al Cíclope atribuye, no, la ofrenda;
no a sátiro lascivo, ni a otro feo
morador de las selvas, cuya rienda
el sueño aflija, que aflojó el deseo.
El niño dios, entonces, de la venda,
ostentación gloriosa, alto trofeo
quiere que al árbol de su madre sea
el desdén hasta allí de Galatea.

31
Entre las ramas del que más se lava
en el arroyo, mirto levantado,
carcaj de cristal hizo, si no aljaba,

a pair of herons abreast the current's flow.
Drifting curtains, fleeting airy veils
the breeze drew soothingly around her couch,
an airy hammock not of knotted cord
but subtly woven of shade, of fine greensward.

28

No sooner in her sleep does the nymph hear
the silver music from the bubbling source,
than springing up she spurns the green bank there,
becoming her own image's destroyer.
She would have fled, but a cold, drowsy fear,
melting through her veins with numbing force,
to the planned escape or sudden flight supplies
shackles of frost, wings weighted with ice.

29

She saw the baskets, fruit, the churned butter
on its bed of reeds, honey, but no donor;
although she recognizes gratefully he's given
to godhead worship and to sleep due honor.
She essayed a thousand times to absent herself,
yet the not negligible mark of feeling
rendered her—though still inclined to flight—
more tractable, less ready to take fright.

30

Not to the ugly Cyclops does she assign
the offering or the thought, nor to any lewd
satyr or his like, whose power to restrain
his actions, might, already undermined
by lust, by her sleeping be totally undone.
The boy-god, he of the blindfold, has in mind
for Galatea's heartlessness to be
the ultimate trophy hung on his mother's tree.

31

Concealed among the foliage of a myrtle,
the one that rises closest to the waters,
he turns the nymph into his sheath or quiver

su blanco pecho, de un arpón dorado.
El monstro de rigor, la fiera brava,
mira la ofrenda ya con más cuidado,
y aun siente que a su dueño sea, devoto,
confuso alcaide más, el verde soto.

32
Llamáralo, aunque muda, mas no sabe
el nombre articular que más querría;
ni lo ha visto, si bien pincel süave
lo ha bosquejado ya en su fantasía.
Al pie—no tanto ya, del temor, grave—
fía su intento; y, tímida, en la umbría
cama de campo y campo de batalla,
fingiendo sueño al cauto garzón halla.

33
El bulto vio, y, haciéndolo dormido,
librada en un pie toda sobre él pende
(urbana al sueño, bárbara al mentido
retórico silencio que no entiende):
no el ave reina, así, el fragoso nido
corona inmóvil, mientras no desciende
—rayo con plumas—al milano pollo
que la eminencia abriga de un escollo,

34
como la ninfa bella, compitiendo
con el garzón dormido en cortesía,
no sólo para, mas el dulce estruendo
del lento arroyo enmudecer querría.
A pesar luego de las ramas, viendo
colorido el bosquejo que ya había
en su imaginación Cupido hecho
con el pincel que le clavó su pecho,

35
de sitio mejorada, atenta mira,
en la disposición robusta, aquello
que, si por lo süave no la admira,

by burying in her breast his golden arrow.
Now the obdurate one, the monster of rigor
looks on the offering more complaisantly;
she even regrets that still the leafy arbor
withholds, invisible, the pious donor.

32
She'd like to call him but stays silent and
is ignorant of the name she yearns to speak;
nor has she seen him, yet a loving hand
already in her fancy sketched his look.
To her foot—now fear's less firmly in command—
the intent's conveyed, and on his field bed
—a field of battle too—where the shade is deep,
she finds the canny youth pretending sleep.

33
The silent form she sees, sleeping, it seems;
and leans, balancing on one foot, above him,
though courtly in her homage to his sleep,
untutored in the rhetoric of his silence.
Like the mighty eagle hanging in suspense
above the fragile nest before its stoop,
feathered lightning poised to strike the chick
cowering in the shelter of a cliff,

34
so now the nymph, in courtesy competing
with the sleeper, not only checks her own
movement, but would have the gentle din
of the dawdling stream cease for his sake. She's grown
aware of what despite the shade she's seeing:
full color added to the outline drawn
on imagination's page by Cupid's art
with the very brush he'd driven through her heart,

35
and changing to an easier position,
she studies that which won't impress by softness,
but in the lines of its rugged composition

es fuerza que la admire por lo bello.
Del casi tramontado sol aspira
a los confusos rayos, su cabello;
flores su bozo es, cuyas colores,
como duerme la luz, niegan las flores.

36
En la rústica greña yace oculto
el áspid, del intonso prado ameno,
antes que del peinado jardín culto
en el lascivo, regalado seno:
en lo viril desata de su vulto
lo más dulce el Amor, de su veneno;
bébelo Galatea, y da otro paso
por apurarle la ponzoña al vaso.

37
Acis—aún más de aquello que dispensa
la brújula del sueño vigilante—,
alterada la ninfa esté o suspensa,
Argos es siempre atento a su semblante,
lince penetrador de lo que piensa,
cíñalo bronce o múrelo diamante:
que en sus paladïones Amor ciego,
sin romper muros, introduce fuego.

38
El sueño de sus miembros sacudido,
gallardo el joven la persona ostenta,
y al marfil luego de sus pies rendido,
el coturno besar dorado intenta.
Menos ofende el rayo prevenido,
al marinero, menos la tormenta
prevista le turbó o pronosticada:
Galatea lo diga, salteada.

39
Más agradable y menos zahareña,
al mancebo levanta venturoso,
dulce ya concediéndole y risueña,

must amaze her by its beauty's manly power.
His hair is scattered, like misty shafts of light
from the sun about to set behind the mountain;
a shadow softly blooms on chin and lips
like flowers that hide their color when light sleeps.

36

The poisonous serpent will more often lurk
in tangled thickets and untonsured ways
than in the groomed and cultivated park
with its playful arbors and protected bays.
Thus Love now sets his sweetest poisons to work,
dissolved in the virile beauty of this face;
Galatea drinks, then takes another step
to drain the cup of poison to the dregs.

37

Acis, fully alert to what's revealed
through the pinhole of his half-closed eyes,
judging her mood—is she frightened or beguiled?—
was an Argos, many-eyed, to scrutinize
her face, a lynx to probe the thought that filled
her mind, even were it shielded by bronze:
for Love to introduce his flames has stratagems
(like the Greek horse) that use no battering rams.

38

Now throwing off the pretence of somnolence,
the young man shows himself in all his glory,
and, casting himself on his knees before her, attempts
to kiss the golden sandal, the feet of ivory.
A forecast storm occasions less offence
to the sailor, just as an end foreshadowed
or catastrophe foreseen is less importunate:
witness how Galatea takes this onslaught.

39

Quite friendly now, less fearful and less skittish,
she raises the young person to his feet,
all smiles and sweetness, pledging what it seems is

paces no al sueño, treguas sí al reposo.
Lo cóncavo hacía de una peña
a un fresco sitïal dosel umbroso,
y verdes celosías unas hiedras,
trepando troncos y abrazando piedras.

40

Sobre una alfombra, que imitara en vano
el tirio sus matices (si bien era
de cuantas sedas ya hiló, gusano,
y, artífice, tejió la Primavera)
reclinados, al mirto más lozano,
una y otra lasciva, si ligera,
paloma se caló, cuyos gemidos
—trompas de amor—alteran sus oídos.

41

El ronco arrullo al joven solicita;
mas, con desvíos Galatea suaves,
a su audacia los términos limita,
y el aplauso al concento de las aves.
Entre las ondas y la fruta, imita
Acis al siempre ayuno en penas graves:
que, en tanta gloria, infierno son no breve,
fugitivo cristal, pomos de nieve.

42

No a las palomas concedió Cupido
juntar de sus dos picos los rubíes,
cuando al clavel el joven atrevido
las dos hojas le chupa carmesíes.
Cuantas produce Pafo, engendra Gnido,
negras vïolas, blancos alhelíes,
llueven sobre el que Amor quiere que sea
tálamo de Acis ya y de Galatea.

43

Su aliento humo, sus relinchos fuego,
si bien su freno espumas, ilustraba
las columnas Etón que erigió el griego,

no pact for sleep but a lasting truce to rest.
An overhanging rock among the trees
offers a shady refuge from the heat,
where ivy, as if furnishing a throne,
winds about the trunks and clasps the stone.

40
Upon a carpet whose variety of tints
the costliest dyes could never reproduce,
for which the silkworm Spring provides both thread
and also the art that puts it to good use,
the two recline, while a pair of amorous doves,
grave with desire, yet buoyant as their plumes,
alight on a handsome myrtle, and their moans
sound in the couple's ears love's call to arms.

41
Acis is aroused by the doves' hoarse music
but Galatea parries his advances,
gently setting limits to his boldness,
witholding from the birds her full approval.
Acis suffers the torments of one fasting
where water is, and fruit in rich abundance:
barred from the fleeting crystal limbs, the pale
round apples—he's in glory, he's in hell!

42
But as soon as Cupid gave the doves permission
to marry the twin rubies of their bills,
the young man dared to lay his thirsting lips on
the open crimson petals of the flower.
All the black violets and white lilies grown
in Paphos and in Knidos now rain down
upon the spot that Love has designed to be a
nuptial couch for Acis and Galatea.

43
With smoking breath, and uttering snorts of flame,
the horses of the sun have moved away
to those gates the Greek erected, where sea foam

do el carro de la luz sus ruedas lava,
cuando, de amor el fiero jayán ciego,
la cerviz oprimió a una roca brava,
que a la playa, de escollos no desnuda,
linterna es ciega y atalaya muda.

44
Árbitro de montañas y ribera,
aliento dio, en la cumbre de la roca,
a los albogues que agregó la cera,
el prodigioso fuelle de su boca;
la ninfa los oyó, y ser más quisiera
breve flor, hierba humilde, tierra poca,
que de su nuevo tronco vid lasciva,
muerta de amor, y de temor no viva.

45
Mas—cristalinos pámpanos sus brazos—
amor la implica, si el temor la anuda,
al infelice olmo que pedazos
la segur de los celos hará aguda.
Las cavernas en tanto, los ribazos
que ha prevenido la zampoña ruda,
el trueno de la voz fulminó luego:
¡referidlo, Pïérides, os ruego!

46
'¡Oh bella Galatea, más süave
que los claveles que tronchó la aurora;
blanca más que las plumas de aquel ave
que dulce muere y en las aguas mora;
igual en pompa al pájaro que, grave,
su manto azul de tantos ojos dora
cuantas el celestial zafiro estrellas!
¡Oh tú, que en dos incluyes las más bellas!

47
'Deja las ondas, deja el rubio coro
de las hijas de Tetis, y el mar vea,
cuando niega la luz un carro de oro,

will rein them in and wash the car of day;
while, blind with love, the giant leans his frame
on the humbled back of a bold promontory,
a cliff, lifting above the rock-strewn shore,
a lightless lighthouse or a silent watchtower.

44

Lording it over the mountains and the strands
from his high vantage point, he brings to bear
on the pipes he joined with wax and hempen bands
the prodigious bellows of his mighty breath;
the nymph would sooner be, when she hears these sounds
a tiny flower, a weed, a clod of earth
than now (a vine with her new tree bonded) and here,
dying for love, and yet half-dead with fear.

45

But (through the crystal tendrils of her arms)
love binds her tight, as terror holds her fast,
to her unhappy elm whom the story dooms
to devastation by jealousy's sharp axe.
And now the caverns and the sloping combes,
forewarned already by the barbarous blast,
are assaulted by the thunder of his voice.
I seek the words, O Muses, aid my choice!

46

"Oh Galatea, beauty, brighter, sweeter
than the fresh carnations that Aurora culls
and whiter than that creature of the air
that, dying, sings, and on the water dwells;
and splendid as the noble bird that bears
as many eyes on its august blue tail
as stars are in the sapphire vault, O you
who summarize their beauty in just two!

47

Give up the waves, give up the fair-haired set
of Thetis' daughters, come to me now and view
the sea, while the gold chariot withdraws its light,

que en dos la restituye Galatea.
Pisa la arena, que en la arena adoro
cuantas el blanco pie conchas platea,
cuyo bello contacto puede hacerlas,
sin concebir rocío, parir perlas.

48

'Sorda hija del mar, cuyas orejas
a mis gemidos son rocas al viento:
o dormida te hurten a mis quejas
purpúreos troncos de corales ciento,
o al disonante número de almejas
—marino, si agradable no, instrumento—
coros tejiendo estés, escucha un día
mi voz, por dulce, cuando no por mía.

49

'Pastor soy, mas tan rico de ganados,
que los valles impido más vacíos,
los cerros desparezco levantados
y los caudales seco de los ríos;
no los que, de sus ubres desatados,
o derivados de los ojos míos,
leche corren y lágrimas; que iguales
en número a mis bienes son mis males.

50

'Sudando néctar, lambicando olores,
senos que ignora aun la golosa cabra,
corchos me guardan, más que abeja flores
liba inquïeta, ingenïosa labra;
troncos me ofrecen árboles mayores,
cuyos enjambres, o el abril los abra,
o los desate el mayo, ámbar distilan
y en ruecas de oro rayos del sol hilan.

51

'Del Júpiter soy hijo, de las ondas,
aunque pastor; si tu desdén no espera
a que el monarca de esas grutas hondas,

which Galatea's two suns will renew.
Come tread the sands, the sands where I delight
in all the shells, silvered by your white foot,
that by contagion with its beauty too
give birth to pearls, without conceiving dew.

48

Daughter of the sea, upon whose ears
my sighs have less effect than wind on stone,
whether you sleep behind a hundred spurs
of crimson coral, sequestered from my groans,
or dance to the clashing rhythm of struck clams
(music that's rough but in the sea well-known)
I trust that one day to my voice you'll listen
because it's sweet, if not because it's mine.

49

A shepherd I am, but one with flocks so great
I can fill the emptiest valleys to the brim,
and make the high hills disappear from sight,
as well as drink dry the course of every stream—
but not exhaust the perpetual floods that spout
from my udders, and from my weeping eyes,
of milk and tears, for I account them equals:
my abundant riches and my passionate ills.

50

My hives, sweating nectar and sweet odors
in secret hollows unknown to the glutton goat
are more numerous than flowers that the bees
sip restlessly and skilfully exploit;
there are spaces too in trunks of bigger trees,
where swarms their amber distillate create
(in April tapped, in May again begun),
on golden distaffs spinning threads of the sun.

51

Son am I of the sovereign of the waves,
although a shepherd; and unless your pride
requires the King, the Lord of these deep caves

en trono de cristal te abrace nuera,
Polifemo te llama, no te escondas;
que tanto esposo admira la ribera
cual otro no vio Febo, más robusto,
del perezoso Volga al Indo adusto.

52
'Sentado, a la alta palma no perdona
su dulce fruto mi robusta mano;
en pie, sombra capaz es mi persona
de innumerables cabras el verano.
¿Qué mucho, si de nubes se corona
por igualarme la montaña en vano,
y en los cielos, desde esta roca, puedo
escribir mis desdichas con el dedo?

53
'Marítimo alcïón roca eminente
sobre sus huevos coronaba, el día
que espejo de zafiro fue luciente
la playa azul, de la persona mía.
Miréme, y lucir vi un sol en mi frente,
cuando en el cielo un ojo se veía:
neutra el agua dudaba a cuál fe preste,
o al cielo humano, o al cíclope celeste.

54
'Registra en otras puertas el venado
sus años, su cabeza colmilluda
la fiera cuyo cerro levantado,
de helvecias picas es muralla aguda;
la humana suya el caminante errado
dio ya a mi cueva, de piedad desnuda,
albergue hoy, por tu causa, al peregrino,
do halló reparo, si perdió camino.

55
'En tablas dividida, rica nave
besó la playa miserablemente,
de cuantas vomitó riquezas grave,

to come himself and hail you as my bride,
answer to Polyphemus, don't be shy:
more husband is on offer, more to admire,
than Phoebus ever witnessed (and more robust)
from the lazy Volga to the stern Indus.

52

When I'm seated, my strong arm can collect
the sweet fruit from the lofty palm's high head;
standing, my body shields from summer's heat
innumerable goats with its ample shade.
It's vain, trust me, for a mountain to compete
by seeking for itself a crown of cloud:
standing on this rock, I reach so high
I can write my woes with my finger in the sky.

53

One day on a tall rock the halcyon
was sitting on its eggs and the blue sea
was a shining sapphire mirror where my person
was reflected: I looked and all I saw was me.
I saw that on my forehead one sun shone
just as in the sky there was but one eye.
The impartial sea was doubting which to believe in:
the celestial cyclops or the human heaven.

54

On other doors the stag avows his years
and the angry beast, whose high back's bristling spine
is like a jagged wall of Helvetian spears,
proffers his long-toothed grin; adorning mine
were once the human heads that travelers
left in my cruel cave. But in your name
it gives the pilgrim sanctuary today,
for him to find relief, though gone astray.

55

A ship, laden with those oriental
treasures the several mouths of Nile disgorge,
was split one day into its individual

por las bocas del Nilo el Orïente.
Yugo aquel día, y yugo bien süave,
del fiero mar a la sañuda frente
imponiéndole estaba (si no al viento
dulcísimas coyundas) mi instrumento,

56
'cuando, entre globos de agua, entregar veo
a las arenas ligurina haya,
en cajas los aromas del Sabeo,
en cofres las riquezas de Cambaya:
delicias de aquel mundo, ya trofeo
de Escila, que, ostentado en nuestra playa,
lastimoso despojo fue dos días
a las que esta montaña engendra arpías.

57
'Segunda tabla a un ginovés mi gruta
de su persona fue, de su hacienda;
la una reparada, la otra enjuta,
relación del naufragio hizo horrenda.
Luciente paga de la mejor fruta
que en hierbas se recline, en hilos penda,
colmillo fue del animal que el Ganges
sufrir muros le vio, romper falanges:

58
'arco, digo, gentil, bruñida aljaba,
obras ambas de artífice prolijo,
y de Malaco rey a deidad Java
alto don, según ya mi huésped dijo.
De aquél la mano, de ésta el hombro agrava;
convencida la madre, imita al hijo:
serás a un tiempo en estos horizontes
Venus del mar, Cupido de los montes.'

59
Su horrenda voz, no su dolor interno,
cabras aquí le interrumpieron, cuantas
—vagas el pie, sacrílegas el cuerno—

planks by a fatal encounter with the shore.
I was employing just then my instrument
to soothe the raging ocean's savage breast,
curbing the waves, although with gentleness,
binding the wind into a tuneful harness,

56
when I saw, amid revolving spheres of water,
a Genoese merchantman surrender
boxes filled with Saba's sweet aromas,
cases stuffed with treasure from Cambaya:
now these delights fetched here from distant lands
were Scylla's spoils, spread out on our sands,
to be mercilessly plundered for two days
by the harpies who harass our hilly bays.

57
A second plank to one of the Genoese
my cave was, to his person and his stock:
the first restored, the other one relieved
of moisture, he told me the story of his wreck.
Choicest fruit from my storehouse he received
and with a handsome gift he paid me back:
a tooth of that beast seen on the banks of Ganges
bearing towers and breaking the foe's phalanges:

58
an ivory bow, that is, and a delicate quiver,
both from a famous craftsman, once donated
by a Malaccan king to a goddess of Java,
according to the tale my guest narrated.
Now you, with one in hand, one on your shoulder,
will emulate the son, surpass the mother:
Galatea all in one will be to this island
the sea's Venus and Cupid of the upland."

59
The horrendous voice, but not the internal pain,
was cut short at this moment by some goats,
that with restless feet and sacrilegious horn

a Baco se atrevieron en sus plantas.
Mas, conculcado el pámpano más tierno
viendo el fiero pastor, voces él tantas,
y tantas despidió la honda piedras,
que el muro penetraron de las hiedras.

60
De los nudos, con esto, más süaves,
los dulces dos amantes desatados,
por duras guijas, por espinas graves
solicitan el mar con pies alados:
tal, redimiendo de importunas aves
incauto meseguero sus sembrados,
de liebres dirimió copia, así, amiga,
que vario sexo unió y un surco abriga.

61
Viendo el fiero jayán, con paso mudo
correr al mar la fugitiva nieve
(que a tanta vista el líbico desnudo
registra el campo de su adarga breve)
y al garzón viendo, cuantas mover pudo
celoso trueno, antiguas hayas mueve:
tal, antes que la opaca nube rompa,
previene rayo fulminante trompa.

62
Con vïolencia desgajó infinita,
la mayor punta de la excelsa roca,
que al joven, sobre quien la precipita,
urna es mucha, pirámide no poca.
Con lágrimas la ninfa solicita
las deidades del mar, que Acis invoca:
concurren todas, y el peñasco duro
la sangre que exprimió, cristal fue puro.

63
Sus miembros lastimosamente opresos
del escollo fatal fueron apenas,
que los pies de los árboles más gruesos

were transgressing against Bacchus in his plants;
seeing such damage done to the tenderest vine,
the angry shepherd responded with shouts, and shots
so thick and fast delivered from his sling
they pierced right through the lovers' ivy screen.

60

Startled from the closest of embraces,
the lovers are abruptly torn apart;
through stones and thorny briars each one races,
seeking the sea as if on feathered feet;
as when to save his crops the farmer chases
the thieving birds away and by accident
separates two hares, a pair of such lovers,
whom different sex unites, one furrow harbors.

61

When the giant witnesses the fleeting snow
slipping silently toward the sea
(for his sight is so acute he can discover
the patterns on the naked Libyan's shield)
and sees the youth as well, he emits a bellow
so resonant it shakes the mightiest tree:
just so, when the dense cloud's about to burst,
a clap of thunder heralds the fatal blast.

62

With irresistible force he tore away
the thickest point of the mighty rock he stood on,
which at once became for one on whom it lay
an outsize urn, a pyramid of no mean
proportions. The nymph in tears implores the aid
of the same sea deities whom Acis calls on:
who all concur, and his body's blood, a trickle
pressed out by the hard rock, becomes pure crystal.

63

Scarcely had the fateful boulder settled
over his shattered, mutilated limbs,
than the feet of all the biggest trees were clothed

calzó el líquido aljófar de sus venas.
Corriente plata al fin sus blancos huesos,
lamiendo flores y argentando arenas,
a Doris llega, que, con llanto pío,
yerno lo saludó, lo aclamó río.

in precious liquid gushing from his veins.
His white bones now to flowing silver turned,
kissing the flowers and silvering the sand,
he comes to the sea, and pityingly by her
is recognized as son, annointed river.

"Thus did he breathe his last; / and she . . . / flung out as if with a catapult / one sigh
and fell on the sword / (such of it as was available)." (*Pyramus and Thisbe*, 459–66).
The illustration, however, does not do justice to the idea that she impales herself on
the point of the sword already transfixing Pyramus. Anon., "Pyrami et Thisbe interitus"
(II.I0I) from *Ovid Illustrated* (1591), engraving. Courtesy J. Daniel Kinney.

·⋊[IV]⋉·
PYRAMUS AND THISBE

Introduction

I have chosen to end with this burlesque piece because it is fun and I think speaks for itself. But also it shows the ability of Góngora's mockery to dignify rather than degrade. The innuendo is not mean and derisive but exhilarating, like good conversation. The true butt is surely not the lovers but literature and language and those who are involved with them closely and sometimes uncritically, including the poet himself.

Góngora started another version earlier, in 1604, but it went no further than a description of Thisbe. He also wrote two similar poems on Hero and Leander. The first, in 1589, starts, "The boy threw himself in the tuna pond" (*Arrojóse el mancebillo / al charco do los atunes*) and ends with an epitaph in which the dead Hero is imagined saying something like, "Love dealt with us like two eggs: he was boiled and I was fried"—the Spanish for a boiled egg being "passed through water" and for a fried egg "smashed," the same word that can describe Hero lying broken on the rocks after throwing herself from the tower. The second poem, from 1610, "Though I know little of Greek" (*Aunque entiendo poco griego*) starts with a description of Hero and her family that is similar to the description of Thisbe here.

In its punning and its bathos *Pyramus and Thisbe* is reminiscent of other earlier poems of Góngora. In 1582 he wrote a satire on the pastoral, "On the stony banks" (*En la pedregosa orilla*), which has a very rustic shepherd addressing a picture of his shepherdess and confessing himself flabbergasted to see how she has "her forehead right in the middle between her temples, and her teeth inside her mouth." In 1585 he parodied a *morisco* ballad of Lope's in "Saddle up my donkey" (*Ensíllenme el asno rucio*) in which a peasant goes off to be a knight.

Romance (1618)

La ciudad de Babilonia,   1
famosa, no por sus muros,
(fuesen de tierra cocidos,
o sean de tierra crudos),
    sino por los dos amantes,   5
celebrados, hijos suyos,
que muertos, y en un estoque,
han peregrinado el mundo;
    citarista dulce, hija
del Archipoeta rubio,   10
si al brazo de mi instrumento
le solicitas el pulso,
    digno sujeto será
de las orejas del vulgo:
popular aplauso quiero,   15
perdónenme sus tribunos.
    Píramo fueron, y Tisbe,
los que en verso hizo culto
el licenciado Nasón,
bien romo, o bien narigudo,   20
    dejar el dulce candor
(lastimosamente) obscuro,
al que túmulo de seda,
fue de los casquilucios

[Pyramus and Thisbe] (1618)

The famous city of Babylon   1
was less for its walls renowned,
whether of terra-cotta
or merely of raw mud,
    than for a pair of lovers,   5
who have become a byword,
and made the tour of the world
skewered on one sword;
    it will surely be a fit subject
(if you sweet, musical muse,   10
daughter of the fair archpoet,
will stand beside my instrument
    and guide my hand upon it)
for the general public's ears;
to be popular, that's what I want,   15
pace my critical peers.
    Pyramus and Thisbe were
the two, that in polished lines
the poet of the outsize nose,
bulbous, Roman or otherwise,   20
    depicted, along with that mulberry,
this brainless pair's memorial,
which gave sweet whiteness up
for a more sombre hue

moral que los hospedó,   25
y fue condenado al punto,
si del Tigris no en raíces,
de los amantes, en fructos.

    Estos, pues, dos babilonios
vecinos nacieron mucho,   30
y tanto, que una pared
de oídos no muy agudos,

    en los años de su infancia,
oyó a las cunas los tumbos,
a los niños los gorjeos,   35
y a las amas los arrullos.

    Oyolos, y aquellos días
tan bien la audiencia le supo,
que años después se hizo
rajas en servicio suyo.   40

    En el ínterim nos digan,
los mal formados rasguños
de los pinceles de un ganso,
sus dos hermosos dibujos:

    terso marfil su esplendor   45
(no sin modestia) interpuso
entre las ondas de un sol
y la luz de dos carbunclos.

    Libertad dice llorada
el corvo suave yugo   50
de unas cejas cuyos arcos
no serenaron diluvios.

    Luciente cristal lascivo
(la tez, digo, de su vulto)
vaso era de claveles,   55
y de jazmines confusos.

    Árbitro de tantas flores,
lugar el olfacto obtuvo
en forma, no de nariz,
sino de un blanco almendruco.   60

    Un rubí concede o niega
(según alternar le plugo),
entre doce perlas netas
veinte aljófares menudos.

     when it sheltered them and was   25
—not by Tigris drowning its roots—
sanctioned for its complicity
through the lovers in its fruits.
     These two Babylonians,
from the day of their birth had been   30
so close that a wall with ears
not abnormally keen
     registered every creak
of their cradles when they were babies,
each burbling sound as well,   35
and their nurses' lullabies.
     It heard, I say, these sounds,
and had therefrom such solace
it was willing in future years
to crack up in their service.   40
     But before that comes let's turn
to the unpolished scratches
of a clumsy goose quill
to paint us their fair pictures:
     smooth ivory at its most splendid   45
interposed (but in modest guise)
between bright golden strands
and a pair of sparkling eyes.
     The gentle curving yoke
of the brows is an eloquent bow,   50
not speaking of the flood's end
but of liberty's overthrow.
     Elastic translucent crystal
(the face, I mean, the skin)
is carnations in a vase   55
mingled with sweet jasmine.
     Like a judge among these flowers
the olfactory sense was sited
in a structure less a nose
than an almond not quite set.   60
     A ruby reveals or hides,
according to how it feels,
a score of dewlike drops,
a dozen flawless pearls.

De plata bruñida, era,   65
proporcionado cañuto,
el órgano de la voz,
la cerbatana del gusto.

Las pechugas, si hubo Fénix,
suyas son; si no lo hubo,   70
de los jardines de Venus
pomos eran no maduros.

El etcétera es de mármol,
cuyos relieves ocultos
ultraje mórbido hicieran   75
a los divinos desnudos

la vez que se vistió Paris
la garnacha de Licurgo,
cuando Palas, por vellosa,
y por zamba perdió Juno.   80

Esta, pues, desde el glorioso
umbral de su primer lustro,
niña la estimó el Amor
de los ojos que no tuvo.

Creció deidad, creció invidia   85
de un sexo y otro; ¿qué mucho
que la fe erigiese aras
a quien le emulación culto?

Tantas veces, de los templos
a sus posadas redujo   90
sin libertad los galanes,
y las damas, sin orgullo,

que viendo, quien la vistió,
nueve meses que la trujo,
de terciopelo de tripa,   95
su peligro en los concursos,

las reliquias de Tisbica
engastó en lo más recluso
de su retrete, negando
aun a los átomos puros.   100

¡Oh Píramo lo que hace,
joveneto ya robusto,
que sin alas podía ser
hijo de Venus segundo!

The shapely swanlike neck   65
is pure silver bullion,
that's both organ of the voice,
and the flute of degustation.
    The breasts belong, if there is one,
to the Phoenix; if it's fictitious,   70
then they are ripening apples
from the gardens of Venus.
    The etcetera was of marble
and its hidden declivities
might do serious injury   75
to those nude divinities
    who paraded the day Paris
to play the judge agreed,
and Pallas was found too hairy,
and Juno too knock-kneed.   80
    This child, then, from the glorious
outset of her days
was held by Love to be
the apple of his missing eyes.
    She grew into a deity,   85
envy of every adult;
how can love not raise altars
to one who is envy's cult?
    How often from public places
she sent them all away,   90
the gentlemen as slaves,
the ladies in dismay!
    Which was understood by the one
who nine months bore the child
wrapped in her womb's velvet,   95
and who, seeing the danger, held
    her out of the public eye,
like a blessed relic sealed her
in the innermost closet,
lest even the air soil her.   100
    O Pyramus, what must it do
to a vigorous young man,
who though without wings could be
Dame Venus's other son?

Narciso, no el de las flores   105
pompa, que vocal sepulcro
construyó a su boboncilla
en el valle mas profundo,
    sino un Adonis caldeo,
ni jarifo, ni membrudo,   110
que traía las orejas
en las jaulas de dos tufos.
    Su copetazo, pelusa,
si tafetán su testuzo,
sus mejillas, much raso,   115
su bozo, poco velludo;
    dos espadas eran, negras
a lo dulcemente rufo
sus cejas, que las doblaron
dos estocadas de puño.   120
    Al fin, en Piramo quiso
encarnar Cupido un chuzo,
el mejor de su armería,
con su herramienta al uso.
    Este, pues, era el vecino,   125
el amante, y aun el cuyo
de la tórtola doncella
gemidora a lo vïudo;
    que de las penas de Amor
encarecimiento es sumo   130
escuchar ondas sediento
quien siente frutas ayuno.

        .   .   .   .

    Medianoche era por filo,
hora que el farol nocturno,
reventando de muy casto,
campaba de muy sañudo,
    cuando tropezando Tisbe   285
a la calle dio el pie zurdo,
de no pocos endechada
caniculares aúllos.

For he was no second Narcissus,   105
that prize flower who gave
his sweet idiot in the deepest
valley an echoing grave,
        but a Chaldean Adonis,
neither hulk nor dandy,   110
with ears concealed behind
kiss-curls that were handy.
        Plus a whispy quiff on the forehead,
a fluffy mane at the nape,
and cheeks that were very smooth,   115
few hairs for the razor to scrape;
        the eyebrows were like two swords,
black but quite beguiling,
turned up at the ends, like rapiers
bent back by the dagger parrying.   120
        In sum, Cupid had made
Pyramus his prick or dart,
the finest tool in his armory,
erect, as befits the part.
        This was the neighbor, then,   125
the lover, even the mate,
of the lost dove who's moaning
like a widower in a state:
        for, to the torments of love
it gives a tremendous boost   130
to listen to water when thirsting,
when fasting, smell a feast.

    .   .   .   .

        It was midnight on the dot,
and, in the sky, night's lantern
was exploding with chastity,
and bragging about her anger,
        when Thisbe ventured forth,   285
setting her left foot forward,
to the accompaniment of a dirge
sung by a canine chorus.

Dejó la ciudad de Nino
y al salir, funesto búho   290
alcándara hizo umbrosa
un verdinegro aceituno.
    Sus pasos dirigió donde
por las bocas de dos brutos
tres o cuatro siglos ha   295
que está escupiendo Neptuno.
    Cansada llegó a su margen
a pesar del abril mustio,
y lagrimosa la fuente
enronqueció su murmurio.   300
    Olmo que en jóvenes hojas
disimula años adultos,
de su vid florida entonces
en los más lascivos nudos,
    un rayo, sin escuderos   305
o de luz o de tumulto,
le desvaneció la pompa,
y el tálamo descompuso.
    No fue nada; a cien lejías
dio ceniza. ¡Oh cielo injusto,   310
si tremendo en el castigo,
portentoso en el indulto!:
    la planta más convecina
quedó verde; el seco junco
ignoróaun lo más ardiente   315
del acelerado incurso.
    Cintia caló el papahígo
a todo su plenilunio,
de temores vellories,
que ella dice que son nublos.   320
    Tisbe, entre pavores tantos
solicitando refugios,
a las rüinas apela
de un edificio caduco.
    Ejecutarlo quería,   325
cuando la selva produjo
del Egipcio o del Tebano
un Cleoneo trïunfo,

As she left the city of Ninus
an owl, bird of ill omen,   290
flew to a shadowy perch
on the branch of a dark green olive.
          Her footsteps led her to where
for quite a few centuries past
Neptune had been spouting.   295
out of the mouths of two beasts.
          She was tired and despite April
it was a gloomy station;
even the fountain's murmuring
grew hoarse with lamentation.   300
          An elm belying its age,
dressed up in youthful foliage,
was wrapped in the loving coils
of a vine already flowering,
          when a bolt from the blue unsquired   305
by attendant light or thunder
destroyed its noble crown
and blasted the loving union.
          It wasn't much, just ashes
enough for a hundred washes.   310
O heaven! how stern your sanctions,
how astonishing your mercies!
          Neighboring plants stayed green,
even dry reeds were exempt
from the touch of the fiery breath   315
of the sudden, swift event.
          Cynthia now draws
her bonnet over her face,
a veil of what she calls cloud
to cover her distress.   320
          Among such terrors, Thisbe
seeking some asylum,
lights upon the ruins
of a decrepit mansion.
          She was about to enter when   325
somehow the forest came up with
the beast that participated
in the Nemaean triumph,

que en un prójimo cebado
(no sé si merino o burdo)
babeando sangre, hizo
el cristal líquido, impuro.

Temerosa de la fiera,
aún más que del estornudo
de Júpiter, puesto que
sobresalto fue machucho,

huye perdiendo en la fuga
su manto, ¡fatal descuido!,
que protonecio hará
al señor Piramiburro.

A los portillos se acoge
de aquel antiguo reducto,
noble ya edificio, ahora
jurisdicción de Vertumno.

Alondra no con la tierra
se cosió al menor barrunto
de esmerjón, como la triste,
con el tronco de un saúco.

Bebió la fiera, dejando
torpemente rubicundo
el cendal que fue de Tisbe,
y el bosque penetró inculto.

En esto llegó el tardón,
que la ronda le detuvo
sobre quitarle el que fue,
aun envainado, verdugo.

Llegó, pisando cenizas
del lastimoso trasunto
de sus bodas, a la fuente,
al término constituto;

y, no hallando la moza,
entre ronco y tartamudo
se enjaguó con sus palabras,
regulador de minutos.

De su alma la mitad
cita a voces, mas sin fruto,
que socarrón se las niega
el eco más campanudo.

330

335

340

345

350

355

360

365

who having just fed on a neighbor
(if merino or just plain sheep,
I know not) was dribbling blood,
polluting the crystal's lip.

        Having more fear of the beast
than even Jupiter's sneezes,
because she received from its look
the most shocking of surprises,

        she flees, and in fleeing loses
her cloak, which horrid faux pas
was to make a perfect fool
of poor Sir Pyram-ass.

        She enters under the portals
of that ancient fortress,
once a noble edifice,
now the domain of Vertumnus.

        Never did skylark press
itself more close to the furrow
on seeing a hawk's shadow,
than she to the trunk of an elder.

        The beast, having drunk its fill,
inspected the cloak, then, leaving it
bloodied and tattered and torn,
vanished into the undergrowth.

        Now the slowcoach arrived
having been stopped by the watch,
suspicious of what he was carrying:
lethal, though clad in a sheath.

        He arrived, treading the ashes
of that sad simulacrum
of his marriage, at the fountain,
the site of their assignation,

        and finding the girl absent,
muttering, half–struck dumb,
he eased his doubts with words,
calculating the time.

        He calls out loud the name
of his soul's partner but his cries
are only mocked, not even
the most eloquent echo replies.

Troncos examina huecos,
mas no le ofrece ninguno   370
el panal que solicita
en aquellos senos rudos.
    Madama Luna a este tiempo,
a petición de Saturno,
el velo corrió al melindre,   375
y el papahígo depuso,
    para leer los testigos
del proceso ya concluso,
que publicar mandó el hado,
cúal más, cúal menos perjuro.   380
    Las huellas cuadrupedales
del coronado abrenuncio,
que en esta sazón bramando
tocó a vísperas de susto;
    las espumas, que la hierba   385
más sangrientas las expuso,
que el signo las babeó,
rugiente pompa de julio;
    indignamente estragados
los pedazos mal difusos   390
del velo de su retablo,
que ya de sus duelos juzgo,
    violos y, al reconocellos,
mármol, obediente al duro
sincel de Lisipo, tanto   395
no ya dismintió lo esculpto,
    como Píramo lo vivo,
pendiente en un pie a lo grullo,
sombra hecho de sí mismo,
con facultades de bulto.   400
    Las señas repite falsas
del engaño a que lo indujo
su fortuna, contra quien
ni lanza vale ni escudo.
    Esparcidos imagina   405
por el fragoso arcabuco
(¿ebúrneos diré, o divinos?
divinos digo, y ebúrneos),

He examines hollow trunks,
but finds not one to offer   370
the honeycomb he seeks
within its rough interior.
    Madam Moon by now
at Saturn's invitation
has put away her coyness   375
and drawn back the curtain
    to allow him to view the evidence,
for fate wants this case published,
though the outcome is prejudged
and the witnesses all perjured.   380
    First there's the quadripedal
marks of the maned phenomenon,
which gives just now a roar,
forewarning of something horrible;
    then the slaver on the grass,   385
where it shines with a redder sheen
than when dribbled from the mouth
of July's roaring sign;
    and then the mangled tatters
of the torn veil of his altar,   390
which now I judge to be
more akin to a veil of mourning;
    all this he recognized,
and never did marble, shaped
by Lysippus, more praise art   395
in denying that it was sculpted,
    than did Pyramus disown life,
poised on one foot like a stork,
reduced to the merest shadow,
just as lively as a block.   400
    He reviews the lying clues
adduced by the cunning wiles
of cruel fate, against which
neither lance nor shield avails.
    He pictures the pieces scattered   405
all over that rough territory
(ivory, call them, divine? I'll
call them divine *and* ivory!)

los bellos miembros de Tisbe;
y aquí otra vez se traspuso,   410
fatigando a Praxiteles
sobre copialle de estuco.
    La Parca, en esto, las manos
en la rueca y en el huso,
y los ojos (como dicen)   415
en el vital estatuto,
    inexorable sonó
la dura tijera, a cuyo
mortal son Píramo, vuelto
del parasismo profundo,   420
    el acero que Vulcano
templó en venenos zumos,
eficazmente mortales
y mágicamente infusos,
    valeroso desnudó,   425
y no como el otro Mucio,
asó intrépido la mano,
sino el asador tradujo
    por el pecho a las espaldas.
¡Oh tantas veces insulso,   430
cuántas vueltas a tu hierro
los siglos darán futuros!
    ¿Tan mal te olía la vida?
¡oh bien hideputa, puto,
el que sobre tu cabeza   435
pusiera un cuerno de juro!
    De violas coronada
salió la Aurora con zuño,
cuando un suspiro de a ocho,
aunque mal distinto el cuño   440
    (cual engañada avecilla
del cautivo contrapunto
a implicarse desalada
en la hermana del engrudo),
    la llevó donde el cuitado   445
en su postrimero turno,
desperdiciaba la sangre,
que recibió por embudo.

of Thisbe's fair limbs, and again
he's gone, lost, translated,   410
challenging Praxiteles
to make his copy in plaster.
    Destiny, now, her hands on
the distaff and the bobbin,
but eyes on (as they say)   415
the book that governs living,
    waved the scissors, at whose
inexorable command
and deadly clatter, Pyramus,
out of his deep swoon waking,   420
    boldly drew from its scabbard
the steel Vulcan had tempered
(and in vats of venomous juices
made lethally effective,
    charged with magic power)   425
and not emulating Mucius
who roasted his own fist,
took a firm grasp on the spit
    and plunged it through his chest.
Idiot! Dimwit! How many   430
turns they'll give to your act
in centuries to come!
    Was life just a bad smell to you?
O heavens! o goodness gracious!
For anything you propose now   435
who'd give a tinker's cuss
    Now with a crown of violets
frowning Dawn arose,
as a most emphatic sigh
(she's unable to tell whose,   440
    but see how the little bird
lured by the caged bird's song,
into the sticky trap
unwittingly rushes headlong)
    beckoned her on to where   445
the spitted idiot lay,
almost done to a turn,
the rich blood wasting away.

Ofrecióle su regazo
(y yo le ofrezco en su muslo   450
desplumadas las delicias
del pájaro de Catulo),
     en cuanto, boca con boca,
confitándole disgustos,
y heredándole aun los trastos   455
menos vitales estuvo.
     Expiró al fin en sus labios,
y ella, con semblante enjuto,
que pudiera por sereno
acatarrar un centurio,   460
     con todo su morrïón,
haciendo el alma trabuco
de un "!ay!", se caló en la espada
aquella vez que le cupo.
     Pródigo desató el hierro,   465
si crüel, un largo flujo
de rubíes de Ceilán
sobre esmeraldas de Muso.
     Hermosa quedó la muerte
en los lilios amatuntos,   470
que salpicó dulce hielo,
que tiñó palor venusto.
     Lloraron, con el Eufrates,
no sólo el fiero Danubio,
el siempre Arajes flechero,   475
cuándo parto y cuándo turco,
     mas con su llanto lavaron
el Bucentoro diurno,
cuando sale, el Ganges loro,
cuando vuelve, el Tajo rubio.   480
     Al blanco moral, de cuanto
humor se bebió purpúreo,
sabrosos granates fueron
o testimonio o tributo.
     Sus muy reverendos padres   485
arrastrando luengos lutos,
con más colas que cometas,
con más pendientes que pulpos,

She offered him her lap,
(and to him on her thigh I allow   450
those featherless delights
of Catullus's little sparrow),
 and she pressed her mouth to his
to sweeten his discomfort,
and took possession of   455
his final remaining element.
 Thus did he breathe his last;
and she, with a face so gaunt,
so chill, a centurion, complete
with helmet, could have caught   460
 his absolute death of cold from it,
flung out as if with a catapult
one sigh, and fell on the sword
(such of it as was available).
 The blade unloosed at once   465
a flood, which though cruel was generous,
of rubies from Ceylon,
 spread on American emeralds.
 Beauty in death reposed
on lilies of Amatunta   470
powdered with fresh ice,
tinged with elegant pallor.
 Not only did the Euphrates
and the proud Danube weep,
and Arakis lined with archers   475
both Parthian and Turk,
 but also the diurnal chariot
was bathed by the flowing tears
of dark Ganges where it rises,
gold Tagus where it disappears.   480
 As for the white mulberry,
sweet garnets were to be both
testimony and tribute
to the purple it had absorbed.
 The pair's most revered parents   485
trailing their mourning weeds
with more tails than a comet,
or an octopus's arms,

jaspes, y de más colores
que un áulico disimulo,   490
ocuparon en su huesa
que el Sirio llama sepulcro,
    aunque es de tradición constante
(si los tiempos no confundo,
de cronógrafos, me atengo   495
al que calzare mas justo),
    que ascendiente pío de aquel
desvanecido Nabuco,
que pació el campo medio hombre,
medio fiera y todo mulo,   500
    en urna dejó, decente,
los nobles polvos, inclusos,
que absolvieron de ser huesos
cinamomo y calambuco.
    Y en letras de oro: "Aquí yacen   505
individuamente juntos,
a pesar del amor, dos,
a pesar del número, uno."

filled the tomb (in Syriac
commonly known as a sepulchre)   490
with marble of more colors
than a palace coverup;
    although there's a strong tradition,
(if it's not anachronistic—
of the authorities, I follow   495
the one who seems most accurate)
    about a pious ancestor
of the deranged Nebuchad-
nezzar, grass-eater (half man,
half beast, all mule) who had   500
    the noble dust enclosed in
an entirely decorous urn,
by Mary's balsam and cinnamon
cleansed of all taint of bone.
    And in letters of gold: "Here lie   505
together and individual,
two, who in love are singular,
and are one, despite being plural."

The poem numbers used here are the numbers of poems in this collection. Line numbers of the English text, where they differ, are given in square brackets. In addition to elucidating obscure passages or references, I hope these notes will indicate the general strategy behind the translations and explain why the English does not follow the original exactly.

The notes are indebted to the work of the various scholars whose editions I have used and those they have themselves consulted. In fact this debt is too general to acknowledge in individual cases; but I have tried to indicate interpretations that depend on my own instinct.

1. Romance (1580)

This very well-known poem is an example of the new, or artistic, ballad, of which Góngora and Lope de Vega were major practitioners. (It is actually a *romancillo*, or little ballad, having lines of six rather than eight syllables.) The new ballad typically uses a refrain (*estribillo*), derived from some popular song or saying, and is usually structured in four-line stanzas. Like the old ballad it has assonance, not rhyme, on the second and fourth lines, generally with the same assonance continued on even-numbered lines throughout the poem. This is a lot easier to do in Spanish than in English.

The topos of a girl speaking to her mother is very widespread in Spanish popular poetry. In this case I feel the girl is protesting rather than just lamenting, in the Spanish literary tradition of women who have to put up with what custom dictates but not in silence. (García Lorca's *Casa de Bernarda Alba* might come to mind.) Some will see the poem as an expression of sexual frustration.

The chief aim of my version has been to retain the brevity and unsentimentality of the original. I have also tried to indicate the verse form by some correspondence of sound between even-numbered lines.

The following notes are rather lengthy for such an apparently simple poem, but "simplicity" can be complicated.

Lines 3–4: The Spanish actually says "yesterday still to be married, now a widow and alone." I have made the change for the sake of brevity.

Lines 9–10: I recognize that I have prejudged an issue in my translation of the refrain: the Spanish is ambiguous between "leave me to" and "allow me to"; the English "let me" would also be ambiguous, but in a slightly different way.

Line 18: Just as the loved one was conventionally described in Renaissance poetry as cruel, it was conventional to equate love with loss of freedom. But Góngora seems to return to this concept especially often (see, for example, nos. 10, 11, and 18).

Lines 23–24: In the Spanish, *oficio* is a job, function, or even office (in the related sense of job, position). The problem here, though, is with the second line, *del dulce mirar*, "sweet-looking." Does it refer to the pleasure of looking at the loved one or to the speaker's appearance? I thought the former, but in a *letrilla* of 1585 Góngora uses the same phrase when speaking of a woman who presumes on her good looks. My translation deliberately tries to preserve the ambiguity.

Lines 31–34: The meaning of "one may be just" is not clear. Some have suggested that "just" should be its opposite, "unjust," which seems to suit the meaning better but not the rhythm; others that there is an implied concessive clause: "although one is just, the other is not." I have chosen the latter solution, but there remains a problem: clearly to blame the girl is unjust, but is it telling her to stop that is just and reasonable, or does this refer back to the fact of her crying: it is just and reasonable for her to cry?

Lines 37–38: The Spanish actually says something like "It would be much worse to die and keep quiet." This is odd: one would expect keeping quiet to come before dying, not the other way around, and one wonders anyway from whose point of view it would be worse. I have chosen to see it as the rhetoric of a protest: she is defending with sarcasm her right not to shut up.

Line 52–53: The eyes represent the lover.

Lines 57–58: More literally, "half my bed is superfluous now."

2. Romance (1580)

Another *romancillo* (lines of six syllables). Here I have not made a serious attempt to reproduce the form beyond trying to keep the lines as short as possible, but I have tried to keep the conversational tone. To those who know Góngora only for giving his name to Gongorism, the directness and simplicity may come as a surprise. Here though the simplicity is not quite transparent: the ending is deliberately shocking and, not surprisingly, was disapproved of by Father Pineda (see introduction, xiii).

Line 3: In Andalusia *amiga* is a school for girls.

Line 11: *palmilla* is a fine cloth made in Cuenca, often blue.

Line 17: *estadal* is said to be a holy ribbon brought back from some shrine, to be worn round the neck. I imagine it would have a holy medal of some kind on it, but the speaker seems uncertain what to call this.

Lines 43–44: These are presumably verses of a popular song.

Lines 53–56: The verb that I have translated as "stoned" is actually an invented word, *anaranjeamos*, "we oranged," meaning "bombarded with oranges."

Lines 81–84: Not all readers agree about the implications of *bellaquerías*, but they are not innocent. Modern Spanish readers I have consulted find the word quite strong, though certainly it is not explicit. I feel quite sure that Góngora enjoyed the ambivalence.

3. Letrilla (1581)

Góngora's *letrillas* are rhyming poems, often with a refrain; many of them are satirical or burlesque. They were set to music (as were many ballads). Jammes (*Letrillas*, 115) sees this early poem, written when Góngora was a student in Salamanca or shortly after his return to Córdoba, as something like his literary *credo*, expressing the view that underlies the later and much more ambitious *Solitudes*. But the posture is traditional and universal, and the nonconformism is quite self-conscious.

I have tried to capture the spirit, without reproducing the rhyme scheme.

Line 22: *the mad king's exploits:* no particular king, just general tall tales from very ancient times.

Lines 24–29: A similar attitude to sea voyages is often expressed by Góngora—for example, in the old merchant's speech in the *First Solitude* (lines 366–502 [374–514]). The interest of a child in seashells on the beach is also mentioned in the *Second Solitude*.

Line 25: The merchant here is clearly to be understood as a trader, perhaps the owner or captain of a ship. The word *soles* is surely a pun: it means "suns" in its most literal sense and is a metonym for worlds or countries, but it can also mean gold coins and a kind of lace and, by extension, novelty goods. All these meanings appear connected if we view these lines in the light of the old merchant's speech in the *First Solitude*, where empire, greed, commerce, danger, and shipwreck are all part of the same picture.

Lines 34–36: Wine, for Góngora, is as much an aesthetic as a physical stimulant, and he is particularly insistent on the visual effect of mixing red and white wine— compare the *First Solitude* (lines 867–871 [888–891]). In a *letrilla* of 1603 he speaks of mixing red wine from Toro and white from Ciudad Real, rubies and gold, and calls wine the greatest antidote to melancholy.

4. Letrilla (1581)

The third stanza is not included in most manuscripts, but Jammes reproduces it and it seems a pity to omit it here. Father Pineda (Jammes, *Letrillas*, 59n.) said something to the effect that it was wrong to blame fate for rewards and punishments, as Góngora does in this poem, because they were meted out after careful consideration by the authorities.

Lines 9–10 *Encomiendas* were originally the titles and perquisites granted by the military orders set up during the period of the Reconquest. *Sambenitos* were the capes that penitents wore after their trial by the Inquisition.

5. Soneto (1582)

This is the earliest of the sonnets I have translated, but it is certainly not an immature one. At first sight it seems conventionally Petrarchan. Yet Góngora adds a more individual twist by suggesting that turbulent waters might upset the perfect (and conventional) image of the loved one as they enter the sea.

Streams and rivers figure often in Góngora's poetry. There may seem to be a contradiction between the slow movement of the stream in the first quatrain and the "swift current" of the first tercet, but the *Solitudes* show how aware Góngora is of the power and the changing moods of water in rivers and sea.

I have made a few changes in order to preserve the overall rhetorical structure. In the Spanish of the second quatrain it is Love who paints the picture of the woman when she looks at her reflection. But the topic ("she" in line 5) is separated from the grammatical subject ("Love" in line 6), a separation that is awkward in English, which normally collates grammatical subject and topic. I have added the "restless steeds," which I think are implied in the mention of reins and crystal bit. I have also made a change in the final tercet: in the original, *el gran Señor*, or Neptune, is the grammatical subject, receiving the image in his depths (or "in his deep bosom," a turn of phrase to delight nineteenth-century English translators). I have lost something here, but the compensation is to put emphasis where I think it belongs, on *confusamente*, which I have translated as "in disarray." I see an element of humor in this concern for the image of beauty (and perhaps also an indication that Góngora places the image rather than the woman on a pedestal) and humor again in the last line, *el gran Señor del húmedo tridente*, "the great Lord of the dripping trident." Góngora often treats mythology and other literary and poetic conventions irreverently.

I do not think anyone would take this sonnet as an expression of passionate feeling. Even as a well-turned compliment it may be somewhat undermined by the sense that the poet is so much in charge. But to discuss the poem in these terms would surely be to return to the prejudices of Romanticism. More pertinent I think are the subversive suggestion of woman's vanity in characterising the river as a mirror and the traditional association between a river flowing into the sea and death. The complex but fluent structure—a single flowing sentence till the middle of verse 9, and then another to the end—gives notice of what Góngora will achieve in later work where conceptual complexity is underpinned by great syntactic control.

6. Romance (1582)

The characters in this ballad are drawn from Carolingian romance, although Count Rudolph should really be Roland. In one of the old ballads, Durandarte (originally not a knight but a sword), dying on the battlefield, says of Belerma: "Seven years I served you, and had no recompense." He instructs his cousin, Montesinos, to cut out his heart and take it to her, and also to remind her of him—twice a week!

The ending presents a difficulty. Góngora was aware of the effectiveness of truncation (the unfinished look) in many traditional ballads (one of the most famous examples of this is *Conde Arnaldos*). In the old ballads it is probably just an accident of oral transmission, but it could be imitated deliberately and often was in artistic ballads. As in Coleridge's Xanadu poem, this effect can create a great sense of mystery, though what to some readers is open-ended will appear to others unfinished. I think Góngora is here using a similar trick for partly comic effect. I am not sure whether this ending with the left-handed page is in imitation of the traditional ballad (the page just happens to be left-handed), or whether something else is implied in *zurdo* (which has connotations of unluckiness or clumsiness). Possibly both. (The question of endings is discussed in Diano Chaffee-Sorace, *Góngora's Poetic Textual Tradition* [London: Tamesis, 1988], chap. 2).

Line 4: *Boquirrubio* has a number of different meanings or connotations, including "young and beardless," "immature," "talkative," and "a fop": I think the general meaning here is "not to be taken seriously."

Line 14: *Estrado* is said to mean a raised area in a room where a lady received visits; *luto*, "mourning," suggests that the furnishings would be black. I have been influenced by a passage in J. H. Eliot's *Imperial Spain, 1469–1716* (London: Penguin, 1985), where he describes how Moorish influence lived on in Spain even after the Moors had supposedly gone. Spanish women, he says, "crouched on cushions instead of using chairs" and "remained semi-veiled, in spite of frequent royal prohibitions" (309).

Line 16: *Neptune's urinals*: this is less unconventional than it sounds in English, but I feel the literal translation matches the poem's general tone.

Lines 27–28: Góngora's puns, which can be serious as well as humorous, are a challenge for the translator. They may be untranslatable, but they cannot be ignored. He is perhaps more addicted to punning than to the complex syntax or learned vocabulary for which he is famed, and he was certainly taken to task for it by his contemporary critics. In *buen pozo haya su alma*, the word *pozo*, "a well," is the same in the Andalusian pronunciation as *poso* meaning "repose or rest." So literally these two lines mean: "May his soul have good rest, and let it be a rest/a well without a bucket." Bucket and well probably have a sexual connotation. I abandoned the attempt to translate all this, substituting two lines that I hoped would fill the space without sounding inappropriate.

Lines 35–36: another pun, "brute" referring also to Brutus, not Julius Caesar's but an earlier figure in Roman history, according to Antonio Carreño (*Romances* 178n.)

Lines 82–84: The phoenix, which burns and is then reborn from its ashes.

Lines 106–109: There were many jokes linking mules, clerics, and sex, and probably Góngora invokes all of them here, but I could not see the way to indicate this.

Lines 109–112: *Broqueles* and *escudos* are shields, both with the same sexual connotation, but I assume the latter to be also a pun on *escudos* = money.)

Lines 113–114: The twelve Peers: Charlemagne's knights. But the Spanish for Peers, *pares*, can also mean even numbers.

Line 127: A four-cornered hat is a clerical hat and hence a synecdoche for *priest*.

Line 132: According to Carreño, (*Romances* 184n.) *zumo*, which I translate as juices, also means sperm.

Line 134: More literally, she "put a knot in it."

Line 135–136: *Came in without knocking*: the Spanish only says he was left-handed. I have tried to suggest that he was inopportune or possibly the reverse.

7. Soneto (1582)

In the sonnet, English and Spanish share the same Italianate tradition, so in general the form transfers quite easily. The fixed rhyme scheme, however, causes problems. Góngora's sonnets have two quatrains rhyming *abba abba* followed by two tercets with some variation in the rhyme scheme. In most of my versions, where it does not interfere too much with the meaning, I have attempted some kind of sound link in the rhyming positions.

Commentators have remarked how in this poem the usually more cheerful *carpe diem* theme changes finally to a cry of anguish at the prospect of annihilation.

8. Romance (1582)

Lines 9–10: More accurate would be "Time weaves its garlands / from flowers that quickly fade," but I preferred the sound of my original version.

Line 17: The flower is *tigridia pavonia,* a bulb that had been imported from the New World. It is sometimes translated as "marigold," which loses the point—that its flowers are so quickly gone.

Line 26: In the original there is a play on words: "The curfew *disarms* you . . ."—it was forbidden to carry a sword after the curfew. This idea leads on to line 30, *mayores de la marca,* which literally means larger than the official limit on the size of a sword. But *mayores* can also mean "older," and I think the intention is clear. This does not excuse my anachronism, but Góngora was not averse to anachronism and mixing registers.

Line 39: *"Rochet"* (pr. *rotchet* or *rocket*): a special surplice worn by bishops, with many pleats (often mentioned in anti-episcopal diatribes of the Reformation).

Line 60: *Opportunity's shown bald:* Books of emblems, like Alciato's (first published in 1531), were popular in the sixteenth century. They featured an illustration of some virtue, vice, or popular saying and a short Latin verse. Opportunity is shown as a woman with a long lock of hair in front but bald in the back—nothing to hold onto once she's gone past. Compare the English "seize Time by the forelock." Góngora again plays with this image in a ballad of 1591, *"Castillo de San Cervantes."* The same figure occurs in Spenser's *Faerie Queene* with a slightly different meaning, because she is called "Occasion" and associated with Furor, or wrath, representing the idea that wrath must have an occasion or cause.

9. Romance (1583)

Góngora started a new fashion by writing several ballads about the galley slave.

Line 5: Dragut was a Turkish pirate, a Greek by origin. Literature tends to conceal the fact that there were many Christian converts to Islam and that some of them prospered at the expense of their compatriots or simply as functionaries of the sultan.

Lines 23–24: The South Sea is the Pacific, so called by the Spanish, who were looking south when they came to it after crossing the Isthmus of Panama.

Line 38: "Sails of the Religion" refers to the galleys of the Knights of St John in Malta who aimed to protect the Mediterranean from Turkish or North African pirates.

10. Romance (1584)

In this knockabout deflation of literary and romantic conventions, one feels that Don Quijote and Sancho Panza are just round the corner. In a temporal sense, they are. *Don Quijote* was published twenty years later, in 1605, but was probably conceived in the 1590s.

Like every concept that becomes associated with a cultural trend or the mood of a historical period, *desengaño,* "disillusionment," is something of a chameleon: it can be related to the cynicism of a Lazarillo de Tormes or to the idealism of the mystic who turns away from the illusions of life to seek spiritual fulfilment. I have found it necessary to translate it differently in different contexts.

Lines 3–4: The metaphor of love as a bondage.

Lines 6–8: It was common to hang objects in churches in thanksgiving for dangers averted or illness supposedly cured through prayer. The word *yerros* here is a pun: it means errors, but *hierros* (same pronunciation) means irons or fetters.

Line 23: Disenchantment is pulled in a carriage like a victorious general of ancient Rome being pulled by captive barbarians.

Lines 39–40: "The precious sweat of the Sabaean tree" is incense, a common periphrasis in Góngora. "Sabaean" means from Saba, more familiar in English as Sheba.

Lines 83–84: Beltenebros, Peña Pobre: this will be familiar to readers of *Don Quijote*. Beltenebros is the name Amadís de Gaula took when he retired to the Peña Pobre to do penance, an episode famously imitated by Don Quijote.

11. Romance (1585)

This is one of several poems Góngora contributed to the genre of the morisco ballad. Such ballads generally portray a chivalric relation between Moors and Christians during the period of the wars between them. Modern historians paint a different picture of relations between the two groups. We should remember, too, that the expulsion of the *moriscos* (Moors who lived on in Spain, nominally as Christian converts, after the fall of Granada) was finally ordered by Philip III in 1609. There is however the possibility that the literary idealization of the Moors is related to the views of some who were opposed to the harsh treatment of the moriscos in the sixteenth century (see L. P. Harvey, *Muslims in Spain, 1500–1614* [Chicago: University of Chicago Press, 2005].

Line 2: Actually the Zeneta, a particular Berber tribe, reputed as cavalrymen.

Line 4: Green grass, red blood—one of Góngora's recurring images.

Line 41: In 1560, the Spanish attempt to capture Djerba, an island off the coast of North Africa, produced a famous defeat and boosted the confidence of the Turkish corsairs in the Mediterranean. The Turkish threat was a continuing worry, which did not go away with their defeat at the Battle of Lepanto in 1571.

Lines 49–53: The Moors of Meliona considered themselves descendants of Arabs who had been expelled from Spain.

Line 72: In some versions instead of ending here the ballad continues for another thirty-five lines or so, in which the Spaniard is so moved by the story that he releases his hostage unconditionally. The shorter version seems definitely preferable.

12. Soneto (1585)

This sonnet seems to have more personal feeling than most, and I have tried to preserve this, even at the expense of the rhyme scheme. It was presumably written while Góngora was staying in Granada.

Line 3: the mighty river is the Guadalquivir, flowing through both Córdoba and Seville; its name comes from the Arabic for "great river." Genil and Dauro (nowadays Darro) are the two rivers of Granada.

Line 4: *even if not gold-bearing*—by contrast with the Dauro or Darro, whose waters were said to carry gold dust.

Line 8: Amongst others, Seneca and the fifteenth-century poet Juan de Mena were from Córdoba.

13. Romance (1587)

Another *morisco* ballad. The ending given here is not Góngora's, according to Chacón, but presumably even Góngora himself could not supply the original one when Chacón edited the poem with him (Romances, ed. Carreño, 263–64n).

Lines 31–32: There is a reference here to the conventional description of lovemaking as a battle; it is paradoxical that *without* him the bed will be a battlefield for her.

Lines 45–52: The substitute ending is based on the concept of simultaneously remaining and leaving, a conventional literary paradox that attempts to reconcile two opposites. One is reminded of the formula the colonists in the New World were said to have worked out for dealing with unwanted royal decrees: "We obey but we do not carry out." This ending may not be Góngora's, but it does echo the poem's opening and its dichotomy of public versus personal allegiance.

14. Romance (1587)

This poem is supposed to have been addressed to some nuns! No doubt it is as dangerous with Góngora as with any poet not to distinguish between the poetic persona and real life, but we do know that he was addicted to cards, bullfights, and music (especially in his university days and his early time in the chapter of Córdoba cathedral, when it got him into trouble). That said, it is clear that the character here is an invented antihero, representing a cynical attitude toward many conventions.

Line 4: The reference is to poem no.2 in this collection.

Line 5: The Spanish probably suggests "so you won't have an abortion."

Line 10: *Filomocosía* seems to have been a nonsense word, used sometimes for *fisionomía*, "physiognomy" and sometimes for *filosofía*, "philosophy."

Lines 14–16: On the pilgrim's route to Santiago de Compostela, that is, one of the most important pilgrimages. *Peregrino* means pilgrim, but it is also an adjective meaning strange, rare, unusual.

Line 24: Water was considered (and doubtless was) unpalatable. Carreño's explanation (*Romances*, 266) is that it was popular to drink water with cherries as an aperitif, but I suspect there is something more. In *Quixote*, II, 35, when Sancho is complaining about his having to be beaten to secure Dulcinea's disenchantment, he adds that since he is governor of an island this unfair punishment is like saying "drink with cherries." In other words, it is even more remarkable or inappropriate, the expression "drink with cherries" being somewhat similar in meaning to "have / put icing on the cake." This does not seem to have any special relevance here, but it would be typical of Gongora to make use of a proverbial saying or set phrase, even if it is not directly relevant.

Lines 31–32: A fig is a rude or defiant gesture, made with thumb and fingers.

Lines 42–44: *Ballestillas* are said to have been instruments like little crossbows used by veterinarians for bleeding horses. I don't understand the reference to "those who sign with their foot," though there seems no problem in relating it to horses.

Lines 47–48: There is doubt whether this should be *gallo* (rooster) or *galgo* (hound). I have chosen the one that seems to make better sense.

Line 88: "Those of Castille" was thieves' cant and refers to con men.

Line 98: *Silva* means a wood (cf. English "sylvan"), but is also a verse form (the one used by Góngora in the *Solitudes*); the word was also used in the title of a famous anthology, the *Silva de varia lección* of Pedro Mexías, published in 1540 and widely disseminated. The English is meant to bring to mind *Tottel's Miscellany,* the great Tudor anthology.

Lines 101–4: These "trees" are rather complicated. What they "bear" is actually "bleach" or "lye" raisins. Lye was used in the preparation of raisins and was produced from ashes; the ashes in this case result from burning dry farmyard straw (manure). Probably Góngora is deliberately confusing here and wants to shock by associating something edible with manure.

Line 108: *Macías* was a troubador from Galicia, proverbial for his unhappy love affairs.

Lines 111–12: *Presa y pinta* is said to have been the name of a card game that was banned in 1597. I imagine these were terms used in play. I have improvised a translation.

Line 113: *Botín* can mean boot or booty. It also has a sexual meaning (see Alzieu et al., *Poesía erótica del Siglo de Oro*, index).

Line 124: Seville was the center of Spanish trade with America, Lisbon the center of Portugal's African-Asian empire. At this time Portugal was ruled by Spain, having been annexed by Philip II in 1580.

Lines 136–37: The English is out of step with the Spanish for two lines here.

Lines 149–50: This actually means "It must be true, Bernia says so."

Line 151: "From the same womb" is, more literally, "shared the same milk."

Lines 157–60: The danger from Turkish galleys was, nevertheless, one of the main preoccupations of the time. The Battle of Lepanto, at which Cervantes was wounded, took place in 1571, but did not eliminate the threat.

Line 161: The "Englishman" is Drake, about whom Lope wrote a rather strange epic, *La Dragontea.* The islands are the islands of the Caribbean. After the Turks, the main perceived threat to Spain and its empire came from the Protestant Netherlands (ruled by Spain but rebellious), and England, which supported them and encouraged piratical attacks on the Spanish colonies and treasure fleet.

Line 166: The usual reading is *coronista,* "chronicler," but in some editions it is *canonista,* or canonist, theologian. Since Góngora is so fond of malapropisms, it is difficult to decide between variant readings on the grounds of sense. I have accepted "chronicler" because it is the greater non sequitur—an interesting case of the less appropriate meaning being the more probable.

Lines 169–72: One of Góngora's most famous puns: *prima,* "prime," early morning, time of the first liturgical office or church service, can also mean a female cousin, which leads to the idea of an evening class with a niece, involving an obvious innuendo.

Line 178: "Humorist" is probably a malapropism, or deliberate mistake, for "humanist."

Lines 195–96: "The Seven Divisions" or *Siete Partidas* were the legal code produced by Alfonso X, a great patron of literature and learning in the thirteenth century. However *Infante* is said to refer to Dom Pedro of Portugal, famous for his voyages of discovery, and in this respect *siete partidas* probably means seven regions of the world. We seem to be getting two literary allusions for the price of one.

Lines 209–11: La Mancha is south of Madrid; I am not clear whether Medina here refers to Medina del Campo, north of Madrid and a great trading center since the

Middle Ages, or Medinaceli in Aragon, which Góngora writes of elsewhere. Either way there would be mountains to cross.

Lines 225–28: *Alzar figura* was casting a horoscope and it was especially popular around this time, if we are to believe Don Quijote, who is very critical of the custom (*Quijote*, II, 25). But literally *alzar figuras*, could mean "raising figures" and one of the meanings of "figure" is any of the playing cards that have human images (king, queen, jack). As so often, Góngora has started with one accepted meaning of a phrase and then switched to an apparently more literal one.

Line 234: *Rosa de Alejandría* was a common purgative.

Line 236: Little round ones: *redondillas* are a traditional verse meter, but I have translated it literally in accordance with the scatological reference of this whole stanza.

Lines 245–48: Fuenterrabía is a town on the border with France. It is not clear why the reference is to the English, not the French, beyond the fact that England was the chief enemy at this time. The main point however is probably the name itself, since it seems to contain the word *rabo*, meaning "tail" or "arse."

Line 258: *Campilla* is said to be a mistake for *capilla*, and *gusto en capillas* must, I think, refer to repressed sexual desire amongst the religious.

Lines 259–60: Appropriately the poem ends with a play on words: *bonete*, "cleric's hat," and *bonita*, "pretty woman."

15. Soneto (1588)

Madrid's river, the Manzanares, is often reduced to a trickle of water in a stony river bed. The Puente de Segovia, however, which is still there, is quite grand. It was designed by Juan de Herrera, architect of El Escorial, Philip II's palace outside Madrid, completed in 1584.

Lines 9–11: The story of the purgative evidently refers to some contemporary event.

16. Soneto (1588)

The date of this sonnet is controversial. The king had received the gift of an elephant and a rhinoceros from the governor of Java in 1581, but 1588 is when Góngora probably visited Madrid. Historians suggest that after the death of Philip II in 1598 royal control of the court was greatly relaxed and nobles, *hidalgos*, and adventurers of all kinds flocked there, causing vice to flourish. But the picture Góngora paints in this sonnet implies that the process was already well under way before that.

Line 1: *Grandes*: this can mean both "large" and "a grandee."

Line 3: I have altered the meaning somewhat: *Gentilhombre de la boca del Rey* was an important post at court, but had nothing to do with being a mouthpiece or spokesman. I feel, however, that the play on words is in tune with the original.

Line 4: The Italian phrase *illustri cavaglier* refers to gentlemen who have given themselves a fancy Italian title. I regret not having managed to work in the *llaves doradas*, golden keys, which refers to the court servants whose badge of office was a key hung on their belt.

Line 5: *Hábitos* suggests the habits of military orders like the Knights of Calatrava, which would have the special insignia sewn on them, but *remendadas* can also mean they are patched, suggesting poverty.

Lines 7–8: Carriages drawn by many horses are ostentatious. *Tiradas*, as well as meaning those who are drawn in the carriages, was slang for prostitute.

Lines 10–11: The attributes of militia and lawyers have been transposed: the former carry legal documents, the latter bear arms.

Line 12: There was a rule at court that those with houses of more than one story had to provide lodging for court servants. Small, one-story houses built to avoid this requirement were known as *casas a la malicia*.

Line 13: *Perejil*, parsley, was slang for excrement. I suppose it could just about be regarded as an elegant euphemism, but Góngora wrote a good many scatological sonnets, and I do not think I have misrepresented his attitude here by being more direct.

17. Romance (1590)

This treats the same subject as no. 1 in this collection.

18. Letrilla (1590)

Lines 13–14: "For eating an egg" (without a dispensation): for breaking the relatively minor rules of fasting during Lent.

Lines 19–23: *Pasa . . . sus cuentas* can mean both telling the beads of his rosary and presenting his accounts, (although clearly the merchant is more concerned about money than piety. I tried to include both meanings because I liked the idea of the rosary as an abacus). Line 21 would perhaps be better rendered as "with an eye on his profits."

Lines 25–30: A strictly literal translation is "passing the narrows, to arrive intact at Collioure." The narrows, *el estrecho*, are the Straits of Gibraltar, and Colibre/Collioure is now in France, close to the Spanish border, so this represents a journey the length of the Spanish Mediterranean coastline, which it would be difficult to complete without being attacked by pirates. But the *double-entendre* relates to a trick for retaining virginity despite the fact that she has two lovers. That is to say, logic seems to require that we interpret this conjunction of *maleta* ("suitcase," also "whore"), *ordinario* and *estafeta* ("express courier," also "scam") as her having two lovers. I am not clear about what *one ordinary and one express* means but it is not hard to imagine possibilities. Melisandre, referred to in the next note, had two Moorish lovers when she was in captivity, "according to Góngora's ballad *Desde Sansueña a Paris.*

Lines 46–47: Don Gaiferos, rescuing his wife Melisandre on horseback after her long captivity, dismounted to relieve himself. This occurs in Góngora's ballad *Desde Sansueña a Paris* of 1588, and if the incident sounds inconsequential (besides scatological), it is deliberately so, the ballad being a parody of Carolingian romance.

19. Soneto (1594)

This sonnet is closely related in language and subject matter to the *First Solitude*. It may or may not be autobiographical. Góngora fell ill during a visit to Salamanca in 1593.

He had gone there on his chapter's behalf to convey their respects to the newly appointed bishop of Córdoba. He wrote another sonnet on this illness and a third addressed to the bishop in which he speaks of his courteous treatment and of his having fallen ill.

On the other hand the topos of a traveler waylaid by a girl in the mountains had long been popular—it is found, for example, in the Marqués de Santillana's *serranillas* and the Arcipreste de Hita's *Libro de buen Amor*.

20. Romance (1599)

Góngora is known to have visited Palencia on business for his chapter in 1588. In this, and a similar ballad written the following year, the fisherman seems to be a forerunner of the "pilgrim" in the *Solitudes*.

Lines 1–8: A different order was needed in English because in the Spanish the opening phrase is the object of the verb at the end of line 6.

Lines 31–32: *fiera* can mean both "proud woman" and "wild beast." Here the man is the hunted, but it is in his power to escape.

21. Soneto (1600)

This sonnet was severely criticized by Father Pineda (Sonetos, ed. Ciplijauskaité, 233) on theological grounds: Góngora was wrong to suggest that the death and Passion of Christ was not his greatest deed.

22. Romance (1602)

Angelica was a character in Ariosto's *Orlando furioso*. It was a well-known story: everyone was in love with Angelica, princess of Cathay, but she was hard-hearted and responded to none of her suitors, until she met Medoro, a noble African.

Lines 23–24: Death is stealing the color from Medoro's cheeks (the roses).

Lines 25–28: The diamond is of course Angelica, because she is so hard-hearted. There was a belief that diamonds could be softened by blood.

Lines 33–34: Sparks from the heart of flint but watery because she is melted by the sight of his wounds and weeps for his plight. Watery sparks from a flint crop up again in the *First Solitude*, lines 578–79.

Line 136: The count is Roland or Orlando, driven mad by her indifference. Don Quijote gives his own account of the count's madness, which endangered the whole countryside and its inhabitants, in *Quijote*, I, 25.

23. Soneto (1603)

The court was moved from Madrid to Valladolid between 1601 and 1607. It has been suggested that the move was instigated by the king's *privado* (his favorite or chief minister) the Duque de Lerma, in an attempt to separate the king from the women of his household, who were Austrian and wanted to influence his decisions in favor of Austrian rather than Spanish interests.

Lines 1–4: By royal decree all visitors had to register with Don Diego de Ayala and obtain a permit for the number of days they wanted to stay.

Lines 7–8: "Enjoying" is of course used ironically: there is no splendor or luxury at this court. We can bear in mind that Spain was frequently bankrupt during the reigns of Philip II and Philip III.

Platón is both the Spanish name for Plato and a big plate or dish.

Line 14: *Grandes y títulos* was a collective term for the upper nobility. *Títulos* here refers to both labels on bottles and nobles with title. The suggestion is that the court is full of people with unjustified pretensions to nobility. Fernand Braudel (*The Mediterranean and the Mediterranean World in the Age of Philip II* [Berkeley:University of California Press, 1995], 713–15) states that Philip III made a considerable number of new nobles, and J. H. Eliot (*Imperial Spain,* 314) speaks of the "inflation of honours" during this period.

Lines 9–11: The Spanish says flattery and ceremony are in mourning: the implication is that they are failing to get what they want. I have taken a liberty with "nabobs" as a translation for *caciques,* said to be originally a native American word, here applying to the ministers or those with power. "Nabob" seems to have come into English from the Indian Mogul empire about a hundred and fifty years later.

24. Romance (1603)

Góngora went to Cuenca in 1603 on business for his chapter.

This poem is a reminder of how essential the blending of myth and everyday Spanish reality was to Góngora's vision. This in turn suggests how his *culto* style arises from the desire to dignify the ordinary rather than to show off his erudition. The changing rhythms of this ballad can also remind us that many of Góngora's poems were set to music, and that he himself composed.

Line 2: There is no adequate English for *serranas,* girls of the mountains. They occur very frequently in Spanish literature.

Lines 11–12: *Plantas* can mean both plants and feet, so there is a pun here; "kiss" has a similar metaphorical meaning in English and Spanish. The expression "I kiss your feet," like "I kiss your hand," was a common salutation in Spanish, implying respect and being at someone's service. This is a small but quite complex joke and it exemplifies the way Góngora personalizes even simple descriptions through his alertness to the ambiguities of language.

Lines 13–16: *Mudanzas,* "changes," is a word connected with music, dance, and song, but it can also refer to the fickleness of Fortune or an unfaithful lover.

Lines 23–26: Blue was symbolic of jealousy in Spanish Golden Age literature. Cuenca was famous for producing a fine cloth called *palmilla,* which was often blue.

Lines 27–44: These are clearly the girls of the wedding party in the *First Solitude,* where we also find the image of skirts lifting to reveal white legs, or at least white ankles, the metaphor of column and base, the white fingers and black stones, the assertion that like Orpheus their singing and dancing can arrest nature.

Line 52: In the Spanish, the girls' white teeth, or possibly their white fingers, as Jones (*Poems of Góngora,* 156n) thinks, are *perlas,* pearls.

Line 61: The eyes of the sun are patches of sunlight between the shadows of the trees (they are in a wood).

25. Romance (1608)

This poem is said to have been written to console the daughter of a friend, whose husband was neglecting her. Unfortunately I have not been able to match the brevity of the original. The refrain, with variations, was imitated many times, and García Lorca wrote his own version of the poem.

Line 3: Blue is again the symbolic color of jealousy.
Lines 5–6: "Jealous" has a narrower meaning than the Spanish *celoso*, which is why I had to introduce "suspicious," linking the meaning to line 29.
Lines 23–30: The conceit of the second stanza compares the girl to dawn because she weeps tears and dawn produces drops of dew. Tears, dewdrops, and pearls are generally interchangeable in poetic language of the period. The girl is also implicitly likened to the sun, because the poem asks her to dissolve mists, as the sun does in early morning.

26. Letrilla (1609)

There is some controversy over both the interpretation and the number of stanzas in this poem. The third stanza is not in most of the early editions, and we are left to imagine the meaning of "the art which so impresses, / the sweetness that consoles." Some readers find this makes it a better poem, more mysterious and suggestive, perhaps to be read as a comment on art in general or as implying a more spiritual message. However, the third stanza strengthens an interpretation in which the little silver bells are the sound of water and the golden trumpets are bees. To my mind, this accords with a general tendency of Góngora's to prefer the more specific and humble elements of a scene to the conventionally poetic ones (in this case birdsong), a preference that plays an important part in the *Solitudes*. Nature is more than just birdsong, he seems to be saying: it is also running water and buzzing bees. If we accept this as a basic meaning, it may follow that close attention to all sense impressions can put us in touch with a higher reality.

Line 7: The "suns" are the eyes of the woman he loves.
Lines 23–24: The "winged violin" and "wandering lyre" are birds.

27. Soneto (1611)

Philip III's queen, Margaret of Austria, was daughter of the archduchess of Bavaria. Góngora wrote three sonnets on the monument in Córdoba. This seems to be the first of them.

Lines 1–2: More literally, all Spain is but a humble dais for her. My version makes perhaps a little more obvious the link with line 11, which refers to the fact that Spain's empire included so many other countries. The opening lines are an example of Góngora's hyperbaton, or unusual word order. The more natural order would be: "*A la que España toda apenas fue humilde estrado y su horizonte (apenas fue) dosel . . .*"
Line 7: *Entenas* = masts, a synechdoche for ships, which in turn are a metaphor for those at court, the rich and famous of the day. I have further extended the metaphor to mariners because it was awkward to speak of ships "recalling."

Line 8: "If the mariners didn't recall too late" (*si han recordado* = if they remembered). One of the best-known poems in Spanish, Jorge Manrique's fifteenth-century *Lines on the Death of His Father*, begins: "Let the sleeping soul remember, / come to its senses and wake up, / contemplating / how life passes, / and death comes / so silently." "Remembering" is linked to the theme of *desengaño* or disillusionment with worldly goods and remembering the need to repent and ask God's mercy before death.

Line 9: "Margaret" means "pearl."

Line 12: *el clarín final* = the Last Trumpet, announcing the Day of Judgment.

Line 14: *desengaños*, literally being undeceived, or seeing through the illusion of human ambitions. This is a general seventeenth-century theme, especially powerful in this period of Spain's economic decline. I find it necessary, however, to translate it in various ways, here as "wisdom" and in the *Second Solitude* as "experience" (see also no. 10).

Line 14: *Peinar*, literally "to comb," is a word Góngora was accused of using too much or in unjustified senses. Here he uses it in something closer to its literal sense, "combing white hair," but also extends it (less obviously) to *desengaños*. As in the *Solitudes*, he is invoking the conventional association of age with wisdom and experience, wisdom, in this case, meaning preparedness for death.

28. Soneto (1611)

According to Jones (*Poems of Góngora,* 13), this is the most unified and successful of the three sonnets on Córdoba's monument for Margaret and therefore probably the last. Neither of the sonnets here is particularly eulogistic, considering they speak of the late queen. Whether or not this shows Góngora's independence is a moot point: his later patrons were on the side of the Duke of Lerma, who was opposed to the queen's influence.

Line 3–4: It is actually *not* a pyramid of fragrant branches, but the purpose of saying so is to introduce the notion of the phoenix. The greater Phoenix is Margaret.

Lines 5–7: The two stars are Castor and Pollux, representing Saint Elmo's fire, which was thought to appear on the ship's masthead during a storm, signifying that the storm's end was near (as readers of *Moby-Dick* will remember). Leda was the mother of Castor and Pollux, but the greater Leda is the Virgin Mary. Góngora uses this image of the fire on the masthead rather frequently in his poetry.

Line 8: Like the Spanish *volubilidad*, an old English meaning of "volubility" is "having the ability to be turned," or being inconstant. Fortune's wheel is a medieval concept that survived well into the Renaissance.

Lines 11–12: The monument is blazing with the light of lamps or candles, but it is a dark shell because Margaret, the pearl, is shut up inside it.

29. Soneto (1612)

This rather cheeky sonnet was deplored by Father Pineda (*Sonetos Completos,* ed. Ciplijauskaité, 192). The occasion was the visit of a French nobleman (the Duc de Mayenne, at the time known in Spanish, rather strangely, as Duque de Humena) to represent the king of France at the funeral of the Spanish queen.

Line 1: A bilingual pun: *grasa*, in Spanish "grease" or "fat," but in Portuguese (*graça*) "grace."

Line 2: *Momo*, an imaginary figure in Latin literature who criticizes the faults of others.

Line 3: Vandomo, le Duc de Vendôme, here standing for France.

Line 6: "Set" because she is a pearl, "in lead" because she is in her coffin.

Lines 7–8: Royal festivities would normally include bull-fights, but not during this period of court mourning. The *Toros de Guisando* are some ancient statues found in Castile. But *guisar* means to cook, so *guisando* could mean cooking. This joke about the French never seems to die.

Lines 9–11: There are several puns here: *estrellarse* could mean "shine like a star" but its normal meaning is "smash to pieces," and *al tope* means placed end to end, but *tope* can also be "a stumble." Some of the diamonds flaunted on the occasion were found to be false. Quevedo also wrote a poem about this affair.

Lines 12–14: The literal translation is actually funnier and even more colloquial: "He's gone at last, and left us the Palace healths so (well) toasted that the next day Their Majesties were sick."

30. Soneto (1614)

Góngora probably knew El Greco through their mutual friend, Fray Hortensio Paravicino (see no. 33).

Line 8: The convention of addressing a stranger when commemorating some famous person goes back to the ancient Greeks. Here Góngora is addressing the "pilgrim" of this sonnet's opening line.

Lines 9–11: Nature has "acquired" art because the artist is dead and has gone back to nature, art has acquired the example of a great artist and so on. Iris is the rainbow, Phoebus the sun, and Morpheus the bringer of dreams (and therefore sleep and night and shadow). The mention of shade is interesting: this was also the age of Caravaggio.

Lines 13–14: More literally, "imbibe tears and all the scents sweated by the funeral bark of the Sabaean tree" (see no. 10, lines 39–40).

31. Soneto (1614)

Although it's untranslatable, I have included this sonnet because it brings back so vividly conversations of the 1950s, when the bullfight played a relatively much larger part in Spanish life (other entertainments being more limited). Bullfighting talk and reports in the press were frequently concerned with the bulls at the current year's festival being too tame, not like they were in the good old days. The poem is notably straightforward in its opening. Góngora was criticized for his interest in the bullfight and other frivolous pursuits: cards, profane poetry, and actors. But it is a reminder that despite his later reputation for learned and difficult poetry he was not out of touch with popular taste. There is some doubt about the poem's date: Chacón gives it as 1614, but there is reason to date it from 1610. Regardless, it must belong more or less to the period when Góngora was concerned with the *Solitudes* and *Polyphemus*, where his style is so different. Bulls, however, also provide him with imagery and symbolism in the *Solitudes*.

An *encierro* is the occasion when the bulls are brought into town and penned before a bullfight and when fans have a chance to view them in advance. It is a social or cultural event that has no equivalent in English.

Line 2: The Nativity is the Christmas manger, usually represented with a few attendant animals.

Line 6: I am not sure why Góngora refers to the ploughing oxen as his "neighbors," unless it is something to do with the old joke about horns. The intention is clearly humorous.

Line 8: I could not translate the pun in this line and have filled in with something I hope is fairly neutral. Two words for "white beard" (*barba cana*), joined together, become *barbican*, or the wall surrounding the bullring. The general idea is that the bull moves so lethargically the writer's beard turns white while he watches.

Lines 9–11: The most usual meaning of *clavo* is "nail" and this might seem, at first sight, to have something to do with goading the bull into action. But *poner un clavo a la rueda de la Fortuna* means to stop the ever-turning wheel of Fortune. This bull is so tame you can even pull it by the tail, so there is no point in trying to stop it.

Lines 13–14: *Bravo* and *Manso*, names of real people (a mayor and a recent president of the Council of Castile), mean *brave* and *tame*, respectively. Don Pedro Manso was made president of the Council of Castile in 1608 and died toward the end of 1610.

32. Romance (1620)

This was transformed from a nonreligious piece, written in 1613, in which the object of the search is a strayed calf; this earlier version was a kind of compliment to a neighbor, whose daughter was represented by the lost calf. I think this accounts for some of its strangeness as a religious poem.

Lines 6–8: The reference is to the Book of Revelation in the Bible, and the book "sealed with seven seals."

Line 12: The two stars are the Christ child's eyes.

Line 30: The sound of this line, *Quedo, ¡ay, queditico, quedo!* accounts for some of the charm of the piece, with its untranslatable diminutive, *queditico*. Diminutives are generally a problem in English, which has no equivalent of their variety in Spanish, even greater in the usage of an Andalusian like Góngora. I have done what I can to imitate the consonants.

33. Soneto (1620)

Father Luis de Aliaga, the subject of this sonnet, was a Dominican who received his post of king's confessor from the Duke of Lerma, the chief minister. The king's confessor had considerable power and Aliaga was apparently ambitious: he later schemed against Lerma, supporting Lerma's son when the latter deposed his father. The Father Hortensio to whom the sonnet is addressed is Paravicino, a close friend of Góngora's, though somewhat younger, an orator and imitator of Góngora's style in poetry. This is as an example of Góngora using the sonnet to convey quite an ordinary experience. Essentially it just describes someone doing his job. Góngora wrote a good many sonnets like this, which are concerned with sending a message to a friend or describing events in his life.

Lines 3–4: More literally, "target and martyr of so many impertinent arrows."
Lines 5–6: Góngora continues the image of the crossbowman shooting.

35. Soneto (1622)

The sonnets written in 1622–23 reflect the increasingly unfavourable circumstances of Góngora's life. His income had declined so he moved to the court in Madrid in 1617 in search of a post or a pension. He took holy orders and obtained the post of royal chaplain. But something happened to each of the courtiers from whom he expected more significant favors—Rodrigo Calderón, the Conde de Lemos, the Conde de Villamediana: one fell from grace and was later executed, one died, one was murdered.

The first stanza represents Rodrigo Calderón, who prospered under Philip III and his favorite, the Duke of Lerma, but was accused of corruption and arrested after the fall of Lerma in 1618. He was later executed after the accession of Philip IV in 1621. The Count of Villamediana, subject of the second stanza, was a courtier and poet. He was assassinated in the street, and it was suggested that some satirical verses he wrote may have been partly to blame, hence the reference to the poetic muse Calliope (Muse of epic poetry, in fact). Góngora must have looked to him to advance his literary reputation at court.

The first tercet represents the Conde de Lemos, who received various important posts (viceroy of Naples, for example) but also fell from favor in 1621 and died not long after.

Line 9: Minerva's tree, the olive, appears white-haired even when its leaves are still green.
Line 10: The Sun: the king.

36. Soneto (1623)

By now, Góngora was not only in poor health but increasingly troubled financially, obliged to sell off furniture to meet daily expenses. Within five years he was dead. Towards the end he is said to have been thrown out of his house in Madrid by Quevedo, who had recently bought it.

Line 1: In the Spanish the name *Licio* is one Góngora habitually uses to refer to himself, so we are to imagine him addressing this warning to himself.
Lines 12–14: The body is consigned to the grave, with its memorial stone; the soul goes up to heaven.

37. Soneto (1623)

The *meta* toward which or aound which the chariot glides is one of three stones in the center of the Roman arena around which chariots raced, one of them also serving as finishing post. It can therefore signify either goal or marker. The chariot wheels were not allowed to touch the marker as they raced around it.

38. Soneto (1623)

Described by a seventeenth-century commentator as containing one of Góngora's most impenetrable passages. The critic rather proves his point with a weird interpretation about an unrequiting lady turning the poet into ashes (see Ciplijauskaité's note, *Sonetos*, 244). Others have had no doubt that the poem concerns ambition, not a love affair. Given the date of the poem, not more than five years before Góngora's death, they are surely right. Nevertheless the poem contains some puzzles, which are interesting because they might shed light on the character of the pilgrim in the *Solitudes*, who declares himself, like Icarus, guilty of a daring ambition and asks to be buried in a peaceful tomb (*Second Solitude*, lines 137–72). The language fits Icarus, one of Góngora's favorite examples of fatal ambition, just as well as the moth, and perhaps it is not entirely unreasonable to think of an underlying reference to an inappropriate and impossible love.

Lines 3–4: Even the phoenix is burnt by the flames, before being born again from its ashes.

Lines 5–6: The moth is fatally attracted by the flame.

Lines 9–10: The moth's tomb is the melted wax of the candle, associated with the sweetness of honey through the work of the bee.

Line 11: But why does supreme bliss correspond to a supreme error? (*Yerro* also often means iron, or bars of a prison, but that doesn't seem to help.) Some have seen a similarity to a poem of Torquato Tasso. But in Tasso's poem a bee *errs happily* in mistaking the girlfriend's lips for a flower, which does not seem relevant here.

Lines 13–14: Smoke is associated with ambition and fame because it is insubstantial, ephemeral, easily blown away.

To the Duke of Bejar

Lines 1–4: Whatever these lines mean (and there has been no lack of discussion) they clearly say something about the whole poem. We surmise that the pilgrim whose steps these lines refer to is Góngora himself as well as the protagonist of his poem. The pilgrim's steps are lost, the verses dictated by the muse and therefore inspired.

Line 5: I have made some attempt to clarify the long sentence that follows, but without breaking it up. I found it necessary, for example, to name the Duke in an apostrophe in the first line, because the imperative verb does not arrive for another eight lines and in English would be difficult to recognize, since the English imperative is not distinguished by a different inflection. Even so I have had to use a somewhat archaic form of imperative. My change can be criticised for oversimplifying a difficult passage, removing some of the initial uncertainty in the Spanish caused by the long wait for syntactic resolution. But I still do not think readers of the English will find it too transparent. I mention this here because it typifies one way in which some readers will find the English version fails to reproduce the effect of reading Góngora in the original.

Lines 6–7: There is ambiguity here: do "the walls of trees" and "battlements of diamond" refer to spears that the huntsmen are carrying or are they another image for the mountains? I have followed Jammes in the latter interpretation (*Soledades* 184–86), but this is not to say that the image of crowded, glittering spears may not be part of the effect.

Line 12: The river Tormes runs through the town of Béjar, the duke's home in the Sierra de Gredos.

Lines 30–37: These lines seem to indicate Góngora's state of mind at the time. His "liberty" was chiefly threatened by financial difficulties, as it continued to be to the end of his life. His pilgrim, on the other hand, is deprived of his freedom by an unhappy love affair, in the traditional way referred to in poems like no. 10. In the *Solitudes* such sources of unhappiness are fused with Góngora's frustration and sense of the court's greed and corruption and with his advocacy for a simpler way of life. Already his burlesque ballads and sonnets had revealed him as a critic of chivalresque and courtly love conventions, sharing the *desengaño*, the disillusioned or cynical mood of his time (which has been linked to Spain's economic decline at this time as well as to a general tendency of the baroque or Counter-Reformation period). But principally, the *Solitudes* represent the positive side of his attitude: a strong sense of the beauty and dignity of ordinary things and people.

First Solitude

Lines 2–6: Taurus, the Bull, whose horns are shaped like the crescent moon. The sun comes into Taurus in April, meaning that the constellation rises with the sun, eating up the stars. The bull is also Jupiter, who took that form in the rape of Europa. I have followed Jammes's reading (see *Soledades*, 196, n4) of *el sol todo los rayos de su pelo* rather than *el sol todos los rayos de su pelo*, because it gives the phrase *el sol todo*, "the whole sun," balancing and contrasting with *media luna*, "a half moon"—typical of Góngora's style. Any echoes of Chaucer and T. S. Eliot are no doubt accidental, but mythological resonance was surely part of Góngora's intention.

Line 7–8 [8–9]: Ganymede, cupbearer to Jupiter.

Line 9 [10]: In the Spanish, more literally, "disdained and absent," the first indication of a motive for the pilgrim's unhappiness. The shipwreck appears almost a result of his unhappiness in love, rather than being itself a cause for his unhappiness.

Lines 11–14: The sympathy of the waves saves him, just as in the classical myth the dolphin saved Arion, impressed by his singing.

Lines 15–18 [15–20]: The pilgrim comes to shore clinging to a plank, a small piece of the broken ship that was made from pine. Elsewhere in Góngora the single word "pine" is used to mean "ship" (as are other words for tree or wood: *haya*, "beech tree," *roble*, "oak," and (as here in line 21) *leño*, "wood."

Line 19 [20]: The pilgrim was rash because he went to sea in a ship. The dangers of sea travel, something of an obsession with Góngora, were of course very real.

Line 28 [29]: Jove's or Jupiter's bird, the eagle.

Lines 38–41: The sun sounds very much like a bull again: the common meaning of the Spanish verb *embiste* is "charges." But it is a paradoxical, oxymoronic bull, both powerful and restrained: its fire is "temperate," and it charges "slowly."

Lines 62–64 [64–66]: A literal translation of the pilgrim's address to the rays of light: "If you are not sons of Leda . . ." The sons of Leda were Castor and Pollux, who were believed to be responsible for Saint Elmo's fire, an electrical discharge that sometimes appeared on a ship's masthead and was believed to herald the end of a storm (see no. 28). I have omitted this mythological reference in order to concentrate on the essentials of the scene: the pilgrim's relief after surviving the storm and climbing the cliff, and his continuing ordeal as he makes his way over the dark heights in the continuing gale.

Lines 70–76 [73–79]: No one seems to know what this nocturnal animal is that carries a jewel on its forehead. In any case, I think it serves its purpose by allowing Góngora some verbal brilliance that lights up this passage.

Line 85 [87]: The Spanish says succinctly *convoca despidiendo*, "summons dismissing," which I take to mean that the barking of the dog, meant to warn the stranger off, in fact helps him to locate the shepherds.

Line 93 [94–95]: The Spanish is *a Vulcano tenían coronado*, literally "they had Vulcan crowned or encircled." Góngora frequently uses "crown" in the sense of "encircle." I have preferred to express this more directly, not because the reference to Vulcan, god of fire, is particularly difficult, but because the scene is so realistic and this first human contact such an important stage in the pilgrim's adventure.

Lines 94–135 [96–138]: I think it is up to the reader to decide whether to take this as expression of the poet's or the pilgrim's thoughts. However it is read, it embodies a pastoral ideal that is central to the *First Solitude*, though we should not assume that Góngora endorses it completely. It is not after all new: apart from classical precedent, there is a strong echo of Garcilaso and Luis de León in the refrain.

Line 96 [98]: Literal translation from the Spanish, "Pales' temple, Flora's farm." Pales was the god of flocks, Flora the goddess of spring, so one would expect Pales to have the farm, Flora the temple. This favorite trick of Góngora's, transposing the gods' attributes, may have various effects depending on the context. But the important point is that his borrowings from mythology, Latin and Greek writers, or the Renaissance in general are never a mere show of learning: whatever he takes, he uses in his own way, for his own purposes, often with some slight but significant adjustment. I have tried to mimic the effect here with two phrases that suggest oxymoron.

Lines 97–100 [99–102]: The Spanish literally says "adjusting the sublime building to the concave of heaven," and this has been taken as referring to a dome. For Renaissance architects the dome expressed an ideal of beauty and unity as well as a return to the classical world, and much effort went into designing them. I do not think Góngora is satirizing this; he is merely making a comment in line with the general philosophy of this first section of the *First Solitude* (or with the pilgrim's thoughts at this moment): simple is best.

Lines 108–114 [110–116]: The descriptions here of personified court vices are traditional, and several can be related to emblems in Alciato (see no. 8). But Góngora's garrulous sphinx is paradoxical (a sphinx should be silent), and she is criticized for making Narcissus abandon the spring (and his own image) and chase after Echo(es), apparently reversing the moral of the classical myth.

Lines 117–119 [119–121]: More literally, "ceremony wastes the powder of important time on irrelevant salvos / greetings." This richly involved metaphor confounded my translation attempts.

Lines 125–128 [127–130]: Compare the image of reefs and shipwreck in poem no. 27, the First sonnet on Queen Margaret's memorial. The sleep is referred to as *canoro*, musical, because it is induced by sirens.

Lines 129–131 [131–134]: The Spanish does not name the peacock, but implies it. The peacock was supposed to be ashamed of its ugly feet, which is why falsehood needs to gild them.

Lines 132–133 [*134–36*]: A reference to Icarus, a symbol of the court favorite, whose ambition is great and fall sudden.

Lines 136–142 [*139–145*]: This invocation of the classical Golden Age, and the description of the country people's hospitality, can be compared with many passages in *Polyphemus and Galatea*. The important point in what follows is the care with which Góngora describes and dignifies ordinary objects, like the milk and the bowl it is served in. I have omitted Alcimedon (line 153) because this reference, as Jammes makes clear (*Soledades*, 228), is only truly significant to readers familiar with the passage in Virgil on which it is based.

Line 160 [*164*]: There is a pun on *vides*, which means "vines" but could suggest "lives," and so contrasts with "death" in the rest of the sentence: "redeemed with his death so many ruined vines [lives]" (which echoes Christ's redemption of humanity).

Lines 203–5 [*209–211*]: I have made this reference more explicit. Amalthea was the name of the goat, or in this case of the nymph who kept it, which gave milk to Jupiter and whose horn became the cornucopia, or horn of plenty. The river resembles a horn in the curves of its course, seen from above, and resembles the cornucopia in the fertility of the land on its banks.

Lines 212–221 [*220–228*]: Góngora gives no explanation for this speech of the goatherd's, though we can deduce from it that he was previously a soldier. I tried to clarify the structure of this passage by announcing at the start who the speaker is.

Lines 243–246 [*247–251*]: In the Spanish this famous passage is very concise and I have had to expand it slightly in the interests of clarity. I hope I have not lost completely the feeling of Góngora's metaphoric language. The girl is scooping up water (liquid crystal) in her hand and pouring it on her face (human crystal and thus beautiful). In the Spanish her hand is literally an aqueduct (*arcaduz*), joining water and face, but part of the Spanish word is "arc" or "arch."

Lines 284–334 [*290–341*]: This procession of youths with wedding gifts may put one in mind of Grecian urns and Keats, but the description of animals and produce is full of observed detail and humor.

Line 298 [*304*]: Apparently the word *copia* here is from Italian and means "a pair," not "plenty" as previously in the reference to the cornucopia. As Jammes (262) points out, it would be difficult to carry more than two goats on your shoulders.

Lines 309–17: I have altered the apostrophe to the turkey because it seemed awkward in the English.

Line 343 [*350*]: The stream is now tamed because it has lost the impetus of its steep descent on the mountain (the pilgrim also, remember, has been going downhill). The description of the stream's music that follows reminds us also about the storm: the roaring of the wind has now ceased, so the stream can be heard. The famous image of the lines of black slate on the riverbed as strings of an instrument, and the trees on the bank as pegs was imitated by Calderón in *El Alcalde de Zalamea*.

Lines 360–65 [*371–76*]: Góngora gives no indication of who this old man is beyond calling him *politico*, which does little more than associate him with the city (the Greek *polis*) or court, not the country. Like the goatherd who had been a soldier, he has experience of a world beyond that of the country people. By calling him "a refugee from court" I may have weighted the issue somewhat in favor of seeing him as a representation of Góngora's own views, but his strictures on greed and suspicion of sea travel, mixed with excitement about the world and about new discoveries, are echoed elsewhere in Góngora's poems. His long speech encapsulates the discovery and conquest of the Spanish empire.

Lines 366–69 [374]: I have written the Hyrcanian tiger out of the action: as a symbol of cruelty it would have been familiar to Góngora's readers, if only from the earlier poet, Garcilaso, but I believe it does little for us. The old man's speech is vital to the poem and I wanted his intention to be clear.

Line 369 [376]: The two seas here would be the Aegean and the Tyrrhenian, the eastern and western Mediterranean, and this probably refers to classical controversy about the when and where of the first sea voyages.

Lines 372–73 [378–80]: This very compact metaphor is a good example of Góngora's methods, almost, one might say, a metaphor about metaphor. Flax was transformed not into a flower but into canvas; the canvas is sails, which are also a sunflower, or more precisely a wind-flower because they turn not towards the sun but towards the wind. But the sails and the sunflower are not named directly: the sails are "canvas," because that is what they are made of, and the sunflower is Clytie, the nymph who was turned into a sunflower by her unhappy love for Apollo. We can add that the sails are a *wandering* Clytie because they are on a ship which is a pine tree, sailed by a captain who is a ploughman ploughing watery fields. Everything is also something else.

Lines 374–78 [381–85]: I am conscious that I have made a slight change here: the original maintains the Trojan horse image throughout, saying that the modern ships have introduced more arms (to other shores) than the wooden horse introduced confusion and fire within the walls of Troy. I have also perhaps modernized the passage slightly by using the word "pain." I tried replacing "pain" with "strife" or "conflict," but these words did not seem strong enough. Clearly the literal translation, "arms," will not do: Góngora is not talking about gun-running. I think my sense that a strong word is needed comes from the fact that it must include not only the sense of modern warfare but also the "confusion and fire" of burning Troy, which it is not just equal to but more than. So I have left "pain" in place, because I think it reflects the seriousness of the criticism in the old man's speech. Similarly I would defend "transported" instead of "introduced" because I see the emphasis not on the comparison with Troy but on the insidious effects of all this early global travel. However, I would not want to suggest that Góngora sees the voyages of discovery only as bad and to deny that he is excited by them as well.

Line 403 [409]: The old man introduces Greed as the motive force behind all these voyages and continues to describe Greed's activities, until line 443 in the Spanish text, which is a direct address to Greed. It can be difficult to recognize that Greed is still the subject of the later sentences, so I have repeated the noun instead of the pronoun. I have also omitted the apostrophe in line 443, which seemed awkward in English, treating it instead as a continuation of the report on Greed's activities. The whole speech is a mix of mythology and historical and geographical fact, but I think readers will have little difficulty in recognizing, for example, references to the compass, to the Isthmus of Panama and the Pacific Ocean, to the Cape of Good Hope, the Straits of Magellan and the spice islands of the East Indies. One of the points that has been made about Góngora is that he is able to describe all this geography without using a single real name, thus avoiding the prosaic name list, which is a pitfall of epics that refer to historical times and places (Ercilla's *La Araucana* is often quoted as example).

Line 466 [477]: In the original the crystal track is the Zodiac: as the sun goes round the circle of the Zodiac, so the ship circumnavigated the world.

Line 496 [507]: There is an untranslatable pun here so I have replaced it with something different. In fact the original meaning is not clear: *clavo* can be both a clove and a nail, but here one of its meanings has to be contrasted with *espuela del apetito*, "spur to the appetite." So it should approximately mean "a hindrance": far from being a hindrance to appetite, the clove stimulates it. As in sonnet no. 31 the reference is probably to a spike or stop put in a wheel to prevent its turning.

Lines 540–549 [554–563]: This famously difficult passage describing the girls is easier to follow when it is compared with the Cuenca ballad (no. 24). The river flows lazily now because they have progressed down from the mountain to the plain.

Line 602 [617]: Although the Spanish says *todos*, it has to be only the men who went on, because we learn a few lines later that the girls remained.

Lines 626–627 [642–645]: "Coagulate snow" is "beautiful girl," like "human crystal." Despite the sun this snow does not melt, and it is not just white but dressed in many colors.

Lines 649–651 [663–666]: More literally, the Spanish says "artfully (artificially) exhales luminous arrows of gunpowder." The usual Spanish for fireworks is *fuegos artificiales*, "artificial fires." In this instance I have tried to follow Góngora in not naming the phenomenon directly.

Lines 697–698 [714–715]: The tree served as a book (literally, paper) because they carved their names, or their lovers' names, on it.

Lines 701–704 [718–721]: One imagines he has in mind formal gardens like those of Versailles or Aranjuez (which were not completed in their present form, however, till the late seventeenth or eighteenth centuries.)

Line 705 [722]: We have had fireworks, dancing, and then sleep, for the travelers, while the villagers continued preparations for the wedding. Now the day of the wedding dawns and increasingly the setting is mythological, with frequent references to Hymen, god of marriage. Some commentators have been surprised that Góngora, so involved with the church, uses no Christian imagery for scenes like this. Perhaps we should see this the other way around: it is precisely because the Christian terminology can be taken for granted that he finds it natural to give it the extra resonance of the classical reference.

Line 720 [737–739]: These "new" hanging gardens are being compared to the hanging gardens of Babylon.

Lines 734–749 [757–770]: This difficult passage describes the pilgrim's state of mind in great detail. It seems psychologically very plausible that meeting the bride-to-be reminds him of his own unhappy love, which presumably he had forgotten during his escape from the storm and reception by the shepherds and villagers.

Line 768 [788]: The groom is contrasted with Cupid, who is blind and has wings. This one will not fly away and leave the girl.

Lines 793–795 [814–816]: These are said to be a lower class of cupid, not Cupid son of Venus who employs his arrows on the other gods, but the offspring of nymphs, whose effect is felt by mortals.

Line 813 [833]: Lucina is the birth goddess. Jammes has an interesting note (362) here, suggesting that in the Spanish the request that she attend *en lunas desiguales*, "on unequal moons," relates to a popular belief that the stages of the moon affect the sex of a baby. Niobe had seven sons and seven daughters, which was considered an ideal state of affairs, but later made the mistake of boasting about it (thus offending the goddess Leto, who had only two) and was punished. Góngora has here invented his own version of her punishment: she is turned to a rock in the underworld river of Lethe. The advantages of having both sons and daughters are explained in the next two stanzas.

Lines 829–830 [850–851]: Another of Góngora's reversals: Hercules should carry the club, Bacchus be crowned with vine-leaves.

Lines 838–843 [861–864]: Her daughters are to weave plain, honest designs, not show off like Arachne, who was turned into a spider for boasting she could weave better than the goddess and for depicting Jupiter's affairs. At the same time, this mythological allusion could be taken as a warning to country girls of the danger of courtiers and seduction by money (Danae and the golden rain) or finery (Leda and the swan).

Lines 867–871 [888–891]: I am afraid I have lost the concise charm of this typically Gongoran passage, but I hope I have kept some of the pictorial quality. In the Spanish the wine that is served is simply "confused Bacchus," because it is white and red mixed and can therefore also be described as "crimson topazes and pale rubies."

Lines 881–882 [900–902]: The olive here is like the olive branch in the Bible, announcing the end of the Flood.

Lines 906–908 [924–925]: First the grain harvest in the height of summer, when days are long, then the grape harvest, in autumn, when days are shorter.

Lines 924–925 [939–940]: Beehives were made out of cork—there are many references to this in Góngora.

Lines 942–43 [957–958]: Literally she seems to be wishing that the tombstone will register *desengaños* ("disillusion" or "wisdom") and "many years be read in few symbols." Carreira (in *Soledades*, ed. Jammes, 390) suggests that in Roman numerals 90 and 100 would be brief: XC and C. But in the context a happy life can be seen as an uneventful life and that seems an equally plausible interpretation.

Lines 948–957 [963–971]: After being reborn, the new phoenix was supposed to collect up the ashes of the old one and fly with them to the Temple of the Sun in Egypt. The King of Rivers is the Nile.

Line 990 [1004]: Ascalaphus, the owl, whom the other birds attack whenever they see him by day. He was turned into an owl for denouncing Proserpine, when she had eaten the pomegranite seed. Góngora brings him out again in the *Second Solitude*, in the company of many other birds. He also provides a sinister ending to what we have of the unfinished poem.

Lines 1061–1064 [1075–1078]: Hercules is associated with various kinds of tree (here elms, elsewhere poplars) so probably the idea is that Hercules might have *been* the tree. The judging is a task he could not have succeeded in, even if every leaf of the tree had been sighted like a lynx.

The Fable of Polyphemus and Galatea

Stanza 1: Thalia, the muse of comedy, was previously the muse of lyric and bucolic poetry. I have not been able to reproduce the wonderful play on Niebla's name in line 5, combining it with the evocation of dawn: *niebla* means mist, so the Spanish literally says, "now that you gild your mist (i.e. ancestral home) with light." This implies that he is in his ancestral home and also that he is like the rising sun. I have expressed only the first part of this. I have also omitted the rustic flute (*zampoña*), but I am less worried by this, since the next stanza again reminds us of the convention that links certain types of musical instrument with certain poetic genres.

Stanza 2: The attempt at persuasion continues: let hunting and falconry make way for poetry, the hunting horn be exchanged for the lute. The Spanish of lines 3–4 literally says the hawk "seeks in vain to deny the bell." The bell is attached to the hawk's leg and like the mastering hand, the horse's bit, and the dog's leash, it is an instrument of control.

Stanza 3: The first stanzas have been leading up to the idea that Gongora's poem will make the count famous. I have changed the verb to the indicative to avoid a succession of sentences beginning with "Let . . ." In the fourth line Góngora is up to his old trick of transposing epithets: "the fierce song of the musical giant" is a transposition of the more obvious descriptive phrase "the musical song of the fierce giant." It makes "musical" ironic, enabling Góngora to avoid any suggestion that this song is soft and melodious—a point that stanza 12 will reinforce.

Stanza 4: Góngora sets the scene, in Sicily, and links the site of the giant's cave with the volcano, Etna, and the classical myths of Vulcan's forge and the Titan, whose assault on heaven was punished by his being buried under a mountain. Commentators have pointed out the associations between the volcano, fire, and love, on the one hand, and the Titan's tomb, ashes, and death, on the other. The linking of these two sets, love and death, prepares us for the fatal (but not necessarily tragic) outcome. Lilibaeum is the westernmost of Sicily's three corners. It is not where Mount Etna is, but Góngora is not too serious about his geography (perhaps his self-characterization in lines 193–212 of poem no. 14 should be taken at face value). Probably he mentions Lilibaeum for the sake of the sound. The last two lines are quite abrupt. I have had to pad this stanza a little, adding "rich" and "broad" (line 1) and "resounding" (line 3). I hope this can be defended as an acknowledgment of the "rich" effect Góngora achieves with sound and rhythm, an effect that one must try to match, however inadequately. Commentators were quick to point out the pleonasm in the Spanish of line 2: "to silver-plate with silver." Most defended it by pointing out that people also said "to silver-plate with gold," so the term *argentar* had lost its original meaning. Apparently in Córdoba these expressions were commonly used of the gilding or silvering of leather boots and shoes.

Stanza 5: The cave, darkness, and black night—these are all associated with Polyphemus. Particularly famous are the last two lines of this stanza (analyzed by Parker in *Fábula*, introduction, 97–98). Line 7 has a double internal rhyme (with the order of syllables reversed): *infame turba* with *nocturnas aves* and line 8 has one: *gimiendo* with *tristes*. I have avoided the word "birds" in my translation in order not to exclude bats from the image. The Spanish *guarnición* can be "garrison" as well as "garnish"—the trees adorn and protect—but I could not find a way to preserve this double meaning. Commentators note the use of a common word (*greña*: "mane") together with some very learned ones (*caliginoso*). Góngora tends to do this, and the fact that modern readers are more accustomed to the mixing of registers may have something to do with the modern revival of his literary credit.

Stanza 6: Stanzas 6–12 describe the giant: his way of life, his appearance, his dominance over nature, his terrible music. In line 1, *formidable* was a learned word, with two meanings: "fearful" and "enormous." It seems to me to have undergone a similar change in modern Spanish to "awful" in English.

The word in line 7 that I have rendered as "living fortune" is *copia*, which really means "plenty" as in "horn of plenty" from the Latin "cornucopia" (see stanza 20, and *First Solitude*, lines 203–5).

Stanza 7: Here Polyphemus is a mountain and in the next stanza "a Pyrenee." The original starts with extreme hyperbaton, the subject being *este cíclope*, "this Cyclops," although nineteen words intervene between demonstrative and noun. Micó (*El Polifemo*, 20) interprets the last couplet as meaning the pine/walking stick is so bent it can only be used as a shepherd's crook. I prefer to think of the giant twirling it around and using it for one or the other purpose. The Spanish says literally it is a "stick so light and reed so thin."

Stanza 8: Through the description of his hair and beard, compared to gales and floods, Polyphemus is associated with the ideas of disorder and violence. Parker (*Fábula*, 98) emphasizes the association with death, reinforced by the comparison with Lethe's waters. There is also an association with fire, because the Pyrenees were supposed to have been formed by fire, their name, it was thought, being derived from the Greek *pyr*. *Adusto* in one of its meanings applies to places that are very hot, and *torrente* may have the suggestion of lava flow.

Stanza 9: "Guile" in line 3 should literally be "speed," but the chance of a rhyme was supported by the fact that "guile" maintains the contrast with other animals that instead defend themselves aggressively. The change does not affect what I take to be the main point of the stanza: the tyranny Polyphemus exercises over the whole of nature. Parker (*Fábula*, introduction, 44) suggests that in the last line the light is doubtful in two senses: doubt*ful* of itself, not sure that it really exists, and doubt*ed* by the peasant, because it contains unknown dangers.

Stanza 10: Lines 3–8 refer to fruit that is picked and placed in hay or straw to ripen. Lines 6–8 compare the straw and the pear with the guardian and his ward: he protects her by keeping her and her fortune away from the world, like a miser, and "gilds" her by increasing her fortune, just as the straw preserves the fruit and helps it to ripen and turn yellow. This image has direct bearing on the situation, in emphasizing the riches of Polyphemus and Sicily and suggesting the giant's possessiveness. At the same time it may be a joke about guardians, reminiscent of Góngora's satirical *letrillas*. In the last line I could not find a way to reproduce the contrast between "miserly" (in the way he guards her) and "prodigal" (in the way he increases her fortune), or the perfect balance of the line.

Stanza 11: The apple is a hypocrite because it looks red but is white on the inside. Acorns are said to have been important food for people of the Golden Age, whose diet was, no doubt, thoroughly organic. When Don Quijote wants to deliver a lecture on the Golden Age he picks up a handful of acorns and holds them in his hand while he perorates (*Quijote*, I, 11).

Stanza 12: In the first line, "disastrously" renders a phrase (*que no debiera*) that was criticized (José Mariá Micó, *El Polifemo de Luis de Gongora*, 27) both for being too colloquial and for adding nothing important to the meaning. But this kind of conversational comment is essential to Góngora's style. I have been unable to bring out the repetitiveness of lines 1–4, which seem to reproduce the cacophony they describe: translated more literally they would be something like: "Wax and hemp bind—worse luck—/a hundred hollow reeds, whose barbarous sound, / by more echoes than the number of pipes which hemp and wax bind, / is harshly repeated."

In the penultimate line, I invented "earless" for the sake of its half rhyme; the Spanish literally says they were "deafened."

Stanza 13: Stanzas 13–17 describe Galatea and two of her suitors.

Venus, symbol of beauty, and Juno, symbol of power and majesty, are united in Galatea. Venus and Juno were normally rivals, but in the perfection of Galatea's beauty they are in harmony. Galatea's eyes are bright, like two shining stars; her skin is white, like the feathers of the swan, bird of Venus. The peacock, Juno's bird, also has beautiful eyes—when it displays its tail. Since Galatea has everything, Góngora switches birds and goddesses, calling her Venus' peacock, Juno's swan. She is also Neptune's crystal (a little confusingly, when Góngora says, "If she is not . . ." he means "She is . . ." the conditional seeming to imply that a description he is proposing is not final: others will follow).

Stanza 14: Galatea has just been associated with light and whiteness. To this, red is now added, the color of roses and of love.

Stanza 15: The portrayal of two sea gods in this and the next two stanzas as Galatea's suitors does not come from Ovid, Góngora's main source. He has added it himself. In the last line, "the silver plain," more literally "silver fields," is the sea.

Stanza 16: I have invented the "bold buccaneer," though Palemon's brow is definitely bound with coral, which according to classical precedent became soft when immersed in water. The adjective *joven*, "young," was surprisingly a *culto* term, mocked as such by Quevedo. The dread lighthouse marks the Straights of Messina, traditionally the site of Scylla and Charybdis and therefore to be feared. Góngora is perhaps identifying Palemon with Portunus, Roman god of doors and of harbors. This would account for his riches, if he owns the whole Sicilian coastline from Messina to the westernmost cape.

Stanza 17: The asp is a reference to the story of Eurydice, the golden apple to Atalanta's race.

Stanza 18: This and the next two stanzas describe the rich fertility of Sicily and its various agricultural products represented by Bacchus, Pomona, Ceres, and Pales, gods respectively of vineyards, orchards, grain, and livestock. It may be worth noting that in Góngora's day Sicily, which was indeed an exporter of grain, was ruled by Spain.

Stanza 20: Line 5 refers again to the horn of plenty or cornucopia (cf. *First Solitude*, 203–205 [211–213].

Stanzas 21: Young people are burning with love for Galatea and duties are being neglected. The island is also burning with the heat of summer and all nature is affected. The whistling of shepherds to direct their flocks and the barking of their dogs occur frequently in Góngora. These are sounds he must have heard constantly on his travels around Spain.

Stanza 22: Unsatisfied desire brings conflict and disorder. Only love can restore order and harmony. The final couplet has puzzled commentators, and none of the explanations seems entirely satisfactory. Micó (*El Polifemo*, 43) prefers to take it as a plea for quiet so master and dog can both sleep, but to me it seems more likely that it concerns the need for a return to order and discipline.

Stanza 23: The tree Galatea rests under is a laurel, the tree which Daphne became when she fled from Apollo. Lines 2–3 are particularly dense and problematic. Literally they say something like: "She gives to a source the same amount of jasmines as the snow of her limbs hides grass." This has been interpreted as meaning she throws herself down beside the spring and covers the grass with the jasmine that is her beautiful body. Others have taken it to mean that her beauty is reflected in the water. I have chosen this latter interpretation, because for me it fits better with stanza 28, which I interpret as saying that by springing up in fear she destroys this reflected image of herself.

Stanza 24: The salamander, like the fire of love, burns without being consumed. The Dog of Heaven is the star Canis, in the ascendant in midsummer, the dog days. "Those two lights" (line 4) are her eyes. The image in the last two lines is very famous: Acis drinks from the spring (*sonoro cristal*, "sounding crystal") and he stares at the sleeping Galatea (*cristal mudo*, "silent crystal"). From here to the end of stanza 42 Góngora depicts the courtship.

Stanza 25: This description of Acis can be compared with the openly phallic description of Pyramus in *Pyramus and Thisbe*. My version is ambiguous, like the original, as to whether "glory of all the sea etc" applies to Acis or to his mother. In the last line, what the oak yields is honey, as can be seen in the next stanza.

Stanza 26: Various myths surround the almond, perhaps because of the whiteness of the young kernel. One of them equates it with the sperm of Zeus.

Stanza 27: The second group of four lines is particularly rich and difficult to render in English. Literally the Spanish says that if Galatea's couch is not (made) of wind, it is made of cool shade and fine turf (the construction "if . . . not" is usually Góngora's way of introducing an alternative description and means something like "as well as"). According to Dámaso to Alonso (see Parker, *Fábula*, 142) there is a reference here to the *cama de viento* or "wind bed," the hammock of the native South Americans, so I have improvised to introduce this idea. The important point however is the sensuous musical quality of the passage.

Stanza 28: The interpretation of the first half of this stanza depends on stanza 23 and also on the first word of the fourth line, *segur*, "reaper," for which some editions have *seguir*, "follow." If we take the word as "reaper," she becomes the reaper of her own beauty ("white lilies"), which if we accept stanza 23 as referring to her image reflected in the water, can mean that by jumping up she destroys that image; if it is *seguir*, it suggests that she gets up and her beauty ("white lilies") goes with her. Either way, I think we must assume that she is startled and jumps to her feet but does not move away. Her disorientation on suddenly waking seems reflected in the fact that the reader too does not at first know whether Acis is still visible or not.

Stanza 29: A special interest of these stanzas that describe the meeting is in the psychological detail. Galatea does not see Acis, only his gifts. These, unlike what Polyphemus offers later, are simple natural products: fruit, butter, and honey. She recognizes this as the kind of pious offering described in stanzas 19 and 20 (*su deidad culta*, "her divinity worshipped"), but also sees the good manners of someone who has not wanted to disturb her or perhaps even assault her (*venerado el sueño*, "the sleep respected") and she is grateful. The recognition of this "no small sign of courtesy" (*de cortesía no pequeño indicio*) balances her instinct to flee (as she fled from the sea gods in stanzas 15–17). She continues to hesitate.

Stanza 30: Had it been the Cyclops or a satyr who caught her off guard, matters would have been quite different. Their lust would have been further enflamed by seeing her asleep. However, Galatea's haughtiness (*desdén*) is an affront to the powers of Cupid. He will transform her, but not by crude force.

Stanza 31: After being hit by Cupid's arrow, Galatea regrets that Acis remains hidden. In more psychological terms, one might say that her curiosity has been aroused. In the last couplet, Acis is *devoto*, "pious" in my version, because like the other young men of Sicily he has come apparently to make an offering, to worship. In the Spanish, the undergrowth that hides Acis is *confuso alcaide*, something like his "tangled guard"—I didn't manage to reproduce this.

Stanza 33: The tables are now turned, as Galatea finds Acis, apparently sleeping. I have rendered the contrast *urbano / bárbaro* as "courtly" / "untutored." Góngora habitually uses *bárbaro* to mean something like "rustic," but in this instance I think it points to Galatea's innocence, so curiously mixed with the sophistication of her courtesy (*urbana al sueño*) in not wanting to wake him. Also of course she is responding to his sleep as he did earlier to hers, as the next stanza makes explicit. We know, as she does not, that he is only pretending to be asleep. His silence and apparent sleeping are "rhetorical" because they have a purpose, but she does not understand this and is therefore *bárbara*, "innocent" or "rustic," in this respect. The "chick" in the penultimate line is specified in the original as a kite's chick. The metaphor seems to suggest a predatory element in love. Galatea's "innocence" is ignorance of the ways of the world, not absence of desire.

Stanza 34: Like the first half of stanza 32, the second half of this stanza emphasizes how Galatea is being led on by what she imagines. We might interpret the effect of Cupid's arrows as a metaphor for this process.

Stanza 35: During two stanzas, Galatea has been hanging motionless over Acis. Now she changes (*mejora*, "improves") her position. The following lines describe the effect on her of his manly beauty. In the last line, the light that sleeps has been interpreted as meaning the eyes of Acis, which are closed in sleep. Parker (*Fábula*, 145–46) argues for interpreting it as sunset, in which case, in the phrase "when light sleeps" it is the sleeping that is metaphorical, rather than the light. I have followed Parker's suggestion, simply because it seems to provide a better way of rounding off the image of the young man's incipient beard and fresh complexion.

Stanza 36: What is natural can have a more powerful effect than what is devised or organized by human culture. This idea is applied to the appearance of Acis to explain its effect on Galatea.

Stanza 37: A more literal version of line 6 would be "even if bronze surrounded it, diamond walled it in," but I could not make that fit. The flames or fire of the last couplet can be taken as both the flames of love and the destruction of Troy by the Greeks hiding in the wooden horse. I have made the reference to the Trojan horse more explicit than in Góngora and "battering rams" is not really correct because the Spanish says "without breaking walls" and refers to the fact that the Trojans had to breach their own walls in order to admit the wooden horse. I think the point about love remains the same, however: it achieves its objectives without open aggression.

Stanza 38: If there is some absurdity (or suggestiveness) in my second line, Góngora too was generally criticized for overuse of the verb he uses here: *ostenta*—perhaps the line could be translated more literally as "he displays his gallant person." I confess to a problem with the second half of this stanza: what is the import of the generalization about lightning prepared for and about predicted or forecast storms? Micó (*El Polifemo*, 67) suggests that Galatea's reaction is in contrast because she was not prepared for the attack. It seems to me more likely that she *is* prepared, otherwise how are we to interpret the opening of the next stanza?

Stanza 39: In line 4 there is "no pact for sleep" and there is "a lasting truce to rest" because love's battle is about to begin and the lovers will not sleep. Góngora repeatedly uses the conventional equation of love with war in his poetry and "a truce to" appears elsewhere with the meaning of "an end to."

Stanza 40: The carpet here recalls *First Solitude*, 614–615 [629–630]. Myrtles are sacred to Venus and doves are her birds, their cooings erotically suggestive—the Spanish calls them *trompas de amor*, love's trumpets.

Stanza 41: Acis suffers the torments of Tantalus, in other words. Only the sustenance denied him is doubly metaphorical: "fugitive crystal" is a metaphor for water but also in this case metaphorically Galatea's limbs.

Stanza 43: The transition is abrupt, and we are tempted to think Polyphemus has already discovered the lovers. But this is not the case: time has passed and the opening line refers not to the anger of Polyphemus but to sunset, the horses of the sun's carriage snorting and smoking as they go down into the sea. There has been something like a cinematic cut after the lovemaking, which began at midday, when Acis and Galatea were both taking refuge from the sun (stanzas 23–24). In the last line of this stanza, the watchtower (or human lookout, since *atalaya* had both meanings) is literally "mute" (being a rock) and therefore, like a lightless lighthouse, not very useful.

Stanza 44: To imagine the effect of the giant's pipes, we should remind ourselves of stanza 12. In the last lines of this and in the next stanza we have Góngora's familiar image of vines climbing up elms, symbol of loving union.

Stanza 45: As in *Angélica and Medoro* (no. 22), the tyrant affects the whole of Nature. In the last line Góngora is asking the Muses to tell it for him. But the poet, when inspired, speaks with the voice of the Muse, so this can be taken as a request for inspiration.

Stanza 46: The swan and the peacock again, something very like the earlier description of Galatea (stanza 13), this time in the giant's words.

Stanza 48: In the pastoral convention shepherds (or courtiers) competing for love were also often boastful.

Stanza 49: Having spoken of his devotion, the giant seeks to impress Galatea with his riches. In line 6, Góngora wrote "eyes" (plural), even if the Cyclops did have only one eye—a problem I suppose of applying language (which relies on being conventional) to exceptional circumstances.

Stanza 50: Honey is one of Góngora's favorite subjects. Critics have admired the artistry of this stanza entirely devoted to it, while perhaps feeling it gratuitous. We might compare the *Solitudes* 321–328 [328–335] and 919–925 [934–940], where he describes honey and cork hives. Perhaps something Góngora has in mind is that the poet also works hard to distil sweetness out of Nature. It might also be relevant that in *Pyramus and Thisbe* Thisbe is referred to as the honeycomb Pyramus fails to find as he searches the hollow tree trunks.

Stanza 51: In this and the next two stanzas Polyphemus seeks to impress Galatea with his connections (he's the son of Neptune) and his personal appearance.

Stanza 53: The halcyon, a mythical bird that was said to lay its eggs on a calm sea, which is why it was regarded as a sign of fine weather.

Stanza 54: In this stanza and the next, Polyphemus seeks to prove that he is a reformed character, his brutality softened by his love for Galatea. No longer does he kill travelers and decorate his walls with their heads. The Helvetian (Swiss) spears (line 3) are really pikes (as carried nowadays by the Vatican's Swiss Guard). Góngora was criticized for the anachronism—Swiss pikemen were famous in his day, but Polyphemus ought not to have known about them.

Stanza 55: Stanzas 55–57, describing the shipwreck, may seem slightly irrelevant— Certainly they contain anachronisms: the Genoese ship, the pirates, even Cambaya, Malacca, and Java, are unlikely to have been uppermost in the mind of Polyphemus, though they were all available to a seventeenth-century consciousness. However shipwreck is an important symbol for Góngora (the *First Solitude*, sonnet no. 27), and we have been warned of the effect Polyphemus has on shipping in stanza 12. Here in the narrative it provides a convenient transition from the giant's protesting that he has become virtuous to his offer of gifts, the final argument in his attempt to win Galatea.

Polyphemus is surely mistaken about the effect of his music (lines 4–8), which we already know (from stanza 12) to be the reverse of calming. It is more likely he has caused the storm (as Micó [*El Polifemo*, 92] suggests).

Stanza 56: The ship of this stanza is in the Spanish *ligurina haya* or "Ligurian beech tree." Like *pino*, "pine tree," this is a synecdoche for "ship," and typical of Góngora. Genoa, capital of Liguria, was a major maritime power in Góngora's day, and he was criticized for the anachronism as he was for the Swiss pikes in stanza 54. It seems more appropriate to note how natural it was for Góngora to fuse the ancient world and the modern. Scylla is of course one half of the marine hazard Scylla and Charybdis, cliff and whirlpool, thought to be located in the Straits of Messina, between Sicily and the Italian mainland. The harpies of the last line remind us that piracy was an ancient and persistent threat in the Mediterranean (see Braudel's chapter, "The Forms of War" in *Mediterranean*, 2: 836–90).

Stanza 57: The "second plank" means a second rescue, implying that this Genoese merchant had escaped from the sea by holding onto a plank, like the pilgrim of the *Solitudes*. In the Spanish of the second line the *h* of *hacienda* has to be aspirated or the line would be a syllable short. Examples like this are cited as evidence of Góngora's Andalusian pronunciation. Line 6 literally describes the fruit as resting in straw or hanging on threads (to keep it dry and preserve it), but I was unable to make this fit.

Stanza 58: Apparently seventeenth-century commentators preferred to think "goddess of Java" meant queen of Java, but as far as I can see it could equally refer to an image in a temple.

Stanza 59: Vines were sacred to Bacchus, which is why the goats "transgress" when (like the old billy goat in the *First Solitude*) they eat or trample them.

Stanza 61: Thunder before lightning? Everyone notes that Góngora got it wrong here in the last line. But this is how his (mainly Latin) sources had it. Also, of course,

Polyphemus's shout (like thunder) precedes his throwing of the rock (the thunder-bolt). His sight is so acute he can look across the sea to North Africa and distinguish the detailed patterns on the Libyan's shield.

Stanza 63: The sea, remember, is Doris, Galatea's mother. If the fleeing Acis wasn't accepted by her in life, he will be as a river after death. We are reminded that in classical mythology a river, like seas, mountains, and other natural features, is a god.

[Pyramus and Thisbe]

Lines 3–4: "Raw mud" to contrast with *de tierra cocidos*, "terra cotta" (lit. "cooked earth").

Lines 9–14: I have had to change the order of these lines. "The fair archpoet" is Apollo.

Lines 19–20: The big-nosed poet is Ovid.

Lines 21–28: The mulberry tree assisted the lovers because they met under its branches. In punishment its fruit, originally white, would turn red with their blood. The point about the Tigris relates to a discussion as to whether or not it passed through Babylon. If it did not, it could not drown the roots of the mulberry. I think that Góngora, as so often, is both showing off his knowledge and having fun with pedantry.

Lines 39–40: *Raja* is a crack, but in *hacerse rajas* could mean "to go to great trouble."

Lines 42–43: A swan's quill is what you would want for writing something dignified; the rougher goose quill is associated with satire and burlesque.

Lines 45–80: The absurd eloquence of this description of Thisbe suggests that Góngora is parodying himself or perhaps just enjoying himself.

Lines 49–52: In the Spanish the brows are a yoke, because they enslave admirers ("liberty's overthrow"), and this yoke is also a bow (as in "rainbow") but not like the one that announced the end of the biblical Flood. Some sources have *luto*, "mourning," instead of *yugo*, "yoke," which seems less interesting, though also pointing towards the tears with which the story will close.

Lines 61–64: The ruby, as usual with Góngora, is the mouth, and the pearls are teeth. Presumably, without worrying too much about the numbers, the larger pearls are molars and the smaller pearls or dewdrops are the front teeth.

Lines 73–80: The Judgment of Paris—when Paris had to decide whether to award the prize to Juno, Pallas Athena, or Venus.

Line 97: The condescending effect of *Tisbica*, diminutive of *Tisbe*, is lost in English.

Lines 122–25: Early commentators noted the erotic reference of these lines: *herramienta*, "tool," was (not surprisingly) slang for penis.

Lines 133–280: These lines have been omitted here. They deal with a black go-between, referred to metaphorically as a *barca de vistas* or ship for negotiations, and the crack in the wall that allows the lovers to speak.

Lines 282–284: "Night's lantern" is the moon, of course. But Góngora has transposed the verbs: you would expect her to be exploding with angry disapproval and boasting about her own chastity like any respectable matron seeing a young girl roaming the streets alone at night.

Lines 285–292: All the auspices are bad as Thisbe sets out: she stumbles (in the Spanish; it didn't seem to fit in the English), she starts on the unlucky left foot, the dogs are howling, an owl appears.

Lines 301–8: The familiar image of the elm and the vine, emblematic of loving union.

Lines 309–10: The ashes of tree and vine produce lye, used as bleach in washing clothes.

Line 317 "Cynthia", the moon.

Lines 325–32: I have made adjustments to clarify the reference to the Nemaean lion Hercules defeated.

Line 327: In the Spanish, another piece of pedantry, which I have omitted in the English: there were many versions of Hercules, but mainly writers distinguished a Greek one and an Egyptian one. The same quibble appears in the *Solitudes*.

Lines 329–30: Like the previous point, the question about what kind of sheep it was brings the poet or narrator more tangibly into the picture, though all along the playful use of words reminds the reader of his presence. He uses the same word here for the lion's victim (*prójimo*, or neighbor) as bulls or oxen in no. 31, suggesting perhaps that we don't always treat our neighbors as religion recommends.

Line 340: The pun is terrible, maybe, but the translation is very literal.

Line 344: Vertumnus, god of orchards.

Lines 349–50: More literally, "the beast drank and left what was Thisbe's veil clumsily rubicund . . ." I could not emulate Góngora's compactness.

Lines 357–59: The sad simulacrum of his marriage is the elm married to its vine, now blasted by lightning.

Line 371: "The honeycomb" is Thisbe.

Lines 387–88: "The sign" of the Zodiac for July–August: Leo, the Lion.

Lines 394–99: A statue by Lysippus is so realistic it seems alive: Pyramus, because of the shock, is motionless as a statue and seems not alive.

Lines 417–19: She has the scisssors to cut the thread of life.

Line 426: Mucius Scaevola, the Roman who put his hand in the brazier to show he was not afraid of pain.

Line 431–48: *Hierro*, which I have translated as "act" means the spit which people will give turns to. But hierro (same pronunciation) is Pyramus's sin or mistake, which people will talk about for centuries to come.

Line 434: The Spanish exclamation *hi de puta, puto*, "son of a whore" is milder than it sounds. Sancho Panza uses it.

Lines 437–60: Dawn is also Thisbe, and the sigh of Pyramus is compared to a coin whose stamp or minting (*cuño*) is unclear, meaning that at first she cannot trace it.

Lines 441–44: In this comparison with a trapped bird, Góngora describes bird lime as "the sister of paste" (*hermana del engrudo*). He was fond of this rather particular kind of metaphor or periphrasis where something is named as brother, sister, son, etc., of something else that it resembles or is connected with.

Lines 467–68: Blood on grass again, red on green.

Lines 489–90: "Colors" here means something like "pretexts," "excuses." "Palace coverup" sounds like an anachronism but is, I think, not far from being literal.

Lines 490–504: Góngora swamps the tragic end with a flood of comic erudition.

Line 497: Another meaning for *pio*, which I translate as "pious," is "piebald," which may account for "mule" appearing in the following characterization.

Line 498: I have taken liberties with Nabuchadnazzar's name, but so did Góngora, shortening it to a familiar "Nabuco."

Lines 505–8: Antonio Carreño suggests that the epitaph might be applied to the poem itself: one text in its artistic unity, but two, in that it tells the story of the lovers but simultaneously sends it up.

Alonso, Dámaso. *Estudios y Ensayos Gongorinos*. Madrid, Gredos, 1960.

Alzieu, Pierre, Robert Jammes, and Yvan Lissorgues. *Poesía erótica del Siglo de Oro*. Barcelona: Biblioteca de Bolsillo, 2000.

Artigas, Miguel. *Don Luis de Góngora y Argote, Biografía y estudio crítico*. Madrid: Tipografía de la "Revista de Archivos," 1925.

Braudel, Fernand. *The Mediterranean and the Mediterranean World in the Age of Philip II*. Vol 2. Berkeley: University of California Press, 1995.

Carreira, Antonio. *Gongoremas*. Barcelona: Península, 1998.

Chaffee-Sorace, Diane. *Góngora's Poetic Textual Tradition*. London: Tamesis, 1988.

Elliott, J. H. *Imperial Spain, 1469–1716*. London: Penguin, 1985.

Góngora y Argote, Luis de. *Letrillas*. Ed. Robert Jammes. Madrid: Castalia, 1980.

———. *Poems of Góngora*. Ed. R. O. Jones. Cambridge: Cambridge University Press, 1966.

———. *Romances*. Ed. Antonio Carreira. Barcelona: Quaderns Crema, 1998.

———. *Romances*. Ed. Antonio Carreño. Madrid: Ediciones Cátedra, 2000.

———. *Soledades*. Ed. John Beverley. Madrid: Ediciones Cátedra, 1998.

———. *Soledades*. Ed. Robert Jammes. Madrid: Castalia, 1994.

———. *Sonetos Completos*. Ed. Biruté Ciplijauskaité. Madrid: Castalia, 1985.

Harvey, L. P. *Muslims in Spain, 1500–1614*. Chicago: University of Chicago Press, 2005.

Micó, José María. *El Polifemo de Luis de Góngora*. Barcelona: Peninsula, 2001.

Parker, Alexander A., ed. *Fábula de Polifemo y Galatea*. Madrid: Ediciones Cátedra, 2002.

Sánchez, Magdalena S. *The Empress, the Queen and the Nun*. Baltimore: Johns Hopkins University Press, 1998.